Cultural Anthropology

A CONCISE INTRODUCTION

Paul V. McDowell

Santa Barbara City College

KENDALL/HUNT PUBLISHING COMPANY

4050 Westmark Drive   Dubuque, Iowa 52002

Brief Contents

Contents

Preface

This is an introduction to cultural anthropology. There are three aims of this book and the glossary that accompanies it. First, the book is intended to be a supplementary text in cultural anthropology classes where an introductory book would otherwise be the main text. It is designed for a course whose instructor would like to rely more on readers and ethnographies than on textbooks. It covers the main themes in the discipline while allowing space for other books and articles, and other media to be assigned. Simply put, the book gets to the point.

Second, in the tradition of Leslie White (1959), the book takes the perspective that anthropology is, or should be, a science of humankind. Thus, there is extensive coverage of biological anthropology related to humankind's capacity for culture, of descriptive linguistics, and of kinship and marriage. While the book accepts in principle that the perspective of the so-called native must be included, as the postmodemists would have it, I also contend that such perspective-taking is itself a part of the scientific enterprise. Harris says as much in his etic-emic dichotomy (Harris and Johnson 2002).

Third, the book is relatively inexpensive. There are no photographs, no multicolored charts, no sidebars, all of which have driven introductory textbook prices to astronomical levels. It simply covers the main principles of cultural anthropology and offers a bibliography for students who would like to consult further works on the discipline.

There is a personal note behind writing this textbook. I teach an ethnography-driven course called Cultures Around the World, a legacy from a locally famous anthropology and sociology instructor at Santa Barbara City College (SBCC), Henry Bagish. On his sabbaticals, he packed his family in a van and took off to Mexico or China or Vietnam, or any of 30-odd other countries around the world, took incredible photographs, made them into slides, and packaged them into this course. It has drawn hundreds of students to the course over the years.

What he didn't include was a guide to the cultures he portrays. Students view the slides and videotapes, read up on some current articles, and answer the questions for each of (now) 43 cultures—but otherwise lack a text. Two years ago, the course added a glossary—but no thematic guide. So, out of a selfish motive that we really needed this guide, I wrote this textbook and, at the same time, expanded the glossary. So here it is. Indirectly, therefore, I have Henry Bagish to thank as an inspiration and, more directly, Dennis Ringer, chair of anthropology and sociology at SBCC, who asked if I would like to teach Cultures Around the World. Of course, I said yes.

This text, however, is intended for a much wider audience than students taking ethnography-driven courses. There are a large number of short courses in cultural anthropology around the country—summer classes, intersession courses, and accelerated programs, such as the Program for Accelerated College Education in the Los Angeles Community College District—which do not meet very often or very long. It is for students who need to get the essentials quickly. And it is for students who want to make sense of the readers and the ethnographies assigned by instructors who, like me, find textbooks far too expensive and bulky for their limited time and the students' limited budget.

The book starts off with chapter 1, which provides an overview of anthropology, its four subfields, and the five elements of culture, then goes on to discuss the basics of anthropological and scientific method and research in chapter 2. Chapter 3 provides extensive coverage of those aspects of human biology related to a capacity for culture, including the neurobiological base of language, the ability to make and use tools, and bipedalism, which frees us all from the distraction of four-limbed locomotion.

The next two chapters address linguistics. Chapter 4 discusses the principles of descriptive linguistics to impart to the student a flavor as to how the linguist goes about her or his work. It covers the vocal tract, articulatory phonetics, phonology, morphology, and syntax. It also gives some overview of Noam Chomsky's model of universal and generative grammar. Chapter 5 covers kinesics and paralanguage, historical linguistics, ethnolinguistics, and sociolinguistics, thereby relating language to culture.

Man may not live on bread alone, but he or she cannot live without bread—we are members of the Animal Kingdom, after all. Therefore, chapter 6 surveys both the two varieties of foraging—simple and complex—and the four major varieties of food production systems, namely horticulture, pastoralism, equestrian hunting, and intensive cultivation. The ecological and evolutionary significance of all these strategies is discussed.

The next three chapters focus on kinship and marriage. Chapter 7 discusses the basics of descent, and includes exercises on tracing bilateral, patrilineal, and matrilineal kin. The importance of gaining a grasp on rules of descent is emphasized, being a key to understanding not only the rest of kinship analysis, but also to the economic, political, and even supernatural institutions of preindustrial societies.

Chapter 8 focuses on sexuality and gender roles, including the question of the incest tabu—why it is so widespread among the world's cultures. Chapter 9 examines the definitions and types of marriage and the varied families that emerge from each type through the varieties of postmarital residence. Chapter 10 covers descent groups and the alliances created by marriage through bridewealth, dowries, bride labor, and cousin marriage.

The book then turns toward political economy from a cross-cultural perspective. Chapter 11, on economic anthropology, reviews the varieties of property, relations of production, and modes of exchange, from reciprocity through redistribution to market exchange. Chapter 12 discusses the political systems of egalitarian societies, including band and tribal societies, and such cross-cutting ties as the age sets and age grades in East Africa, and the bachelor and men's houses in Papua New Guinea. Chapter 13 examines the political systems of ranked and stratified societies, including chiefdoms and states. Caste systems in India are considered and explained. The concept of peasantry is included, emphasizing its links to the state.

Although cultures emphasize groups of persons sharing a language and a set of worldviews, technology, and practices, individuals also play important roles, and so chapter 14 covers psychological anthropology. The elements of personality are spelled out; then discussion turns to enculturation, which includes language acquisition and cognitive development. Explanations for individual cognitive maps and behavior are also advanced, and the chapter concludes with ethnic variation of mental disorders.

All cultures have to face the unknown that precedes birth and follows death, so chapter 15 focuses on the supernatural, and the various ways human cultures have dealt with the unknown. Worldviews of the unseen are covered, as well as the practitioners and the institutions involved with them. Revitalization movements conclude the chapter.

Finally, in addition to the familiar levels of sociocultural integration—band, tribe, chiefdom, state—we now have a new level, worldwide in scope. We hear of it every day as jobs are being bundled up in the United States and shipped abroad. Chapter 16 focuses on this reality. It examines the global system of production that underlies this new level, and the military and legal mechanisms that reinforce it. Applied anthropology is discussed in light of this new reality, and we see one reason that the famed Vicos Project appears not to have caught hold in the rest of Peru. Attempts to resist the globalization project are also briefly covered.

An epilogue evaluates the potential of anthropology to resume its function as a science of humankind through holism and cross-cultural comparison—if only anthropologists have the will to synthesize those findings that have the potential to test generalizations about the behavior of individuals and groups. It is a call to get on with the task.

Many people had considerable input into this book. In addition to Professor Bagish and Ringer, I wish to thank the support services of Ms. Janice Chase, who manages the day-to-day operations of Cultures Around the World; Mr. Joe Wells, who suggested I send a manuscript of this dual project to Kendall/Hunt; Ms. Carrie Maro, who has seen this project from beginning to end; and the many members of the Kendall/ Hunt editorial staff who rendered these scratchings into readable text.

Paul V. McDowell
Instructor in Anthropology
Santa Barbara, California
March 14, 2005

Chapter 1

INTRODUCTION TO ANTHROPOLOGY

As the title of this textbook indicates, this is a concise introduction to cultural anthropology, and as such, we will get down to cases. The word *anthropology* is derived from two Greek words: *anthropos*, which means "man" or "human," and *logos*, which means "the science of," or "the study of," or "the logic of." There are hundreds, if not thousands, of definitions of anthropology. We'll stick to one definition to which most of the others would agree: **Anthropology is the comparative and holistic study of humankind**. That means that anthropology is the study of human groups throughout the world, and that is the focus of all four major subfields of anthropology: **physical anthropology** (also known as biological anthropology), **archaeology**, **linguistics**, and **cultural anthropology** (also known as sociocultural anthropology and ethnology).

a. *Physical anthropology* is the **comparative study of the biological aspects of humankind**. It involves both comparing the human species with related species—such as the great apes and the fossil prehuman and early human forms—and comparing different human populations. It also is the comparative, biological study of existing human populations. Forensic anthropology relies on the knowledge of contemporary human population—from physical morphology to DNA analysis to serology—for its work.

b. *Archaeology* is primarily the **comparative study of cultural remains of human societies**, although understanding the physical remains of prehuman and human forms is important in that field, too. Archaeologists try to understand past cultures by excavating, mapping, and analyzing the artifacts and layout of a site and **retrodicting** who and what were there, what life was like, and what the material culture consisted of, based partly on what is known about cultures today or of the recent past. To reconstruct the events at a crime scene, forensic scientists use many of the techniques that archaeologists use to reconstruct the cultures from long-abandoned sites.

c. *Linguistics* is the **comparative study of spoken language**. Because the overwhelming portion of the world's languages has never been written, linguists have to uses special techniques to (a) learn the speech sounds of particular languages, and (b) construct their morphology ("word forms"), their syntax (roughly, sentence structure), and their grammar (overall rules that govern a language). Linguists also study the historical development of language families (glottochronology), the tone of voice and gestures that accompany languages (paralanguage and kinesics), and the relationships between a language and its culture (ethnolinguistics and sociolinguistics).

d. *Cultural Anthropology* (also known as **socio-cultural anthropology** and **ethnology**) is the comparative study of human behavior according to the rules, usually implicit, of the society of which individuals are a part. Let's take a closer look. You have probably all heard buzzwords such as "diversity" and "multiculturalism." If we stick to the definition of anthropology as the comparative study of humankind, then we should be concerned with the comparison of human cultures.

Why should we be studying different cultures? There are three reasons for doing so.

First, every culture has its standards of correct behavior. As examples, let's take two tabus in the Middle East. One is that, when sitting cross-legged, you do not aim the soles of your feet at your neighbor. Soles are dirty; they pick up everything from soil to animal feces; thus, to aim your sole at anyone exhibits contempt. That is an issue of etiquette. Another is that at a meal you never pass food with your left hand. Why? The left hand is used throughout to perform—um—sanitation functions. Therefore, not only is this a matter of etiquette, but it is also a matter of health. Elsewhere, an A-OK signal in the United States becomes an obscene gesture in Brazil. Belching in Asia is a compliment to the chef, not a vulgar act as would be construed in North America. So it is a matter of diplomacy to know these things if you want to get along with your neighbor or co-worker from another culture.

Second, there are cultural universals, creating questions that need answering. For example, why do people engage in gift-giving just about everywhere? Why do people, with few exceptions, go to war? Why do smiles represent the same emotion worldwide? Any explanation would have to be tested by cultures not just in Europe or North America but in South America, the Middle East, South Asia—in short, among cultures just about everywhere. Anthropologists seek to explain not only differences among cultures, but also commonalities across them.

Third, there are practices that are seemingly strange to the North American. Why, for example, do Yanomamö marry their cross-cousins, while doing so here could land you in jail in some states? Why are the Japanese reluctant to sue while Americans hold the world's record on lawsuits? Why is it that murder is punished by blood wealth compensation in some societies, revenge killings in others, and executions in our own? Only by comparing two or more cultures can you start looking for the answers.

Defining Culture and Its Attributes

Definitions

What, then, is culture? Most certainly, culture is not what you get at concerts at the Dorothy Chandler or Carnegie Hall, or the paintings at the Los Angeles County Museum of Art or New York's Metropolitan Museum of Art. There are hundreds of definitions in the literature—Alfred E. Kroeber and Clyde Kluckhohn, two early anthropologists, collected some 100 definitions (1952). At the risk of getting bogged down by the multiplicity of definitions, we have to start somewhere.

Perhaps it is just as well that we start with the definition offered in 1871 by Edward Burnett Tylor, the British founder of anthropology as a formal discipline: "that complex whole which includes knowledge, belief, art, law, morals, custom, and any other capabilities and habits acquired by man as a member of society" (1976 [1871]). Haviland offers a definition that reflects the modern emphasis on behavior: "the values, beliefs, and perceptions of the world shared by members of a society that they use to interpret experience and generate behavior, and that are reflected in their behavior" (2002:34). To Haviland, what is cultural must be *observable* and *measurable*, both concerns of today's social science in any field. Anthropologically, then, culture concerns human behavior as guided by rules of the society of which they are a part; it is not just about individuals or even groups, but of entire societies. Such societies may be small, such as the Chumash, who once lived in the Ventura and Santa Barbara areas, with a hundred or so people making up a group. They may comprise entire nations, as Japan with its millions sharing the same language and culture.

What, then, is society? Again Haviland offers a definition: a group of persons who "have a common homeland, are interdependent, and share the same culture" (2002:34, 492; see also Scupin 2003: 43–44, Ember and Ember and Ember 2002: 16, and Nanda and Warme 2004; 4 for similar emphasis on territory in defining "society"). We may point out that this definition has its own loose ends, such as the major diasporas, or dispersed peoples sharing a common culture, such as the "ethnic" Jews, the Afro-Americans, or the Armenians. Even so, there is a structure. One might compare society to a skeleton. If you didn't have a structure of bones to hold you up, you wouldn't, well, hold up. Each bone has a function, from pelvis to femur to rib cage to skull. Put together, your skeleton is your structure, your mainframe. The same principles apply to the circulatory system, the digestive system—and to cultures, and so on.

Similarly, every society has a structure. No culture is a hodgepodge of this or that feature, any more than you and I are just bags of bones, or buckets of blood. So a social structure consists of the overall relationships among people in a society that hold it together. It includes the economy, the government (or some other means of social control), and, especially in preindustrial society, kinship. (We're setting aside four chapters on that topic—that's how important it is.)

Attributes of Culture

So far, our definition of culture shares many features with nonhuman species. Ants and termites both form societies, and most species of animals form groups: schools of fish, herds of cattle, prides of lions, and troops of chimpanzees. All these share a space, and share behavior patterns as well. Culture has at least five attributes that separate human groups from nonhuman ones.

1. **Culture is learned**. Culture entails learning rather than genetic transmission. Ants, fish, termites all acquire their behavior through the genes. That does not mean that nonhuman animals lack learning. For example, dogs do learn, but their behavior is the product of conditioning, or repeated training with rewards. Humans, on the other hand, apply their learning to new situations. In anthropology, *enculturation* refers to the transmission of a society's culture from one generation to the next; sociologists call the same process *socialization*. To a lesser extent, nonhuman primates also learn certain behaviors that roughly may be described as culture.

2. **Culture is based on symbolism**. *Symbolism* is the capacity to bestow a meaning to a thing or event (e.g., speech) which has no inherent relationship to the thing itself. Symbols can be reflected in a stop sign, or a cross, or a Star of David; there can be negative associations, such as the hammer and sickle in the now-disintegrated Soviet Union, or the swastika in Nazi Germany. These are commonplace meanings of symbols.

From a cultural standpoint, the most important form of symbolism is language. As you can see and hear for yourself, there is no meaning to the letters [k] or c or [æ] or a or [t] or t. Puzzled by the letters in the square brackets? These are letters from the **International Phonetic Alphabet**, or **IPA**, used to standardize spoken sounds on paper (more in chapter 3). Language acquires meaning only when these letters are strung together to form words. By themselves, c, a, and t mean nothing. Strung together, *cat* means something in English—a feline creature, or perhaps a make of bulldozer. Strung together another way, *act* means performance on the stage. Although this seems a trivial example, language is the basis of culture. Without language, there is no culture. Picture symbolism as water, and we're the fish. Without the water, we are nothing, and we have nothing. We'll return to this important matter in chapter 3.

In contrast, **signals** or **signs** are sounds or gestures that have a self-evident meaning, such as a pointing finger to mean "this," or a tear to indicate sorrow, or screaming to indicate anger, excitement, or fear. In fact, these are the main elements of nonhuman animal communication. For reasons we'll also cover in chapter 4, species that rely on signals *only* are lacking in culture, except in the most rudimentary form.

3. **Culture is shared**. It may be shared among a group of people who speak a common language and a common set of customs. Such groups may be as small as 50 persons in a !Kung San (Ju/'hoansi) band or a dispersed assemblage of Inuit families—or as numerous as 117 million people in Japan, which is probably the least ethnically diverse nation in the world. (The largest indigenous minority in Japan are the northern Ainu).

The matter becomes complicated when a society contains more than one culture, or there are different groups whose cultures are not entirely distinct. The latter are called *subcultures*, or groups showing a distinctive set of standards and behavior patterns by which a group within a larger society operates. Haviland cites the Amish as one example. They differ from the dominant U.S. culture in many ways: rejection of modern technology and the material world itself, use of a distinct language (German), and 17th-century clothing styles. Still, they also share elements of dominant society: belief in thrift and hard work as virtues, independence, value of family life. (2002:36, 38).

Nevertheless, the matter is much more complex than this. For example, North American Native people are regarded as belonging to separate cultures, yet many speak English, all wear North American clothing, several drive North American cars, and many even believe in Christianity. Then, how about Afro-Americans, who through slavery and discrimination have lost virtually all their culture—language, myths, kinship ties—yet many are searching to "rediscover" their heritage? Are the Native peoples and the Afro-American a subculture of North Americans, or do they comprise distinct cultures in their own right?

There are the ranges of behavior that may fall outside a culture, that is regarded as "weird" or, as sociologists call them, "deviant." The so-called drug culture, organized criminals, and countercultures are all familiar examples. To take another culture, the Cheyenne of the Midwestern Plains valued bravery in warfare among their men, but they also had **berdaches**, who adopted the behavior and clothing of women. Even so, they did not form a true subculture.

These examples point out the importance of learning. To be Cheyenne or Amish or even Afro-American in culture (though perhaps not in biology) is not to inherit these attributes genetically but to learn them. No language is genetically inherited; the offspring of Chinese or Eastern European or Indian immigrants generally speak flawless English. No cultural trait is inherited; why shouldn't a former horseman learn to drive? A woman born in India, Kalpana Chawla, became an astronaut in her tragically short life that ended with the accidental disintegration of the *Columbia*. To paraphrase Shakespeare's *Julius Caesar*, our fate is not in our genes, but in our culture—that is, ourselves. Perhaps we should see subcultures as transitional forms.

4. **Culture is patterned or integrated**. One aspect of a culture reflects other aspects of society as well. For example, the !Kung (or Ju/'hoansi) observe a sharing ethic that reflects the changing fortunes of the hunt. Because of their hunting technology—bows and arrows tipped with a weak poison—game is hard to come by. If you share your game today, someone else will share his tomorrow. The "owner of the arrow" that first penetrated the animal "owns" the animal—but only to give it away. Elderly may "own" the arrow and play that role of distribution. Sharing is king when it comes to game. Meantime, women provide most of the food (via gathering roots, nuts, and berries), and, partly for that reason, they have a large say as to where the band should move to next.

Another example concerns the Kapauku of New Guinea, recounted by Leopold Pospisil (1963:51–52) and described in Haviland (2002:41–42). Although reliant primarily on sweet potatoes, the Kapauku have little protein to consume; pigs are the most important source of protein. Pigs are also the most important form of wealth and, for that reason, are an important source of prestige. The so-called big men establish their prestige by holding a feast periodically, usually every ten years. Pig raising involves a lot of work, a lot of food (especially sweet potatoes), and therefore a lot of gardening—which only women perform. Guess who raises the pigs!

This kind of work is more than one woman can handle, so *polygyny*—marriage of one man to more than one woman—is one way to obtain and hold female labor. Polygyny works best if there are more women than men. That is where traditional warfare comes in; men are killed but not women. (These were the days before women served in the military.) Finally, polygyny works best if women live with their husbands, so several women are involved in gardening and pig breeding. All this is not to say that the Kapauku plan this overall cultural pattern; rather, if Pospisil is correct in his analysis, this case study shows how elements "fit in" with each other (Pospisil 1963).

5. **Culture is generally adaptive.** !Kung are in a relatively impoverished environment that could not sustain anything more complex than hunt-

ing and gathering; private ownership, legally known as *fee simple,* would militate against survival. An attempt by one band of !Kung to herd goats proved disastrous (see the video *Bushmen of the Kalahari* by John Marshall).

Here's another example. Tropical environments allow for settled communities among Kapauku, but they live in a largely protein-poor environment. One proposition, set forth by Marvin Harris (1974) for the Yanomamö of tropical South America, is that warfare reflects competition for protein resources (in this case, game). Napoleon Chagnon, the ethnographer who has visited the Yanomamö for some 66 months over a dozen years, disputes this interpretation (1997).

Conclusion

Cultures around the world handle the same issues of life in different ways. As animals, we all have to eat. Different cultures go about it in different ways. Humans reproduce. Different cultures have different rules of sexual behavior, different forms of marriage (if marriage ceremonies take place at all), and different ways of rearing children. Some cultures have governments, others do not, but all cultures have some form of social control. Yet one question underlies all anthropological inquiries: How is it that one species of humankind—*Homo sapiens*—can spawn such diverse cultures throughout the globe? The remainder of this book offers some of the answers to this question.

Chapter 2

ANTHROPOLOGICAL METHODS

Introduction

At a theoretical level at least, there are two competing views of social science in general and anthropology in particular. The dominant one is a *scientific approach*, which seeks to explain things or events with hidden but universal and unchanging principles, or laws. To reach this ideal, anthropologists are expected to regard all explanations with skepticism and to take a rigorous approach to their work while in the field. The second approach to anthropology views it as one of the *humanities*. Many anthropologists think that to understand another culture, you must not only observe it, but you must experience it as well.

In actuality, successful anthropologists are mindful of both approaches. No anthropologist can treat a field situation as if it were a controlled laboratory. Everyone in a culture is a volitional being, capable of telling the truth or lying, capable of participating in a study or refraining from doing so. Sometimes the field situation may prove dangerous, as Chagnon reports for the Yanomamö when he mentioned the name of the deceased relative of an informant—strictly tabu in that culture. The agitated informant threatened to kill him. In that respect, fieldwork cannot but be experiential. At the same time, however, the scientific ideal must remain foremost in the fieldworker's mind. What matters is the reliability of the information that the ethnographer reports. This is where methods become important.

This chapter first discusses the principles of anthropological method, and then describes some of the basics of social research. The chapter then discusses the scientific method, including a test that involves the acceptance or rejection of propositions, anthropological or otherwise. A few case studies then illustrate the limitations that the field situation imposes on the ideal study.

Principles of Anthropological Method

As we stated at the beginning, anthropology is the comparative and holistic study of humankind. We therefore begin with these concepts and others associated with them.

Holism

A fundamental principle in anthropology, **holism** posits that aspects of any culture must be viewed in the broadest possible context to understand their interconnections and interdependence (Haviland 2002:14). This ties in with the view that culture is patterned; the question is, then, how does every aspect of a culture fit in with every other aspect? We have already illustrated this with the sharing among the !Kung and the prestige economy of pigs among the Kapauku (chapter 1).

In reality, this principle is ignored in practice. Like other social science disciplines, anthropology has become hyperspecialized, to the extent that anthropologists in one subfield rarely communicate with those in other subfields. It will take generalists to integrate their findings and to provide answers to the "so-what" questions that overspecialized research elicits, but few positions are open to them.

Cross-Cultural Comparison

Cross-cultural comparison involves the comparison of two or more cultures with regard to a certain trait or complex of traits. If any generalization is to hold up for all the peoples of the world, then it must be tested with instances from several cultures. To do so, there must be some commonalities among the two or more cultures. Hunters and gatherers, for example, have much in common: almost total reliance on natural sources of subsistence, the fluctuation of resources that accompany such reliance, and a naturally occurring carrying capacity. Only with a common base can differences among hunters and gatherers be appreciated. Similar principles apply for comparing more complex societies.

Cultural Relativism

Cultural relativism refers to the idea that, because all cultures are unique, they can be evaluated only according to their own standards and values. Many anthropologists, such as the eminent British anthropologist Edmund Leach, argue that no two cultures can be compared—cross-cultural comparison is an unrealistic enterprise.

The opposite concept to cultural relativism is **ethnocentrism**, or the belief in the superiority of one's own culture over all others. Members of all cultures are ethnocentric. Expressions of patriotism, regardless of country, reflect ethnocentrism. Closely related but not identical is the notion of one being **culture-bound**. From birth and enculturation, all of us harbor assumptions that are derived from our culture. Many of these assumptions are unconscious. Eating dog meat is not something we think of—until it is actually done by a neighbor, as when Cambodians who include dog in their meals were arrested in Long Beach, California, for this "crime." In another context, we reckon kin through both sexes—our mothers and our fathers, our sisters and our brothers—unaware of cultures that reckon their kin through a line of males only, or through a line of females only.

Not all anthropologists subscribe to the notion that cultures cannot be evaluated by criteria other than their own. In his volume *Sick Societies: Challenging the Myth of Primitive Harmony*, Edgerton argues that such a notion betrays an unwarranted romanticism among non-Western cultures, and cites numerous examples of ways that such evaluations are not appropriate—ranging from the mutual neglect among the nomadic Siriono of Amazonian Bolivia, to clitoridectomy among preadolescent and adolescent females throughout Africa and the Middle East. Cannibalism and headhunting are among the examples that cultural relativists have had to explain away. Scupin (2003) in his textbook introduces the concept of **ethical relativism**, defined as tolerance of practices harmful to the body or psyche of the victims.

In reality, cultural relativism may be interpreted in two ways. One involves the so-called **noble savage complex**, the belief, first postulated by the French philosopher Jean-Jacques Rousseau, that "primitive" cultures uncorrupted by civilization represent ideal models for all peoples to emulate. The second interpretation would regard cultural relativism as **scientific detachment** and open-mindedness, cast in anthropological terms. It is one thing to abhor cannibalism—or to explain it away in noble savage terms. It is quite another to ask what role cannibalism plays in the functioning of societies in which it occurs—the Mundurucu of Amazonian South America, for example, or the Aztec (Mexica) of 15th-century central Mexico. Viewed in this way, the concept of cultural relativism is a useful, if not mandatory, research orientation.

Cultural Universalism

Finally, there is the question regarding the absolute notion of cultural uniqueness. In fact, universals are found in every culture, or almost every culture, on the globe. Paralinguistic phenomena are one example: smiling to indicate happiness or amiability; frowns that reflect disapproval or an unhappy state; weeping to indicate sorrow. Another is the so-called incest tabus. Why, with rare exceptions, is sexuality between primary kin (father-daughter, mother-son, brother-sister) universally condemned? Why is the giving, receiving, and repaying of gifts, whether between individuals or groups, found everywhere? **Cultural universalism**, then, refers to the opposite idea that all people, regardless of culture, have many attributes in common.

Anthropological Research Techniques

Basics of Research Techniques and Methods

Research techniques do not automatically assure results. They have to be selected; some are appropriate and others are not. The question of selection, then, hinges on another question: What is to be researched? What is the problem or issue to be studied? To answer this question, one needs to know the basics of methodology and the methods that spring from it.

Research techniques refer to the actual means of gathering information, whether observed facts, assertions made by informants, or data gathered from statistical surveys. In most other disciplines, surveys are the principal sources of data, involving questionnaires and statistical analysis of the results. Experiments involving observations of individual responses or interpersonal interactions under controlled conditions are also common. Both of these are *closed-ended* techniques, so called because the number of possible responses is limited. Their main value rests in testing hypotheses that have been formulated in advance, and cannot elicit new information. Any information that might have been overlooked cannot be acquired except by other techniques.

Open-ended techniques serve to elicit new data from any sources; they do not involve preconceived ideas derived from prior research. In fact, such techniques serve to elicit information that may have been overlooked before. Indeed, the first order of business among anthropologists is to collect information for an **ethnography**, or description of a culture based on firsthand work in the field. Open-ended techniques include **observation**, which entails watching the behavior of people within a culture, with not only the aim of describing one detail or another, but also asking how it fits in with the rest of the culture. It may involve learning the language and observing how that language structures the reality experienced by the people being observed. **Participant observation** involves taking part in the activities of the people under study: wearing native dress, engaging in production activities, participating in ceremonies—the list is endless. **Open-ended interviews** comprise yet another

major source of information. Often, one may rely on **key informants**, at least initially, to gain some sense as to what is going on, but relying on a few informants does involve the risk of bias. Informants should be representative: women as well as men, people of all ages, members of all religions, and other factions. As you may surmise, the ethnographer relies on all of these techniques.

Other means are used as needed: filming, videotaping, recording; what works best is situational, as you may well see from reading ethnographies, viewing documentary films, or even attempting fieldwork on your own. The field situation dictates the method you will use. If you are trying to construct a modal personality within a culture (see under "Psychological Anthropology" of this book), you may used a culturally modified version of the Rorschach Inkblot Test or Thematic Apperception Test. Ethnic dances and public ceremonies clearly call for a video camcorder. Determining the dietary importance of protein might entail weighing game animals like porcupine or tapir as they are carried into the village, as Kenneth Good did among the Yanomamö. To use that tired cliché, "it depends."

Research and the Ethnographer

Finally, the quality of the data and information depends upon the personal qualities of the researcher himself or herself. One reason that replication in restudies can never be precise is that one ethnographer will have perceptions, attitudes, and personalities different from those of another ethnographer.

For example, Chagnon's first several months on the field with the Yanomamö of Bisaasi-Teri was no picnic. He was badgered mercilessly for his goods until he found how to fight back—and in so doing actually gained respect. When queried what he was eating—peanut butter—he retorted "Guess!" Queries about eating Vienna sausage elicited a similar response. The turning point came when he lost an axe. Read about his setbacks and eventual rapport with the Yanomamö, especially the leader Kaobawä, and the outsider Rerebawä (Chagnon 1997).

To take another example, the Harvard Chiapas Project involved research of the Tzotzil Maya of Zinacantán, Chiapas: the benefits of a longitudinal study involving more than (by now) 200 anthropologists conducting microstudies in such areas as cargo (office) participation, local lawmaking and conflict resolution, corn farming and marketing, joking behavior, mythologies, weaving, child delivery, and so on. Many have criticized the project for contaminating Zinacantán with a surfeit of anthropologists and paying informants for their services, artificially stimulating the local economy and drawing a larger-than-normal population into the community (Vogt 1969).

Basics of Scientific Methodology

The scientist begins with a **hypothesis**, or tentative explanation of the relationship among certain things or events, or phenomena. Then he or she gathers various data or information that seem to support this generalization and, equally important, by showing why alternative hypotheses may be falsified, that is, eliminated from consideration.

Repeating this procedure several times—formulating and testing hypotheses, and retaining those that are validated—the scientist arrives at a system of confirmed hypotheses, or **theory**. No theory is ever confirmed once and for all. A better method may come along, or better information or data, or a new hypothesis that does a better job explaining the data. That means that all theories are probabilistic, some more probabilistic than others; there is no theory that is absolute.

Evaluating Hypotheses: Lett's Six-Way Test

How, then, do we evaluate the validity of propositions or statements purporting to explain certain cultural attributes or events? Perhaps one of the best ways is a six-way test proposed by James Lett, Professor of Anthropology at Indian River Community College and author of the *Human Enterprise: A Critical Introduction to Anthropological Theory* (1987). Appearing originally in *The Skeptical Inquirer* in 1990, the article sets forth the principles summarized in the acronymic memory device FiLCHeRS, each capped letter forming the first letter of the test—which serves as a reminder that many false statements are attempts to "filch your belief" (Lett 1990).

Falsifiability

Any hypothesis must include or imply the conditions under which that hypothesis is to be rejected or subject to *falsification*, in other words, be falsified. Examples include the well-established law that water should boil at sea level at 212 degrees Fahrenheit. If water did not boil at 212 degrees Fahrenheit at sea level, this hypothesis would be rejected. (This statement is obviously simplified; air pressure would have to be controlled for, and so on.)

For example, say a healer claims that crystals restore harmony and balance. How do you define harmony and balance? The healer offers no test of this harmonious state. Or say that a faith healer offer says you must have faith. You express faith and die anyway. Have you died because of lack of faith? How do you know? You don't, so the faith healer is off the hook.

Another nonfalsifiable ploy is the multiple out. Say I tell you I created the world five minutes ago. You object (if you have managed to stop laughing meanwhile) that you were here five minutes ago. Then I tell you that when I created the world, I included everyone's memories in it. You and I know the proposition is ludicrous—yet try to disprove it with all these logical trapdoors surrounding this demented fool. (By the way, did you know that some evangelicals use dinosaur bones and other evidence of life in the millions of years as a test of faith?)

Logic

Any argument offered as evidence in support of any claim must be both **sound** and **valid** to meet the standard of **logic**. In other words, a set of propositions must be factually true. The major premise (the most comprehensive proposition) must be such that the minor premise (the narrower proposition) follows from the original proposition and the conclusion follows from both.

Some examples should clarify the terms *sound* and *valid*.

1. Example of argument that is both valid and sound:
   - Major Premise: All dogs are mammals (true)
   - Minor Premise: Xavier is a dog (true)
   - Conclusion: Xavier is a mammal (valid)
2. Example of an invalid argument
   - Major Premise: All dogs are mammals (true)
   - Minor Premise: Xavier is a mammal (true)
   - Conclusion: Xavier is a dog (invalid: does not follow)

3. Example of an unsound argument
   - Major Premise: All dogs have fleas (false)
   - Minor Premise: Xavier is a dog (true)
   - Conclusion: Xavier has fleas (unsound, true or not)
4. Example of both an invalid and an unsound argument:
   - Major premise: All dogs have fleas (false)
   - Minor Premise: Xavier has fleas (true, for argument)
   - Conclusion: Xavier is a dog (invalid: could be a flea-ridden cat; unsound; not all dogs have fleas)

To sum up, any claim must be (1) **valid**—the **minor premise** must follow from the **major premise**, and the **conclusion** must follow from both major and minor premise; and (2) it must be **sound**—both premises must be true.

Comprehensiveness

Under the rule of **comprehensiveness**, the evidence offered in support of any claim must be exhaustive; that is, all of the available evidence must be considered, not just that which supports the theory. Unfortunately, lawyers and politicians routinely advocate one side or the other, and their arguments tend to emphasize the facts that support their case. If either were true scientists, they would consider *all* the facts, supportive of their case or not.

Examples run the spectrum from quack medicine to anthropological theory. Here are a few:

According to biorhythm theory, for anyone to perform best at any task, one has to be at the highest point of three cycles—intellectual, emotional, and physical. You get each cycle by getting the person's (a) date of birth, and (b) date of measurement; (c) divide the difference by 33 (intellectual), 28 (emotional), and/or 23 (physical). Falsifiability is very evident here.

Applying this principle to airline pilots, the biorhythm practitioner would tell us that an airplane crashes whenever the pilot is at the low point of all three cycles. The problem, Lett points out, occurs when research covers only those cases involving low biorhythms; if one considers *all* airplane crashes, which other studies reveal, frequency of crashes involving low biorhythms are no greater than chance.

Here is another example, taken from the so-called protein debate about the Yanomamö that raged between Napoleon Chagnon and Marvin Harris. According to Harris, who had never visited the Yanomamö, low availability of protein in a tropical rainforest environment (in other words, a low number of game—animals available for hunting in that environment) tends to foster warfare.

In refutation, Chagnon shows that Yanomamö and other forest Indians in South America consume higher amounts of protein than do people in industrialized nations. (Average amount of protein was 64.4 grams; Harris said that if Chagnon found average protein intake of forest Indians to exceed a Big Mac, or 30g of protein, he would eat his hat of unknown protein content), and higher than minimum daily requirements. Yet, they are all warlike. Therefore, these cases should reject the theory. This issue has not been settled, by the way. Chagnon's ex-student, Kenneth Good, tends to buy the protein argument.

Honesty

The term **honesty** refers to the principle that evidence offered in support of any claim must be evaluated without either self-deception or intent to deceive colleagues or the public. There is no choice but to accept the results, whatever they may be.

Though this rule is straightforward, its observance involves complications that are often unrelated to the subject at hand. Several studies have demonstrated that once one has one stated a hypothesis, one is strongly motivated to verify it, and this can cause one to overlook negative evidence, not to mention other information which, I might add, could lead to better hypotheses, that is, which better explain the facts. Cases are now coming to light where even hard scientists have been found to "cook" or modify their data to conform to their hypotheses. Detailed case studies can be found in a book entitled *Betrayers of the Truth: Fraud and Deceit in the Halls of Science* (Broad 1983), among several other sources.

Replicability

If the evidence for any claim is based on experimental results, or if the evidence offered in support of any claim could logically be explained as coincidental, then it is necessary for the experiment to be repeated. In experimental science, the study must be repeated involving identical procedures and identical laboratory conditions. A second positive result strengthens the hypothesis.

The anthropological version is a *restudy*, or the study of a culture previously studied by another anthropologist. Tepoztlán, a village located 75 miles south of Mexico City, is a classic example. First studied in 1926 by Robert Redfield, Tepoztlán was characterized as a sleepy, harmonious community. Oscar Lewis, who studied the same village in 1943, found a very different Tepoztlán: a fractious community, dominated by *caciques* (political bosses) whose factional rivalry could be traced back to the outbreak of the Mexican Revolution in 1910.

A less perfect example concerns American Samoa. Margaret Mead established her fame via the study of female adolescent sexual behavior on the Island of Ta'u in the eastern part of the chain. Although she spent only five months on the island, and that in a missionary school for girls, Mead claimed that female adolescents engaged in promiscuous sex and, for that reason, lacked the mental stress affecting the more restricted female adolescents of North America. The book arising from the study, *Coming of Age in Samoa* (1961 [1927]), was a perennial best seller for several decades.

Derek Freeman, a New Zealander anthropologist based at the National University of Australia, disputed her findings in 1980. He had conducted studies in Western Samoa prior to the outbreak of World War II and then, after serving in the military during the war and conducting research among the Iban of Borneo, returned to Western Samoa in 1966 to conduct his study primarily at Sana'apu. His findings about female adolescence were radically different from Mead's; their sexuality was puritanical, to say the least. He based his conclusions on both his own work and on travelers' accounts of Samoans during the 18th and 19th centuries. He pointed out the flaws of confining research to missionary school girls, of failing to broaden her inquiries to include other Samoans in the village, and of failing to perceive that the girls might be practicing "recreational lying." Mead clearly had reported on what she wanted to believe.

Was Freeman's work entirely replicative? There is reason to believe not. His study was conducted in a different locale, and in the commonwealth half of Samoa at that. His primary informants were talking chiefs and other males of high status. His only contact with the people of Ta'u were two girls from the missionary school, now well into their eighties, who claimed to have lied to Margaret Mead (1989).

Since Mead's day, ethnographers are expected to spend a year in a community, not five months. Preferably, they try to conduct a longitudinal study, or at least revisit their community periodically. The study of Zinacantán, a Tzotzil Mayan community in Chiapas, is ideal from that standpoint. Since 1957, there has been at least one anthropologist in residence, and 90 professional and student ethnographers had studied the community by 1969. Yet there is another side to the story: Are anthropologists contaminating the community by their very presence?

Sufficiency

Evidence must be adequate in support of any claim, and this adequacy is governed by three stipulations: (a) The burden of proof for the claims rests on the person making the claim and no one else. (b) Extraordinary claims demand extraordinary evidence; predicting heavy snowfall tomorrow in coastal Southern California would be an extraordinary claim. (c) Evidence based on testimony of an authority is always inadequate for any claim, particularly if the issue at hand is outside the expertise of that authority.

In conclusion, it should be stressed that even if propositions passing this sixfold test are true, disconfirming evidence can later appear. Rather, any proposition failing any one of these tests cannot be accepted.

Conclusion

It is plain to see that ethnographic fieldwork and analysis combine the careful recording of information expected from a scientist with the ingenuity of an artist. Ethnography requires both inductive and deductive reasoning. Through careful observation, the ethnographer may detect patterns of individual and group behavior that contribute to a culture, but such observation may prove misleading. Therefore, important as hunches are in generating hypotheses as to how a culture operates, these hypotheses must be rendered testable. This is where deductive reasoning comes in. If the statement meets the six criteria suggested by Lett, then it is likely to become a confirmed theory, acceptable until new information is gathered that refutes it. Clearly, anthropology has the attributes both of science and of art.

Chapter 3

HUMAN EVOLUTION: BIOLOGICAL AND CULTURAL

Introduction

One of the attributes of culture we defined in chapter 1 is its adaptability. For good or for ill, the species we know as *Homo sapiens* (to some, *Homo sapiens sapiens*) is found everywhere on the globe, from the Arctic to Antarctica and everywhere in between. The Inuit and their cousins in Greenland, Lapland, Siberia, and other parts of the circumpolar region adapted very well to a frigid climate that lasts ten months out of the year. Africans and their cousins in Amazonia managed to thrive in a hot climate that is hostile to topsoil upon which trees and brush—indeed, the entire biota—depend. Nomadic herdsmen trod the arid environment of the Sahara or Saudi Arabia or survived in the heat of the savanna grasslands of East Africa or managed their herds in the freezing steppes of Central Asia. We, the genus *Homo* and the species *sapiens*, have thrived everywhere.

In our ability to adapt to varying climes, we owe much to our culture, our ability to create the necessary techniques for survival. This is an ability few of our mammalian cousins possess. Chimpanzees adapt well in the forested environments of Tanzania or West Africa. They can build sleeping platforms, fish for termites, and establish social relations with one another. But no chimpanzee troop will survive the woodlands of eastern North America, let alone the

boreal forests of the Canadian Shield. As for *Homo sapiens*—been there, done that.

How did we get so adaptive? This chapter reviews the main lines of our ancestry, from unknown apes or apelike creatures in the Miocene to the first Australopithecines in the late Pliocene and early Pleistocene to the first hominids, oh, say 2.5 million years, give or take. We start this chapter with a brief taxonomy—how we, the sapient hominids, fit into the general scheme of the animal kingdom and, in particular, the Order Primata. We also cover some general principles of **speciation** and **natural selection**. We then make a general foray into comparative hominid-pongid anatomy—how our anatomy compares with our distant cousins the chimpanzees, the bonobos, and the gorillas, and what the differences say about the evolution of ourselves.

We then trace our ancestry, from the earliest known humanlike forms—*Ardipithecus*, for example—through the major Australopithecine forms to the first toolmaker we know for sure, *Homo habilis*, its successor, *Homo erectus*, and its probable descendants, archaic *Homo heidelbergensis*, our probable cousins *Homo neanderthalensis*, and at last to ourselves, modern *Homo sapiens*. We also look at the tools that co-evolved with our ancestor: the first choppers of the Oldowan tradition, the finer stone axes and the associated flake tools of the Acheulean tradition, the even finer flakes knapped from prepared cores of the Levalloisian tradition, and so on, into the highly specialized tools of the Upper Paleolithic, made not only of stone but also of antler, wood, bone, and ivory.

Behind every invention of a new toolmaking and tool-using technique lurks the question: When did we cease depending on our genetic make-up, our biological characteristics and start depending on what we could do ourselves—hunt, gather or grow food, construct shelters, and wear clothing that would protect us from the elements? In other words, when did culture replace biology as an adaptive mechanism, how was it done, and how long did it take?

Taxonomy

A Few Principles of Taxonomy

Let's start with the basics. Regardless of the current administration's attitude, we are not alone in this world—never were and never will be. If we blow ourselves up in the end, other species will survive; cockroaches come to mind. So let's see where we fit in the **taxonomy** of organisms, or a classification system based on similarities and differences, arranged hierarchically from the general to the specific. More specifically, the term refers to the science of categorizing organisms using a **nomenclature** (naming principles) that reflects their relationships. An individual category within a classification system, general or specific, is known as a **taxon** (plural, **taxa**).

Because biological anthropology, like all other branches of the discipline, are changing, you should know that there are two systems of classification competing for dominance. The first is **phenetic taxonomy**, or one which is based on existing **phenotypes** or physical characteristics (see below under "Mechanisms of Evolution") and their adaptive **traits** (or physical characteristics); the second is **cladistics**, or a classification system based on order of evolutionary branching based on genetics instead of present similarities and differences.

Phenetic taxonomy is the older system of the two, dating back to Carolus Linnaeus, also known as Karl von Linné (1708–1777), a Swedish botanist who in 1758 published a systematic classification design that remained—some say until recently—the prototype of today's taxonomy. Cladistics lays less emphasis on physical appearance, preferring to base taxonomy on the order of evolutionary branching, as reflected in genetic data. For example, phenetic taxonomy would place humans in a separate cate-

gory from pongids (the great apes), whereas cladistics would lump humans with chimpanzees, bonobos (close relatives of chimps), and gorillas in a broader hominid (humans and their close relatives) category, but separate from the orangutans. That is because only 2 percent of the genes separate us from the chimpanzees and more separate us from the orangutans. We are separated from the chimpanzees by the neologism *hominini* as a "tribe"; gorillas and chimps are categorized as of the tribe *gorillini*. For an excellent summary comparing these two schemes, see Park (2002:131–137).

There is one other issue of which you should be aware. All taxonomists (including biological anthropologists) do not agree on how individual forms should be categorized, especially when it comes to fossil forms. For some, Neanderthals would be split apart from modern humans; thus *Homo neanderthalensis* versus *Homo sapiens*. These taxonomists are the so-called **splitters**. Others see few essential differences, if any, between these two hominids (see definition below), so that they would lump the two together in one species, *Homo sapiens*, and categorize them as *Homo sapiens neanderthalensis* versus *Homo sapiens sapiens*. These taxonomists are the so-called **lumpers**.

There are also conventions for identifying groups, including individual lifeforms. All categories are identified in Latin. A "dead" language, Latin is unlikely to change. The generic identifiers are lowercased, but their specific categories are capitalized: thus, phylum Chordata, order Primata. However, their English glosses (equivalents) are lowercased: chordates, primates. The genus (plural genera) and species are italicized, with the genus capitalized and the species lowercased: *Homo sapiens*. If a variety is added, it is also italicized and lowercased, such as the lumper nomenclature for humans, *Homo sapiens sapiens*. ("*Sapiens*," by the way, means "wise"; ironic, when you consider the Nuclear Age.)

From Phylum to Class

The remainder of this chapter will use the **phenetic** system of taxonomy, partly because **cladistics** is counterintuitive, and partly because most or a plurality of biologists still use the phenetic scheme. We use phenetic analysis mostly because cladistics requires assumptions of evolutionary relationships among species that are yet to be demonstrated. One can also argue that humans and their ancestors share far more traits—full bipedalism (locomotion on two feet and legs), for example—than do chimpanzees and their close cousins, who are semi-bipedal (capable of bipedal locomotion only some of the time) at best. Nothing further will be discussed on the issue of cladistics versus phenetics, but you should be aware that it exists. One should also note that the categories are ever-changing, one of the rationales for biologists to argue for cladistics in the first place.

We begin with the broadest **taxon**, or biological category, the **kingdom**. There are five kingdoms, but we focus on the two broadest ones: the **plant** (Plantae) **kingdom**, those forms capable of producing their own food through the process of photosynthesis; and the **animal** (Animalia) **kingdom**, those forms that cannot produce their own food but must feed on other lifeforms, plants or animals, to thrive. We are animals in that sense, and the implications of that fact are discussed in chapter 6, on subsistence systems. We are animals also in that we are capable of independent movement, an attribute lacking in plants.

Of the 30 or so **phyla** (singular, **phylum**) we belong to the phylum **Chordata** (animals with a spinal cord running up and down our backs; this separates us from the starfish, sponges (how Spongebob Squarepants gets around bipedally is a mystery), insects, and spiders. We belong to the **subphylum Vertebrata** (vertebrates) because, unlike the tunicates, we have a protective bony (others have cartilagenous) spines protecting our spinal cord. We belong to the **class Mammalia** (mammals) because our females have lactating (milk-secreting) mammary glands, we have a self-regulating system, making us "warm blooded"; we give birth to live young, have hair, and have relatively large, complex brains. The complexities of mammal classification—the spiny anteater and the duckbilled platypus, both mammals, lay eggs rather than give birth to live young—are discussed by Park (2002: 133). As he notes, the "real world does not always make things easier for those of us who try to describe it" (2002:133). This is true for the rest of anthropology, as you will see.

Order: Primata

Among the 19 or so existing orders within the mammal class is the **order Primata** (primates), which include the prosimians (lemurs and tarsiers), the pongids (great apes, such as the chimpanzees, their cousins the bonobos, the gorillas, and the orangutans), the hylobates (lesser apes, such as the gibbons and siamangs), and the Old and New World monkeys—not to mention us modern *Homo sapiens* (humans, remember?). Once upon the time, primates included the tree shrew, but that form has been shunted over to the insect eaters (insectivores).

We the primates share many attributes. First is our visual orientation. We rely on **stereoscopic vision**, which involves the angling of our eyes in the same direction, thus enabling us to see things in three dimensions—depth perception, in other words. (Compare the angle of your eyes with the nearest convenient dog's; notice its eyes are not angled forward but to the sides.) We also see in color, while dogs see in black and white. In fact, we are more visual than other mammals, such as dogs, who rely on smell, or bats or dolphins, who rely on sonar; even so, our vision is not so acute as birds of prey (hawks, eagles, owls), who can spot their prey a mile away.

Second, primates have prehensile digits in the hands, and except for humans, in the feet. We can manipulate objects, and some of the great apes are capable of **brachiation**, or moving arm over arm in tree branches. We also have an **opposable thumb**, or a thumb that is capable of rotating around so that it comes in contact with the palm of the hand or the index finger. Except for us, most primates also have an opposable toe. It is mostly the twin abilities of finger flexibility and opposable toe that enabled us humans to become toolmakers and users. (Chimpanzees, whose East African members use termite sticks, have a rudimentary form of this ability.)

Third, we have a distinct pattern of **locomotion**. Although most primates are quadrupeds, in common with rodents, hoofed animals (deer, cattle), and felines (including big kitty cats known as tigers and lions), primates are also capable of bipedalism at least some of the time. We humans are the only habitual bipedal primates—and mammals. (We might pluck a chicken and say a human is a featherless biped—but how many chickens have you seen make and use tools, even a termite stick? Besides, they're birds—class Aves—not mammals.)

Fourth, primates' reproduction patterns are different. Compared to cats or dogs, females bear relatively few young and nurture their offspring for a relatively long time. (The same can be said of cattle and horses, but unlike primates, calves and colts can stand up shortly after birth—they don't need long periods of nurturing. See how complex nature really is?). Learned behavior also takes a longer time to acquire.

Fifth, compared to other mammals, primates have larger and more complex brains. The brain-to-body ratio is greater among primates than among other mammals. Sperm whales have brains of about 20 pounds; ours is about two. Still, a whale's body is 500 times the size of ours. Human brain size is three times the size one would expect for a primate of our body weight. In addition, the primate brain is more complex than other mammalian brains; the neocortex, that part of the brain where memory, abstract thought, problem solving, and attentiveness reside, is greater in primates. Primates have a longer learning period than other mammals, but their mental capabilities are greater.

Finally, primates are gregarious. Most other mammal species are solitary, and even those animals that move in groups—wolves in packs, antelopes in herds, or lions in prides—lack the complex gestures, calls, and touch that primates possess. Grooming, or combing the hair of another chimpanzee or baboon to remove dry skin, parasites, and dirt, is also a sign of reassurance lacking in other mammals. Primates interact in other ways: reassuring touch, large repertoires of vocalization, and facial expression. Only one species in this order possesses an efficient communication system we know as language: *Homo sapiens*.

Anthropoidea to Homo Sapiens

The taxonomy of ourselves takes us to a new level, so to speak. We part ways with suborder Prosimii, prosimians (literally, "before the simians, or monkeys and apes")—the lemurs, the lorises, the tarsiers—who don't look much like us and join the **suborder Anthropoidea,** ("humanlike") who do look like us. They include Old World and New World monkeys, great apes, (chimpanzees, bonobos, gorillas, and the somewhat more distantly related orangutans), lesser apes (gibbons and siamangs), and humans (including those that are now fossils). These subgroups vary considerably, but resemble each other more than they resemble prosimians.

The New World monkeys (infraorder Platyrrhini), besides the fact that they all live in the tropical rainforests of the New World, all have flat noses (hence the name platyrrhines, which means, well, "flat nose"). Their nostrils are widely spaced and separated by a broad septum (part of nose between the nostrils). They also have dental patterns different from their Old World counterparts; some New World monkeys have four extra premolars, while others have four fewer premolars; all Old World anthropoids have two premolars only. Finally, some New World monkeys have prehensile tails, which wrap around tree branches; none of the Old World monkeys has a prehensile tail.

The Old World monkeys and apes belong to **infraorder Catarrhini,** or anthropoids, whose nostrils are close together and face downward. They include members of superfamily Cercopithecoidea, comprising about 75 species of monkey. In addition to having the nasal shape and tooth number of all Old World anthropoids, most have nonprehensile tails. Also unlike the platyrrhines, cercopithecoids have fully opposable thumbs. Finally, unlike their New World counterparts, most are adapted to a wide range of habitats: tropical rainforests, open plains, even mountains (as is the case of Japanese macaques); the New World monkeys are found only in tropical rainforests.

Apart from cercopithecoids, Old World anthropoids include the **superfamily Hominoidea,** which includes the larger apes and humans. All hominoids lack tails, they have larger brains (both absolutely and relative to body size), and the neocortex of their brains are larger, meaning that they are capable of abstract thinking and a wider variety of communication modes. They also have a sophisticated ability to suspend from trees, with a flexible shoulder joint and appropriately placed scapula (shoulder bone) and clavicle (collar bone). Although we do not have the sophisticated ability to brachiate, as gibbons and the great apes do, we do have a similar structure, as gymnasts on high bars or rings inadvertently remind us. We reserve further discussion of their attributes for the section "Pongid-Hominid Comparative Anatomy."

Hominoids are grouped into three **families: Family Hylobatidae** include the so-called lesser apes, namely the gibbons (*Hylobates* with several species) and siamangs (*Hylobates syndactylus*), of Southeast Asia and Malaysia. Both the hylobates are the smallest of all the hominoids, both with a well developed **brachiation** mode of locomotion in trees, and both with an unusual form of social organization in that they live in male-female pairs and their offspring and not, unlike other hominoids, in larger groups.

The second subgroup is **family Pongidae,** or the great apes that comprise the orangutans (*Pongo pygmaeus*), who also live in Southeast Asia, and the chimpanzees (*Pan troglodytes*), the bonobos (*Pan paniscus*, sometimes known as "pygmy chimpanzees"), and the gorilla (*Gorilla gorilla*), all of Africa and all of whom live in arboreal (forest) environments. Some biologists have found a significant difference in the molecular composition between the orangutan and the African apes, and so have reclassified the chimpanzees, bonobos, and gorillas as **family Panidae,** leaving the orangutan the sole member of the pongid family.

Pongids, or panids, if you like, are larger in body size and weight than either the Old World monkeys or the hylobates; they have larger and more complex brains, and though quadrupeds, they have the ability to stand and walk on two legs briefly. All pongids are intimately familiar with their food sources, some of which grow seasonally or occur only in limited areas. Chimpanzees and bonobos eat meat on occasion, in addition to the fruits, nuts, and vegetables that all four species eat.

All pongids, including orangutans, have a wide repertoire of calls and, under experimental conditions, have learned to use the American Sign Language and other nonvocal versions of languages. Some also use tools, but not in all places at all times. Use of a stick for termite fishing, observed among the chimps at Gombe Stream Reserve, has not been observed in West Africa, although the chimps there do capture ants by using a branch. One could argue that this is one of the first signs of culture.

The third subgroup is **family Hominidae**, of which modern *Homo sapiens* is the sole survivor, although there are six billion of us and rapidly growing. We form a **species** because we are capable of reproducing fertile offspring, unlike horses and donkeys, whose offspring, mules, cannot reproduce. All other hominid species are extinct, known to us only through fossil forms.

Human physical characteristics are discussed and compared with pongid forms under "Comparative Pongid-Human Anatomy," and their evolution is discussed in two sections on early and late hominids. For now, we can summarize the distinct characteristics of *Homo sapiens*. First, we are naturally bipedal; we are the only primate with this ability. Much of our anatomy, not least because of our doubly arched feet, is centered around this ability. Second, we have the largest brain-to-body ratio among primates and, for that matter, all animal species. Third, and most important, we have the most complex brain, with the most highly developed neocortex, among all

species. Fourth, and as a product of brain complexity combined with a well developed speech mechanism, we are the only living species with a language. Fifth, we have the best developed hand structure, most flexible fingers, and most fully opposable thumb among all primates. Sixth, we have the ability to make and use tools, from handaxe to computer, partly because of the complexity of our brain and the complexity of our hands. Bipedalism also helps.

What about our forebears? From remains ranging from bone fragments to partial skeletons, we know that they walked on two legs—evidence of bipedalism goes as far back as 3.5 million years ago (m.y.a.). On the other hand, we have no idea when language developed among hominids, because brain matter and the important mechanism of speech—tongue, lingual nerves, even the small bones involved—decayed long ago. Tools give us a better idea—provided they are made of stone. The first confirmed tools in association with toolmakers are dated about 1.5 m.y.a. All of these are discussed below. First, we must know something about two aspects of human biological evolution: genetics and natural selection.

Mechanisms of Evolution

Human beings, like all other contemporary animals, are products of evolution. Although culture is the product of learning rather than genetics, our *capacity* for culture springs from our genes. Our genetic content changed in interaction with environmental forces over eons and eons. Therefore, we need to know something about genetics and then about natural selection.

Genetics

First things first. The basic building block of all life is the **cell,** or the smallest unit capable of performing all functions of a living organism. The billions upon billions of cells make up all the functioning parts of our bodies: brain, blood, muscle—the list goes on. The cell consists of two basic parts: (1) the **nucleus,** the structure inside the cell that contains the **chromosomes** that comprise, in turn, the **genes;** and (2) the **cytoplasm,** all the material found in a gelatin-like substance between the membrane of the nucleus and the wall of the cell.

Chromosomes are strings of hereditary material, which is made up of segments known as **genes,** which code for specific traits of the organism. In actuality, chromosomes and genes are strings of **deoxyribonucleic acid**—the DNA that you hear about in crime investigation shows and crime news. Unfortunately, space does not allow discussion of the molecular biology of genetics.

We can say, however, that each parent contributes half their genetic traits to their offspring. To understand the process, we need first to discuss the two major types of cell division, then show how traits are passed from parent to offspring.

Cell Division

In the process of **mitosis**, or division of **somatic** or body cells, division begins with the chromosomes (DNA) doubling in number (in humans, from 23 to 46 pairs). They then line up at the center of the cell as the walls of the nucleus dissolve. Fine fibrils then pull each pair of chromosomes toward the opposite end of the cell. Toward the final phases, a wall forms to separate the daughter cells, and two nuclei form around each pair of the new chromosomes.

The process of cell division is different for the **gametes**, or sex cells, of the organism: Gametes are **sperm** among the males and **ova** for the females. Sex cells divide initially in the same way as somatic cells. They then divide again, but this time without the chromosomes, or DNA molecules, replicating themselves. Half the number of human chromosomes remains in each sex cell, and so gametes are named a **haploid** cell. This process is known as **meiosis**. When the sperm fertilizes the ovum, a **zygote** (fertilized egg) forms with its complement of 46 chromosomes and develops into a human infant by mitosis, as described above.

Genotype and Phenotype

Chromosomes, or DNA, and their genes, determine the **traits**, or physical appearances of each life form. The term **genotype** refers to the genetic composition of the organism. The traits that actually appear are said to be its **phenotype**. How, then, does genotype translate into phenotype?

Remember that parents donate half their chromosomes to their offspring and that their chromosomes and their constituent genes are paired. Each gene is known as an **allele**. To take an oversimplified example, if the genetic attributes, say, for eye color, determine the same color, then phenotypically they are that color—blue or brown. The individuals are then said to be **homozygous**. If, however, one set of genes determines blue and the

second set determines brown, then the phenotypic eye color is most likely to be brown. The individuals are said to be **heterozygous** for eye color. In the Punnett Square below, consider the outcome of a brown-eyed (dominant allele B) person mating with a blue-eyed (recessive allele b) person:

	B	B
b	Bb	Bb
b	Bb	Bb

All the offspring will have brown eyes. The set of alleles for brown are said to be **dominant** and those for blue eyes are said to be **recessive**. Brown, not blue, appear as phenotypes, and only in the third generation will two recessive genes combine to appear as blue eyes; there is one chance in four for that outcome, as this Punnett Square shows:

	B	b
B	BB	Bb
b	Bb	bb

In actuality, several genes are involved in eye color, and other colors of eyes occur: green, gray, and various other shades.

Sometimes the two traits may be **codominant**. For example, four o'clocks, a species of flower, blend their respective colors. A red and a white four o'clock yields pink four o'clocks in the next generation. In the third generation, the chances of red, pink, and white flowers appearing are, respectively, 1:2:1.

Mutation

Ever so often, an "error" is made in the replication of cells. Sometimes genes may switch position, or a chemical change creates a new gene. Aging is thought to reflect cumulative mutation; cancer is the product, ultimately, of mutation as formerly healthy cells turn malignant. Such changes, however, are confined to individuals and do not necessarily pass to the next generation—unless the gametes are involved.

What affect populations are mutations in the gametes, or sex cells. Any change in the genetic composition of a sperm or ovum carries on into the next generation. Usually, mutations are **deleterious**, inasmuch as they render the individual maladapted to the environment. Persisting deleterious traits are usually recessive, so that persons with hemophilia have two recessive alleles for that condition. This gene survives, however, because it is "masked" in heterozygotes. Indeed, populations heterozygous for sickle cell anemia have immunity against malaria.

Much more rarely, mutations may prove highly adaptive, especially if an environment is changing or if they fill an empty niche in the environment. Mutations alone, however, are not sufficient to trigger evolutionary change. For this to happen, natural selection enters the picture.

Natural Selection

Popular conceptions attribute the theory of evolution to Charles Darwin. Actually, Darwin's contribution was his observations that environments favor some lifeforms over others, and that these spread at the expense of less adapted lifeforms. This summarizes the principle of **natural selection**, which we may formally define as genetic change in the frequency of certain traits in populations because of differential reproductive success between individuals. Sometimes the disadvantaged individuals die out and even entire species become extinct. Mutation proposes; natural selection disposes.

The combination of mutation and natural selection contributes to the process of **speciation**, or the process by which new species are developed from earlier ones. Usually, two populations of one species will become isolated in some way—one group may migrate, or a river may shift to separate one population into two. Over several generations, the populations have undergone enough mutations to render themselves mutually incapable of reproduction.

Other factors of evolutionary change include **gene flow**, the introduction of new genes to an existing population through migration. For small populations, **genetic drift** may increase the frequency of certain lifeforms by chance alone; genetic drift may also eliminate existing lifeforms.

For early hominids, one selective factor appears to have been the decimation of rainforests as rainfall decreased and savannas, or tropical grasslands, replaced the forests. The new hominids, enjoying the advantages of bipedalism, probably were able to avoid approaching predators, to peer over the grass in search of game, and to free their hands for making tools and weapons. This issue is taken up later in this chapter.

Pongid-Hominid Comparative Anatomy

The next question on the table is this: How do we know what we know about our ancestors? All we have from the past are skull fragments, perhaps some teeth, maybe what is left of limb bones or the digits of hands or feet. Once in a while we are lucky, and we recover 40 percent of the skeleton belonging to an *Australopithecus afarensis*, or a nearly complete skeleton of *Homo erectus*. We may be truly lucky and find a long-frozen body in the Alps around Northern Italy, with even its eyeballs intact.

The answer involves two elements: (1) thorough knowledge of human anatomy and anatomy of our closest relatives, the pongids (or panids, if you like); and (2) some long-shot assumptions as to the possible transition from early forms that looked like apes to forms that look human. Often the findings run counter to our expectation, and the search for the "missing link" is a stretch at best. Still we have to make the best use of what we have, and we do have a thorough knowledge of pongid and human anatomy. We first compare the skulls and particularly the **crania** (sing. **cranium**) or braincases of humans and chimpanzees. Next, we look at their facial features and jawbones. Finally, we compare their **postcranial skeletons**.

Human Skull and Braincase

The first noticeable characteristic is that the braincase, or **cranium**, of humans is rounded with a high forehead. The facial skeleton is located directly below the forehead. Pongids, in contrast, have a sloping forehead, suggesting a relatively underdeveloped **frontal lobe** of their brain, a topic discussed below. In humans, the forehead ends where the eye sockets begin, marked by a very slight **supraorbital torus**, or brow ridge. Chimpanzees and other pongids have a very heavy brow ridge in comparison. Furthermore, there is no **postorbital constriction**, unlike the pongids, whose depressions behind the brow ridges are very pronounced. Finally, we lack a *sagittal crest*; some pongids, especially male gorillas, have such a crest, to which some of their chewing muscles attach.

The skull itself is divided into four main bones, divided by sutures and each named corresponding to the part of the **cerebrum**, described below. The **frontal bone** is, as the name implies, located in a region from the forehead to the middle top and side of the skull. The **temporal bone** is located on the side of the skull, which we know as the temple. The **parietal bone** ranges from the middle top and side of the skull to the middle back. Finally, the **occipital bone** is located toward the lower back and base of the skull.

The presence of a forehead and rounded skull betrays the presence of a highly developed brain. For one thing, the braincase is the highest among the primates: an average of 1400 cubic centimeters (cc), as compared with roughly 400 cc among chimpanzees and 535 cc among gorillas. (Note that this is the size of the braincase, not the brain itself.)

In calculating the cranial capacity, one must also take body size into account, and by that measure, the human brain-to-body ratio is well beyond that of other primates, including our close pongid relatives. The proportion of brain relative to some other measure, such as body size, is known as **encephalization**. More precisely, the term refers to increases in brain size beyond that which would be expected given the body size of a particular species.

More to the point than brain or braincase size or body-to-brain ratios is the *structure* of the brain. This requires some background. The brain is divided into four major functional parts. The first part is the **brainstem**, which is involved with some of the body functions essential to life—breathing and the heartbeat for example. The second part is the **cerebellum**, immediately above the brainstem, which regulates all aspects of body movement, including balance and body position. The third part is the **limbic system**, which is involved with other basic bodily functions plus such impulses as sexual desire and self-protection through flight or fight.

Where a parting of the ways between ape and human takes place is the fourth part of the brain, the **cerebrum**, which is much more developed in humans than in pongids and other anthropoids. The cerebrum covers the top part of the brain and obscures the other parts. It is divided into two halves, or **hemispheres**. The **right hemisphere** controls the left side of the body and is also involved with spatial abilities, whereas the **left hemisphere** controls the right side of the body and also deals more extensively with language production and reception than does the right hemisphere. The two hemispheres are connected by nerve fibers that make up the **corpus callosum**.

Covering the entire cerebrum is the **cerebral cortex**, a layer about three millimeters (0.125 inches) thick; this part is also known as the **neo-**cortex, which governs abstract thought. The layer contains numerous convolutions, which increase the surplus of the cerebral hemispheres. Each of the two hemispheres is divided into four lobes by deep grooves; each lobe corresponds to the bones of the skull described above.

The **frontal lobes** (one to each hemisphere) constitute the largest part of the cerebrum. Located at the front underneath the **frontal bone**, this is the part that deals with purposive behavior. Behind the frontal lobes and ranging from the middle to the back part of the brain are the **parietal lobes**, which receive and process sensory information from the body. Located on either side of the brain are the **temporal lobes**, which process perception and memory; a section of this lobe, the **auditory cortex**, deals with hearing. Finally, at the low back of the brain are the **occipital lobes**, which handle visual information and are often called the **visual cortex** for that reason.

No discussion of the human brain can be complete without a review of the part of the brain that governs language. As stated above, most language activity is conducted in the **left hemisphere** of the brain. Two regions in particular are involved: **Broca's area**, which is involved with the production of spoken language; and **Wernicke's area**, which is involved with the perception of spoken language. The two areas are connected by a bundle of nerves known as the **arcuate fasciculus**, which connects Broca's and Wernicke's areas. In addition, there are **association areas** that are composed of thousands of neural (nerve) connections that integrate information from various parts of the cerebral cortex. For example, information related to senses of vision, smell, touch, and hearing is first combined and then sent to Broca's area for speech production. This and other integrative roles are performed by the **angular gyrus**, located in the parietal region, whose role it is to integrate multimodal (i.e., sight, sound, touch, taste, and smell) information from the senses.

Facial and Dental Anatomy

This is where the anatomical aspects of the face come in, much of which is involved in speech production. The face includes the **nasal bones**, which support the nose's structure; the **maxilla**, or upper jaw; and the **mandible**, or lower jaw. Moreover, the jaw does not jut out; in other words, there is little or no **prognathism** among humans, in contrast with pongids and early hominids, the jutting of whose jaw is very prominent. The mandible is reinforced with a **chin** rather than, as in apes, a bone structure in the inside curve of the mandible called a **simian shelf**.

Turning to the teeth, humans and pongids have different tooth characteristics and arrangements. First is the large size of the **canine tooth** among the apes—so large, in fact, that a gap is present in the opposite jaw known as the **diastema**. Second, pongid teeth are arranged in a squarish **dental arcade**, with the back teeth (**premolars** and **molars**) in parallel rows and the front teeth (**incisors** and **canines**) rounded toward the front. Also, unlike humans, the front teeth of pongids are placed at a forward angle rather than vertically. The enamel caps of the teeth of many pongids are thinner than those of humans. There is one similarity, however: all Old World anthropoids, apes and humans included, have the same **dental formula**, or same numbers of tooth types: two incisors, one canine, two premolars, and three molars (2.1.2.3) in both the upper and lower jaws.

Speech Anatomy

More important from the standpoint of human evolution are the lingual nerves and muscles related to speech. The specific mechanisms of speech will be covered in chapter 4 on descriptive linguistics. However, there are some developments that provide background to **articulatory phonetics** and the **articulators**, especially the tongue. First, both humans and chimpanzees have a **hypoglossal nerve**, which runs from the brain through an opening as one of 12 cranial nerves that do not pass through the foramen magnum. It ends up under the tongue (hence the term, which means "under the tongue") and branches out into several nerves that serve the muscles of the tongue. The hypoglossal nerve in humans is three times the size of a chimpanzee's, and involves many more nerve endings for the tongue muscles. This enables humans to make many more utterances—speech sounds or **phones**—than the chimpanzees.

Also important to speech is the very small and fragile **hyoid bone**, which anchors muscles connected to the tongue, the larynx, and the jaw. The **larynx**, or voice box, contains **vocal cords**, important to the voice in speech production. It is located far down in the throat, compared to that of the chimpanzee and other pongids, thereby allowing greater resonance in the mouth during utterances.

Hand and Arms

One of the attributes that have been thought to be distinctly human is the ability to make and use tools. Indeed, a title of a supplementary text issued in the 1960s is *Man the Toolmaker*. Since then, studies carried out by Goodall in the Gombe Stream Reserve have shown that chimpanzees are capable of making and using simple tools, such as a termite stick, a sponge wadded from leave to absorb water, and even sleeping platforms (Goodall 1986). Nevertheless, pongid-made tools lack the sophistication of even the earliest stone tools, let alone house construction, combustion engine manufacture, or computer assembly.

Much of it involves a sophisticated brain that is capable of conceiving the design of a tool or product. This conception, called **displacement**, involves the ability to speak about, and therefore think about, objects that are not present, that are abstract, or that do not even exist. This is discussed further in chapter 5, on descriptive linguistics.

No less important is the ability to make fine manipulations with their hands and fingers (**metacarpals** or hand bones, and **phalanges,** or fingers), articulated with our lower arms (**radius** and **ulna**). If we compare the human with the chimpanzee hand, we find that we have far greater ability to manipulate objects than do other primates. First, the thumb is much larger in humans than in chimpanzee hands. Second, although the thumbs of both humans and chimpanzees are opposable, the product of a saddle configuration that allows the thumb to be directly opposed to the other fingers, the human thumb has a higher degree of movement than the pongids'. Moreover, the pongid fingers are curved, reflecting an ability to move around in the trees; the human fingers are straight. Third, both pongid and human hands are capable of making a **power grip**, whereby the individual grabs an object between the palm and the fingers; grasping a hammer is one example. They both can make a **precision grip**, whereby the animal holds an object, say a pen, between the thumb and forefingers, thanks to the opposable thumb. However, humans have developed *precision manipulation*, neither found nor possible among other primates. The wider range of thumb opposability and the noncurvature of human fingers are partial factors.

Toolmaking is facilitated with the **clavicle**, or collar bone, and **scapula**, or shoulder bone. Their structure is such that we are able to rotate our upper arm, or **humerus**, and so can move large and heavy objects such as wooden beams or boulders. Try doing this with a dog or cat—or better yet, don't. That would be cruelty to animals.

Bipedalism, Quadrupedalism, and the Postcranial Skeleton

A sentence describes the postcranial skeleton of humans and pongids: The human skeleton is oriented toward **bipedalism**, or the ability to walk on two feet, whereas the pongid skeleton is oriented toward **quadrupedalism**, or the ability to walk on all four feet. Discussion of the adaptations of a postcranial skeleton to either of these modes of locomotion could take up the entire book, indeed several books. We confine our comment to the most important adaptations here.

We start where it begins: the feet. The human foot is supported by a dual **arch**, in which the **metatarsals** (bones on the main part of the foot itself) form a **longitudinal arch**, starting with the ball, or first metatarsal of the foot, forming an arc between the five metatarsals and the first and second cuneiform (two of the inner bones of the **tarsals** or ankle bones) and ending in the **calcaneus**, or heel bone. The second arch begins in the outer fifth metatarsal bone and gradually arises to the elevated first metatarsal at the inner side of the foot. Furthermore, unlike the chimpanzee, the largest toe (**phalange**) of the human foot is nonopposable. Given the arch and the rigidity of the foot at large, the human individual is capable of walking on two feet. Indeed, she or he has little choice, the defining characteristic of **obligate bipedalism**.

Unlike the human foot, the chimpanzee has an opposable big toe, enabling it to move about in the trees as well on the ground; it can grasp branches with both hands and feet. Second, the chimpanzee lacks an arch, thereby compromising its ability to walk bipedally on the ground—although it can do so with difficulty.

Moving up, we find that the **pelvises** of the two species are also different. The human pelvis is short, with an **ilium**, the upper blade of the pelvis, forming a large surface on which the **gluteus maximus**, an extensor of the leg (**femur** or thighbone), that allows for running and climbing, is attached. (Be respectful of your rear end; you can't move without it.) Other muscles, the **gluteus minimus** and **gluteus medius**, serve as abductors, which move the thigh away from the midline of the body and maintain balance while walking. The pelvis is bowl

shaped, enabling it not only to permit bipedal mobility, but also to support the upper trunk of an upright body. The front part of the pelvis is formed by a **pubic bone**, which reinforces its bowl-shaped structure. Finally, the **femur** (thighbone) angles inward from the pelvis toward the **patella** (kneecap), bringing the knees together for better balance.

In contrast, the chimpanzee pelvis is elongated rather than curved, and lacks a bowl-shaped structure. The chimpanzee ilium is far longer and narrower than the human one, and its muscle attachments are consistent with quadrupedal locomotion. The chimpanzee must bend its leg at the knee, which humans need not do. It doesn't help that the thighbone does not angle inward. Consequently, the bipedal gait of the chimpanzee is awkward at best. Both the chimpanzee and the gorilla are more proficient at **knuckle walking**, whereby the knuckles of their hand form part of the locomotion.

Going upward still, we find that the human vertebrae adapt to a bipedal stance by developing an S-shaped curvature, and by the increase in vertebra size from the top, or **cervical** (neck) **vertebrae**, down to the larger **thoracic vertebrae** at the rib cage, and downward still to the largest **lumbar vertebrae** below the rib cage, and so to the pelvis. This configuration enables the vertebrae to support the trunk upright, although lower back pain is a common complaint. In contrast, the chimpanzee's vertebral column is bow shaped, similar to other quadrupeds, and the size of the vertebrae do not increase in size from the thoracic to the lumbar regions as the human one does.

Reaching finally to the top, parts of the skull reflect the human ability to walk on two legs. The **foramen magnum** ("big hole"), is located at the base of the skull, far forward of that of any other species of primate or mammal; the large **spinal cord** passes through it. In contrast, the chimpanzee's foramen magnum, as with other partial and full quadrupeds, is angled further back. The **occipital condyles**, smooth knobs on either side of the foramen magnum, articulate the skull with the **cervical vertebrae**, the topmost vertebrae that support the skull and the neck. Neck muscles connect with the **nuchal ridge** and the area where the **nuchal muscles** (muscles of the back of the neck) are attached. In quadrupeds, including pongids, the foramen magnum and occipital condyles are angled further toward the back, and the nuchal crest is larger, allowing more area for the nuchal muscles to attach to support the head of a quadruped.

To sum up, the human skeletal and muscle structure reflect the human ability to stand up and walk on two feet. This frees their hands for other purposes, including making and using tools. An increased cranial capacity and a restructured brain allows for language and an ability to think—and thereby a capacity for culture.

Early Hominids: The Way We Were

Contrary to much of the beliefs throughout the Bible Belt, we were neither created in six days nor were our ancestors spitting images of ourselves. Furthermore, paleoanthropologists do not argue that humankind descended from the apes. In fact, there is much reason to believe that at some point in time, the great apes and we had a common ancestor. who may be as elusive as the so-called Missing Link.

In the next two sections, we trace the likely lines of hominid evolution from the fragmentary evidence of *Ardipithecus* through *Australopithecus* and the robust *Paranthropus* to *Homo habilis* and *Homo erectus* to the archaic *Homo heidelbergensis* and *Homo neanderthalensis* to modern *Homo sapiens*. In the section following, we discuss the tools in possible association some australopithecines and the confirmed association between tool traditions and various species of the genus *Homo*. The chapter ends with a discussion of human physical variation that folk taxonomists call "race."

Our journey begins with the oldest known member of the family Hominidae, *Ardipithecus*, which, based on fragmentary evidence, is the most apelike of the hominids. *Ardipithecus ramidus* (the genus meaning "ground ape" and the species name meaning "root" in the Afar language) is represented by 17 fragments found in Aramis, Ethiopia, including two skull bases, a child's mandible, and some teeth and arm bones found in 1992 and 1993 (Gee 1995:272).

Dated at 4.4 million years ago (m.y.a.), *Ardipithecus ramidus* is considered a hominid because the foramen magnum is placed further forward than those of apes, and the vertical root of the canine is hominid, unlike the angled placement among apes. The arm bones also suggest they were not used in locomotion; this and other skeletal attributes hint at **obligate bipedalism**. Other attributes are apelike: the canine teeth are larger than in other hominids, and the foramen magnum is placed toward the back compared with modern humans; also, apelike are a flattened cranial base and the thin enamel on the molar caps (Wolpoff 1999).

The remaining early hominids are collectively known as **australopithecines** with two genera: **Australopithecus** and the much more robust (though not larger) **Paranthropus**. The oldest of the australopithecines is *Australopithecus anamensis* (the genus name meaning "southern ape-man" and the species name meaning "lake"; its remains were found at Lake Turkana, Kenya). Dated between 4.2 and 3.8 m.y.a., the remains consist of jaws, teeth, a skull fragment, a tibia and fibula (two lower leg bones) and other leg bones, and a humerus (upper arm). Although they resemble an ape with its large canine and parallel tooth rows, *Australopithecus anamensis* also has important hominid traits. The tooth enamel is thicker than in pongids, the teeth vertically placed, the knee and ankle joints consistent with bipedalism, and the fibula intermediate between a pongid and hominid. Experts differ on whether A. *anamensis* is a direct hominid ancestor and *Ardipithecus ramidus* represents an evolutionary side branch. (Leakey and Lewin 1995; C. Ward et al 1999).

The next oldest, and one of the best documented, australopithecine hominids is *Australopithecus afarensis*, the species of the much-celebrated Lucy. Lucy, named after the Beatles song "Lucy in the Sky with Diamonds," is a female hominid found in 1974 at an extinct lakeside in Hadar, Ethiopia, by Donald Johansen and his team. Because about 40 percent of her skeleton (practically all postcranial—there were few skull fragments) was intact, and because of the 300 other fragments since discovered (including a nearly complete skull found in 1995), there is much that can be said about Lucy and her kind. The range of dates falls somewhere between 3.7 and 3.0 m.y.a. (Johansen 1974).

First of all, evidence abounds that they were all bipeds. Five sets of footprints found in Laetoli, Tanzania, imprinted on volcanic ash that later hardened, and dated 3.7 m.y.a. clearly established the bipedalism of their owners, probably A. *afarensis* (M. Leakey 1979).

The reconstructed A. *afarensis* specimens had common characteristics, The dual arch (transverse and longitudinal) was plain to see, and the big toe was nonopposable to the other digits. The pelvis was bowl shaped, and the vertebrae suggest an

S-shape, characteristic of hominid bipeds. Nevertheless, the toes and fingers were curved, suggesting they spent at least some of their lives in the trees. Their arms were, in proportion to their height, longer than human arms, another apelike feature, and like the chimpanzees', their thumbs were short.

Turning to the skull, it was clear, as Johanson puts it, that A. afarensis was no smart ape (or hominid, for that matter). The cranial capacity ranged from 380 to 500 cc, with the mean average standing at 440 cc (the chimps' cranial capacity averages 400 cc). There is a constriction (or depression) behind the brow ridge called the **postorbital constriction**, betraying an underdeveloped frontal lobe of the brain. The forehead sloped from back to front, indicating a small frontal lobe in the cerebrum. The face showed a significant *prognathism*, or jutting jaw; a chin was absent; the teeth were large, there were large canines and corresponding **diastema**, and a slight sagittal crest at the top of the skull, all consistent with pongids. On the other hand, the dental arcade was more rounded than that of apes, the foramen magnum was placed forward, in common with other hominids (a bipedal attribute), and the teeth were heavily enameled.

Australopithecus africanus, dated between 2.3 and 3.0 m.y.a., comes later than A. *africanus* but seems to bear many attributes as hominids. Found mostly in South Africa with a couple of likely East African sites (Lake Turkana and Omo), A. *africanus* is less prognathous than A. *afarensis*, its jaws are more rounded, and it lacks a sagittal crest. On the other hand, its average cranial capacity, at 440 cc, is no different from A. *afarensis*, though one specimen measures at 515 cc; its canines are larger than those of Lucy and her kind, and it may have longer arms and legs than its *afarensis* counterpart. Otherwise, its pelvis, its lower legs and feet, and the placement of its foramen magnum are consistent with bipedal locomotion.

A peculiar set of hominids belong to the genus *Paranthropus*, although scholars differ about evenly whether they should belong to the genus *Australopithecus* instead. Because of their morphology and robustness (large bone size) compared with their other australopithecine counterparts, I will use the genus *Paranthropus* here. Called *Zinjanthropus* ("dawn man") by Louis Leakey after his wife Mary discovered its teeth—much larger than human teeth—this form has many hominid and pongid attributes, yet its date ranges between 1.0 and 2.2 m.y.a.—almost one million years *after Australopithecus africanus* made its appearance.

There are at least three major species of *Paranthropus*: P. *aethiopicus*, P. *boisei*, and P. *robustus*. Some would regard P. *aethiopicus* as ancestral to the other genera of *Paranthropus*. At 410 cc, its cranial capacity is one of the smallest among adult hominids, yet its sagittal crest is the largest, and its face the most prognathous, with a very large area in the jaw to accommodate its back teeth (which were not found). This skull, found at Lake Turkana in Kenya, and the bone fragments found in Ethiopia, are dated between 1.8 and 2.2 m.y.a, somewhat later than A. *africanus* (2.3–3.0 m.y.a.).

The other two species differ somewhat from their presumed ancestor—cranial capacity, for one. The one skull found of P. *robustus* measures 520 cc. P. *boisei* specimens, to which *Zinjanthropus* was later reclassified, have cranial capacities ranging from 500 to 530 cc, with a mean of 515. Both P. *boisei* and P. *robustus* have a relatively flat face, unusual for an australopithecine and a stern reminder that not all "apelike" versus "humanlike" attributes move along a smooth evolutionary continuum. In contrast with A. *africanus*, but somewhat like P. *aethiopicus*, the robust forms have heavy, large jaws, large back teeth, and large sagittal crests, all apelike attributes. Their arms are also long. On the other hand, they have hands similar to modern human forms, and feet consistent with bipedal locomotion.

There are other species of *Australopithecus* and possible other genera. For example, Maeve Leakey, granddaughter of Louis and Mary Leakey, and her team discovered a unique specimen—distorted cranium and mandible—dated at 3.5 m.y.a. Called *Kenyanthropus platyops* ("flat-faced man from Kenya"), this specimen has the cranial capacity, dental features, and details of nasal structure similar to australopithecines. Its face, however, is flat (hence the species name); it has a tall, vertically oriented cheek area, and lacks the depression behind the brow ridges one finds in australopithecines—hinting at a better developed frontal lobe (M. Leakey et al. 2001). Other species have been found in distant association with tools. *Australopithecus garhi*, for example, was found at the same level of a site as stone tools, leading some to speculate that the individual may have sliced off the meat of game, whose remains were also found at the site. The association between australopithecine and tools was not close enough to be conclusive (Heinzelin et al. 1999).

To sum up, the australopithecines showed many human attributes: skeletal structures consistent with bipedalism; hands not unlike human ones, with a possible potential to make and use tools (but no conclusive evidence); some dental evidence, such as a rounded jaw; and the like. On the other hand, they showed many apelike characteristics: long arms relative to the body, large teeth (including large canines among *afarensis*), prognathous faces, sagittal crests in some, and relatively small cranial capacities. Were they toolmakers? There is no direct evidence—only speculation. Given chimpanzees' abilities to make termite or ant sticks, to hunt cooperatively, and to construct sleeping platforms, it is reasonable to suggest that australopithecines may have had similar abilities. Direct evidence is lacking, however.

Late Hominids and Their Tools: What We Became

It is only with hominids of the genus *Homo* that we find the first confirmed evidence of tool manufacture. We begin with *Homo habilis* ("handyman" or perhaps "handyperson") the first confirmed maker and user of stone tools. We also look at the tradition associated with them: the so-called Oldowan tradition, namely choppers and other **core tools** and the **flake tools** that they **knapped**.

We then look at *Homo erectus* ("erect man," harking back to the days when experts thought they were the first hominid who stood erect and called this species *Pithecanthropus erectus*, or "erect apeman"), which was the first to make tools with the sophistication of handaxes, though not all populations had them, nor were they all cores. We include *Homo ergaster*, thought by some splitters to warrant a separate category.

Finally, we look at the early variants of archaic and modern *Homo sapiens*, namely *Homo heidelbergensis*, *Homo neanderthalensis*, and, at last, our own kind, *Homo sapiens*. They all in turn created ever more sophisticated tools: We look at the **Levalloisian tradition**, in which flake blanks were knapped from cores prepared specifically for that purpose, then fashioned for their specific function. This technique is generally associated with *Homo heidelbergensis*. We then examine the **Mousterian tradition**, often associated with *Homo neanderthalensis*, with an assemblage of 63 types of tools. Finally, we look at the tools in the *Upper Paleolithic* and **Mesolithic**, and the increased specialization they entailed as modern *Homo sapiens* gained ascendancy worldwide.

Homo Habilis and the Oldowan Tradition

After it became clear to everyone that *Zinjanthropus* was not the "dawn man" or even the first toolmaker—with massive jaws and muscles to chew tough stems, roots, and nuts with their hard shells, who needs tools?—it became evident that the choppers and flake tools must have been created by some other hominid. After searching around their site at Olduvai Gorge (for which the Oldowan tradition is named), Mary Leakey again made an important find in 1961: a second hominid from the same level at Olduvai as the first. They named this hominid *Homo habilis*, or "handyman" (or "handyperson") because of its close association with hundreds of core and flake tools they had known about since Louis first visited Olduvai Gorge in 1931.

In many respects, *Homo habilis* and related hominids (such as *H. rudolfensis*, which splitters put in a separate taxon) are similar to australopithecines; their cranial capacities overlap (at 500 cc) with the robust australopithecines, the teeth of some are similar to *A. africanus*, their arms are relatively long, and they are still prognathous, though less so than their predecessors. Their brain-to-body ratio is similar to those of australopithecines, though their brains are generally larger.

On the other hand, the average cranial capacity of *H. erectus* is 680 cc, fully 160 cc greater than the average cranial capacity of robust australopithecines (515 cc), and 240 cc greater than that of *A. africanus* (440 cc). Their faces are flatter, with less of a sloping forehead and less of a postorbital constriction than the australopithecines—an important indication that the frontal lobe may have been more developed. They have no sagittal crest, unlike the robust forms. Most important of all, *H. habilis* is the first hominid whose association with stone tools is confirmed. The time period for *H. habilis* ranges between 1.6 and 2.4 m.y.a.

Flintknapping. Compared to modern technology, or even with stone tools that later proliferated, they were nothing to write home about. Often, it is difficult, even among experts, to distinguish cores and flakes knapped by humans from those that broke off naturally. Nevertheless, the selection of stones to knap, the planning involved before striking the first blow, and the hand-eye coordination the process requires involve hominids who have the mental and the manual coordination to pull it all off. So far, all evidence points to *H. habilis* as the first to meet these requirements.

First, the **flintknapper** (one who produces stone tools by the **hard hammer**, **soft hammer**, or **pressure technique**, even if the material is other than flint) has to select an appropriate lump of stone. Such stone has to be **crystalline**, that is, with a repeating arrangement of its atoms, so that its fracture is regular when the stone is struck. **Flint** is one of the most common crystalline rock, the glasslike **obsidian** is highly valued for that quality, and so is the pale colored *chert*. Other crystalline stone includes agate, jasper, basalt, and even the more fragile slate.

Second, the flintknapper has to judge exactly the correct angle by which to hit the **striking platform** (point of impact) of the rock to be fashioned into a tool or prepared core. The angle cannot exceed 90 degrees, and the stoneworker has to be aware of the pattern of fracture that will be created thereby. Fractures are conchoidal in shape, something like the conch shell of a limpet or other object shaped like a shallow cone. This comes with practice, something modern humans can learn, but which might have been difficult to grasp among australopithecines.

Third, the flintknapper has to know when to use the **hard hammer technique**, or the technique whereby he (or she) strikes the lump of stone to be knapped with another stone (the **hammerstone**); and when to switch to a **soft hammer technique**, that is, to use antler, ivory, or wood to start doing finer work. Finally, at some point, the flintknapper has to use an implement—a sharpened piece of wood or bone, perhaps—to employ a **pressure technique** to remove the rough edges of the worked piece and otherwise **retouch** it.

As one can see, at some point there was a quantum leap from stripping leaves of a twig and inserting it into a termite hill, then withdrawing and licking off the termites clinging onto the twig, to actually manufacturing a stone tool that took much planning and skill. Until we find evidence to the contrary, this quantum leap took place between the most advanced australopithecines and the least developed member of the genus *Homo*.

Oldowan Tradition.   The first known tools consisted of two types: **core tools**, or the lumps of stone

that themselves were fashioned into tools; and **flake tools**, those chips that were knapped and were themselves fashioned into tools. Of course, not all flakes were made into tools. Some were **debitage**, or **waste flakes**, that were disposed of or otherwise unused. Then there are **prepared cores**, cores that are themselves not intended to be tools but rather those that are knapped to certain shapes so as to knap flakes, which will then be fashioned into tools. At first, authorities thought that Oldowan tools might be all cores, leaving the flakes as debitage. Further analyses have established that flake tools were important, perhaps more so, for the flintknappers identified with the Oldowan tradition.

What, then, is the **Oldowan tradition**? This tradition refers to the relatively simple technique of knapping a few flakes, anywhere between two or three up to ten. First, the flintknapper strikes off the flake on one side of the stone being worked, turns it over, and strikes the second side. After a few more blows, the flintknapper has a core tool with a sharp edge (albeit with a lot of **cortex** or unworked surface left) with which to cut the meat or break the bone of an animal to get at its marrow. There are several sharp-edge flakes left, too, which the flintknapper can use, also. Microscopic analysis showed that the edges of many flakes had a polish, demonstrating that they had been used for a variety of tasks, such as cutting meat, stripping meat off a bone, or sawing wood and bone. Cleavers, scrapers, and unidentified discoid tools have been found at Oldowan sites, both at Olduvai Gorge (Tanzania) and such sites as Lake Turkana in Kenya, Omo in Ethiopia, Uraha in Malawi, and possibly Sterkfontein and Swartkrans in South Africa.

Homo Erectus and the Acheulean Tradition

The next major shift in both biological and cultural evolution of hominids takes place between 1.78 and 0.1 m.y.a (i.e., 1,780,000 and 100,000 years ago; henceforth expressions in thousands will be referred to as B.P., or before the present). This shift is represented by the several variety of *Homo erectus*, although there are **splitters** who would divide this genus up to six species. One such are the hominids located on the eastern and western shores of Lake Turkana, Kenya; the best known is the so-called Turkana Boy (labeled KMN-WT 15000, which translates as the 15,000th find at West Turkana in the cataloguing system of the Kenya National Museum). This specimen is one of the best preserved skeletons, including skulls, in the history of biological anthropology so far.

Starting with the skull, the cranial capacity of *Homo erectus* ranges from 800 to 1250 cc, with a mean of about 1000 cc, an average exceeding that of *H. habilis* by 320 cc. More important, the frontal bone of the *H. erectus* skull slopes less than does that of *H. habilis*, and the postorbital constriction is reduced, both features indicating that the frontal lobe may have developed. The dentition is closer to modern humans; the dental arcade is rounded, and the diastema is absent. The entire postcranial skeleton is modern. The length of the arms is proportional to the body, as in modern humans, parting ways with *H. habilis* and the australopithecines in that respect.

Nevertheless, some apelike characteristics are still present in the skull of *Homo erectus*. For example, there is a sagittal keel, but it is not anything like the sagittal crest of its robust australopithecine counterparts; indeed, chewing muscles probably did not reach that high in the skull and it lacked the massive back teeth of the robust forms. Furthermore, there is still a pronounced brow ridge, and though reduced, the postorbital constriction is still present. The skull also has a pronounced **occipital torus**, a reminder that the earlier forms once had massive nuchal muscles and a highly placed nuchal crest of earlier hominids—and pongids. The face is still significantly prognathous, and there is still no chin at the mandible.

The *Homo erectus* remains at Lake Turkana (including "Turkana boy") are categorized by some as *Homo ergaster* (meaning "work man," in reference to the numerous tools also found at the site.) Their justification for creating a new species lies in the fact that one skull is thinner and higher in profile. However, the thinness of the skull may reflect **sexual dimorphism**. A similar skull from East Turkana is much more rugged in construction, and may have been a male. In all other respects, the skulls are similar in morphology; their average cranial capacity is 850 cc, well within the range of *H. erectus* sizes. The nearly complete skeleton of Turkana Boy differs little from other specimens outside the region.

There is another characteristic: *Homo erectus* did not stay in Africa; it migrated to the Near East, to Europe, and to Asia in China and southeast Asia. Indeed, the first find of *H. erectus* was made by a Dutch military physician, Eugene DuBois, in 1891 at Trinil, Java, a province of what is now Indonesia. Thinking he had discovered the "missing link" between apes and modern humans, he named his specimen *Pithecanthropus erectus* ("erect ape-man"), a term that stuck until about the 1970s. Why they could migrate such a distance is, as they say, another story.

Acheulean Tradition.   What we do know about *H. erectus* is that the tools it made far exceeded the quality of work of Oldowan tools. The classic artifact is the **Acheulean handaxe**, although handaxes were not the only tools *H. erectus* made, nor was this type of handaxe found everywhere. Furthermore, Oldowan tools were found in association with *H. erectus* remains.

Acheulean handaxes are usually teardrop shaped, with the entire cortex removed. Some compare it with a Swiss Army knife, with its several types of blades and tools in one instrument. The axe is pointed at one end, which may have been used for piercing; the edges may have been used for cutting, and the rounded end, also sharpened, may have been used for chopping. Compared with Oldowan choppers, usually made with ten strikes or fewer, the typical Acheulean handaxe involves anywhere between 50 and 100 strikes. There are indications that transitional types evolved during the 1.5 million years between Oldowan chopper, through the asymmetrical **Abbevillian** design, to the symmetrical pattern of the Acheulean variety.

Not all *H. erectus* populations had handaxes; indeed, there is a imaginary line drawn northward from central India, known as the **Movius line** (after the archaeologist Hallam Movius, who first described it), east of which the handaxes are absent. No satisfactory explanation has been advance to explain why. The caves at Zhoukoudian, located near Beijing, China, represent a classical site associating the remains of more than 40 *H. erectus* individuals, together with thousands of animal remains and a tool assemblage that included burins (engravers), scrapers, projectile points, and even choppers reminiscent of the Oldowan tradition—but no handaxes. With the outbreak of the war in 1937, excavations ceased and the fossils were lost in 1941; their whereabouts are unknown to this day. Some *H. erectus* sites in Asia yield no tools at all, including Trinil, Indonesia. Whether the inhabitants used tools of perishable materials, such as bamboo, bone, or wood, is unknown, but none of stone has been found.

Another possible innovation of *H. erectus* involves the use and control of fire. The earliest evidence of fire may have been at a site in Swartkrans, South Africa, where burnt bones, though no hearths, were probably present 1.3 m.y.a. Fire may have been present at the Zhoukoudian site, again as indicated by burnt animal bones, but no hearths were found in the caves themselves.

Homo Heidelbergensis and the Levallois Tradition

We now come closer to *Homo sapiens* as we know the species today. In fact, so diverse are the so-called archaic *Homo sapiens* forms that various authorities have come up with various names. They range from lumping archaic with modern forms as one species, to assigning a wide variety of species names; one of the latter is *Homo heidelbergensis*, after a site near Heidelberg, Germany. A plurality of paleoanthropologists have assigned this name to cover all archaic forms other than Neanderthal, and so I will adopt it here.

The specific characteristics vary by location: some have greater prognathism than others; some have thicker skull or long bones than others. Common attributes include greater robustness than modern forms, with slightly lower average cranial capacities than modern forms—1280 cc as compared with 1400 cc—larger brow ridges in some specimens, and various degrees of roundness of skull. That localities differ considerably is shown by the fact that at the Ileret site in Kenya, the cranial capacity of one specimen is 1400 cc, but with heavy brow ridges. It is dated as 300,000 B.P. On the other hand, the Ndutu cranium in Tanzania has a cranial capacity of 1100 cc and shows a much more rounded profile than the Ileret or other specimens; it is dated as 200,000 B.P., 100,000 years later than the Ileret specimen. Similar variation is shown at other African sites, in Europe, and in Asia.

Levallois Tradition. Early *Homo sapiens*, or *Homo heidelbergensis*, forms continued to use all kinds of tools invented earlier: Oldowan choppers, Acheulean handaxes west of the Movius line, and flakes of various levels of quality. The new technology generally associated with *Homo heidelbergensis*, however, is the **Levalloisian tradition.** This entails first preparing a core, as described above, for the express purpose of making specialized flake tools.

Once the core is prepared, the flintknapper strikes a series of flakes.

Compared with the Oldowan or even the Acheulean tradition, the Levalloisian tradition reflects finer control over the form and function of the flake. How the core is prepared depends on the kinds of flake tools the maker wants: projectile points, knives, burins, scrapers. The flintknapper then retouches the flake as desired. The technique also reflects a more efficient use of the stone module, compared with the Acheulean tradition. One study shows that as many as five flakes could be knapped from a single Levallois core (Bradley in Gamble 1986).

Neanderthals and the Mousterian

Probably no presapient specimen has received worse press than *Homo neanderthalensis* (or as the splitter would have it, *Homo sapiens* and neanderthalensis, thereby placing it in the same species as modern humans). Neanderthals are named after the Neander Valley, Germany, where early specimens were found and identified. The stereotype of the stooping brute wearing animal skins, club in hand, ultimately came from an arthritic specimen. It is true that Neanderthal forms were larger boned than modern humans, had a protruding face (though not as prognathous as *H. habilis* or *H. erectus*), larger eye brows, sloping forehead, and a large mass of bone to the rear of the skull. It also lacked a chin.

However, the cranial capacity of Neanderthals averaged 1450 cc, slightly higher than the 1400 cc of modern humans; when brain-to-body ratio is factored in, the difference is insignificant. Furthermore, the postcranial skeleton, apart from the larger size of most bones, was indistinguishable from modern humans.

Mousterian Tradition. The question regarding the phylogenic status of *Homo neanderthalensis* in part hinges on its cultural products, particularly tool manufacture and use. The **Mousterian tradition**, one in which a wider assemblage of specialized tools emerges, is generally associated with *Homo neanderthalensis*. Francois Bordes identifies 63 varieties of tools in this tradition, including notched tools (possibly used to smooth spear shafts—no bows and arrows are found in association with Neanderthals). Other tools include denticulate implements (those with two or more notches), burins, scrapers of several kinds, projectile points for spears, and a handaxe known as the Mousterian of the Acheulean type. Bordes offers a five-fold functional categorization of these tools: cutting, slicing, piercing, scraping, sawing, and pounding.

Besides tools, other cultural attributes are found in association with Neanderthals. There are signs they were compassionate beings. Thus, at Shanidar Cave, Iraq, a male skeleton showed several serious but healed bone fractures; despite apparent blindness in the left eye, amputation of the lower right arm, and signs of a diseased right leg, he had survived to middle age, suggesting that he received care over several years. Mortuary practices are also indicated by the flexed position of the body, unmodified animal remains, ochre (a red paint), and tools; they are found at Shanidar, at several sites in France, and at three sites in Israel, among others. On the other hand, there are also signs of cannibalism, as indicated in Krapina Cave, Croatia, where human bones had been burnt, split for extracting marrow, and disposed of in the same way as animal bones were disposed of.

Language. One of the poorest paleoanthropological pieces of evidence is that for language, or other physical indicators of capacity for culture. One conclusive bit of evidence that Neanderthals did have language is found at Kebara Cave, Israel, where a humanlike hyoid bone was recovered from a Neanderthal specimen. Although we need the kind of corroborating evidence that is hard to come by, this does give us some indication that Neanderthals may have had a sophisticated system of communication, if not a language.

Modern Homo Sapiens and Their Culture

We now reach the present. In the fossil record, modern humans emerge sometime between 200,000 and 160,000 B.P. By then, the human skulls lacked the robust attributes of their premodern predecessors: the heavy brow ridges reduced or gone, the skulls fully globular, the chin present, the occipital bones all but disappeared. Transitional forms between archaic and modern humans are found at Ilaret, Kenya, dating back to 300,000 years B.P., and Floresbad, South Africa, back to 200,000 B.P. A classical site is Klaeses River Mouth, South Africa, whose fragments range between 84,000 and 120,000 B.P.; the fragments include a mandible with a chin, unmistakably modern human. Liujiang, China, contains modern human remains dating back to 100,000 B.P. When our direct ancestors first appeared depends on the available evidence and how it is interpreted. As one wag indicated, the earth is stingy when it comes to yielding skeletal remains (he might have added that the funding sources are equally stingy, precluding much work that could have been done).

Upper Paleolithic and Beyond

The material culture associated with these finds is richer, emphasizing the fact that human biological evolution becomes less important than human *cultural* evolution. In effect, the tools, the food-getting techniques, the clothing, the shelters all form a buffer between the human organisms that we are and the environment on which we depend—and by virtue of which we might perish.

Thus, tools of the Upper Paleolithic period become more sophisticated, more specialized, and more subject to local and regional variations. **Blade** flaking technology—one in which flakes are produced that are at least twice the length of their width—is invented and diffused. Microliths—very small stone tools—are created. Fine laurel leaf points of the Solutrean tradition make their appearance. In the Magdalenian period, we witness not only a proliferation of previously specialized stone tools—needles, knives, awls, ever smaller projectile points—but also tools made of other materials, such as ivory, bone, or wood.

Nor are all artifacts functional. We see in the caves throughout Spain and France finely detailed **murals** of animals (humans, if portrayed at all, are stick figures). Portable art also appears, from the Venus figurines famous for their oversized breasts and stomachs (signifying fertility perhaps) to a mysterious set of female figurines discovered at Dolni Vestonice in the former Czechoslovakia, which, despite their dissimilarity, may portray the same person whose face was paralyzed on the left side. Ornaments reflecting a diversity of sites also appear.

Migration of Modern Homo Sapiens

Migration also plays a major role in the prehistoric eras of humankind. *Homo erectus* had already covered every part of the Old World, from Africa to Europe to China at the Zhoukoudian caves to

Indonesia at Trinil. Waves of archaic humans followed, although Neanderthals did not range much further than Europe and the Near East.

Now modern *Homo sapiens* begin to travel—but the question is from where and when? Two basic explanations seek to provide answers. The first is the **Replacement** or **Out-of-Africa model**, which stipulates that hominid populations first evolved into fully modern humans in Africa alone, then migrated through the Near East into Europe and the rest of Asia. In so doing, they displaced any remaining *Homo erectus*, *Homo heidelbergensis*, and *Homo neanderthalensis* populations. The second is the **Multiregional** or **Continuity model**, which contends that modern humans evolved from their regional *Homo erectus* forebears, and maintained unity of the species by exchanging genes. Feder (2004: 183–211) provides a six-way test for evaluating these theories, plus a third, "middle ground," model that emphasizes **gene flow** as the factor displacing genes of archaic species with modern ones. The relative lack of data prevents any one model trumping the others.

Whichever model ultimately retrodicts the actual migration pattern, almost all authorities agree that presapients (i.e., hominids preceding modern *Homo sapiens*) did not evolve in the Americas or Australia. Though authorities differ on the dates of migration, they generally agree on the main routes the migrants took. For North America, peoples from Siberia and Asia migrated across Beringia, the land bridge formed when an advanced ice age lowered the sea level, from northeastern Asia to what is now Alaska. They differ as to the southward routes after that, some suggesting a sea or coastal route along the Pacific, and others suggesting a break between two ice shields further inland. Most estimates place the date of migration at 15,000 B.P., but many argue that 25,000 to 30,000 B.P. is closer to the mark.

For Australia, the migration model has to factor some kind of floating craft into the equation. When the sea levels fell, Australia merged with New Guinea to form the continent of Sahul (New Zealand remained an island). Even then, a waterway called the Wallace trench (after Alfred Russel Wallace, Darwin's rival on the theory of natural selection, who first described it) remained; migrants thereby had to reach Sahul from southeast Asia by raft, canoe, or boat. Migration took place between 50,000 and 40,000 B.P. and the Lake Mungo site was populated by 30,000 B.P.

Race and Polytypic Variation

However we migrated, *Homo sapiens* (and the splitters would categorize us all as *Homo sapiens sapiens*) became and remains a single species. The concept of **race**—the categorization of breeding populations by such characteristics as skin color, hair texture, nasal structure, body morphology (tall and thin or short and stocky), and an infinite number of others—lacks validity in biological anthropology. This is because we are all capable of interbreeding, reproducing fertile offspring who are themselves able to produce fertile offspring. This means that we are all of one **species**, and the splitters would go so far as to say that we are all of one subspecies or variety as well.

To be sure, there is some ontological foundation for identifying diverse groups based on physical differences. What evolved are **polytypic populations**, which comprise diverse local **breeding populations**. Nor is it inconceivable that, had they remained mutually isolated for a long period in time, they might have evolved into separate species, mutually incapable of interbreeding. There have been some trends about the interaction between environment and physical attributes, such as melanin content and body surface. Thus **Gloger's rule** predicts that within the same species, there is a tendency for heavily pigmented populations to be located in the equator (given the length of sunlight) and for lighter pigmented populations to be located in northern regions. **Allen's rule** predicts that within the same species, the relative size of protruding parts of the body, such as nose and ears, and the relative length of the arms and legs, increase as the average environmental temperature increases. If true, we might have the beginnings of reproductive isolation leading to speciation. Yet, why are Inuit brown skinned while many southern European populations are light skinned? Why do we have Swedes who are tall and African so-called pygmies who are short? Even these "rules" have important exceptions.

There may even be some benefit to knowing human variations based on genes. Sufferers of **sickle cell anemia**, many of whom are indeed Africans and African Americans, might benefit from medical treatment for a condition in which oxygen-deficient red blood cells that are sickle shaped (sickle cells) are genetic in origin. The same holds for **Tay-Sachs disease**, whose sufferers, mostly groups of ethnic European Jewish descent, are afflicted with an enzyme deficiency of lipid metabolism, which leads to death in childhood.

Nevertheless, the concept of race is not so much a valid biological category as a **folk taxonomy**, in which physical characteristics have more of a sociological significance than a biological one. Clearly, we look different, but this difference is what governs the behavior of members of one breeding population toward those of another. **Racism**, which is guided by skin color or other attribute, is the demeaning of one population by another on the basis of these characteristics. **Eugenics** was (and is) a **pseudoscience** that attributes differences in behavior or personality characteristics, such as intelligence, to differences in physical characteristics. The most recent attempt is a book, *The Bell Curve*, which argues that intelligence differs among East Asians, Anglo-Europeans, and blacks, using techniques that have since proven methodologically invalid and unsound (Murray and Herrnstein 1994). Even census methods employ a folk taxonomy that mixes ethnicity with "race" (Hispanic, Native American, African American, non-Hispanic white—the list goes on). Earlier censuses used Negroid, Mongoloid, and Caucasian, ignoring not only East Indians or Native Americans who don't fit neatly in these cat-egories, but also mixed peoples, such as the Mulatto, who are offspring of black and white parents. Anthropologists who expunge the concept "race" from the anthropological lexicon have a well founded biological reason for doing so.

Reprise and Conclusion

This chapter discusses the biological foundations for humans' capacity for culture. We have looked at the mechanisms of evolution that gave rise to this capacity, the development of a brain that allows for conceptual thought and is the prerequisite for language, and the development of bipedalism and manipulative fingers and hands, which allow us the freedom to make and use tools.

These are the biological roots of culture. Now we turn to language, and through language, the elements of culture itself. It is only partly in biology that we can ask what the universal elements of culture are—such as marriage, family, and kinship. It is also partly through biology that we may try to explain why cultures are so different. If there is one thing that human biology has allowed us, it is choice. We, unlike the bees or the ants, are not programmed to behave in certain ways. We have free will, and we don't have to wait for some mutation to change our culture, or way of doing things.

Chapter 4

ANTHROPOLOGICAL LINGUISTICS: DESCRIPTIVE LINGUISTICS

Introduction

Language is the mediator between our culture and the environment in which we live. We use language without thinking; if we were all suddenly mute, our culture would collapse as surely as oil depletion would mean the end of our society as we know it.

We start this chapter with a discussion of language as symbol, and how symbols differ from signs. Next, we survey descriptive linguistics, analyzing articulatory phonetics, phonology, morphology, and syntax. In the next chapter (chapter 5), we discuss six features of communication that our language shares with communication among other animal species—and one that it does not. Then we turn to the relationship between language and culture: paralanguage and kinesics; historical linguistics and how languages branch off into different directions; ethnolinguistics, or how culture affects our perception of the world through language; and sociolinguistics, or how language is influenced by society. We conclude by tracing how our capacity for language probably evolved.

Symbols and Signals/Signs

Language is based on symbols, and forms the basis of culture. Indeed, it is fair to say that if there are no symbols, there is no culture. As we said at the beginning (chapter 1), we rely heavily on symbols

for our culture, and language is highly symbolic. The term **symbol** refers to the process of bestowing a meaning to a thing or event that intrinsically has nothing to do with that meaning. There is a great deal of evidence to indicate this quality. For example, stop signs have no inherent meaning to "stop." A century and a half ago, a red octagon would mean nothing. Only through learning do we associate this symbol with the command to stop. Similarly, black has no inherent meaning of sorrow or death. In much of Africa, white, not black, symbolizes death.

Another bit of evidence is the diversity of words for the same thing or event. Whereas we English-language speakers refer to the ordinary canine—*Canis familiaris*—as a "dog," the word becomes *chien* in French, *perro* in Spanish, and *Hund* in German. (If *Hund* sounds strangely like *hound*, it is only because there is a historical link between German and English.)

Signals (sometimes **signs**) are sounds and gestures that do have a natural, self-evident meaning. Facial expressions are signals; so is chest-pounding among gorillas, displays and screams among chimpanzees, and so on. Signs will be discussed in the next chapter.

The importance in difference is this: Signals are more or less "married" to their meanings; symbols are not. Because of the tremendous combinations one can make of a few sounds, language has a great deal of communication potential.

The Nature of Descriptive Linguistics

The core of language is its sounds and the principles governing their arrangement. No understanding of anthropological linguistics can be achieved without understanding **descriptive linguistics**, the nuts and bolts of the field. Covered in this section are the anatomy of speech, articulatory **phonetics**, the study of **phones** or speech sounds; **phonology**, or the study of **phonemes**; **morphology**, or the study of **morphemes**; and **syntax**, the study of sentence structure. Collectively, the study of all these aspects of a language is known as **descriptive linguistics**.

Structural Duality: The Core of Descriptive Linguistics

Any legitimate study of descriptive linguistics must take into account a language's **structural duality**, which refers to the quality, distinct to human languages, of two sets of language structure: nonmeaningful sounds and meaningful arrangements of sounds. So far as is known, no other animal communication system has the dual structure that language has. Table 4.1 summarizes the parts of a language and where structural duality fits in.

As a concept, structural duality is difficult to grasp and to explain; to do both, it is necessary to explain how a language works. We start with an overview, as represented in Table 4.1, and start from the bottom of the chart and work up.

Language requires some understanding of the mechanisms of speech, which we discuss under the heading "Articulatory Phonetics": the tongue, the lips, the teeth, and the roof of the mouth (see Level 7 of Table 4.1). We then turn to speech sounds, or **phones** (Level 2, Table 4.1). These comprise consonants and vowels, but also other elements, such as tones of voice that are important to Chinese, clicks that are important to southern African peoples, and glottal stops that we find in German and other European languages.

We then turn to the main elements of the first linguistic structure, **phonemes** (Level 3, Table 4.1), whose definition hinges on the differences among speech sounds, or clusters of speech sounds, that speakers of a given language can hear. No two languages have exactly the same set of phonemes. Therefore, what defines a phoneme is the phone, or phones, that the speakers of a language can distinguish from other phones. A phoneme may comprise one phone, or more than one. The exercise that follows should clarify this point. Because phonemes involve contrasts, they form an overall structure, as we shall also see.

We then go on to examine the elements of the second linguistic structure, **morphemes**, (Level 4, Table 4.1), which are approximately words. We say approximately, because most suffixes also carry meaning, and they are morphemes too. We continue with the other part of the second linguistic structure, **syntax** (Level 5, Table 4.1), or phrases and sentences. They are involved in the structure of meaning because they have a bearing on the meaning of the morphemes that form phrases and sentences.

Finally, we reach the intersection between the linguistic and nonlinguistic world (Level 6, Table 4.1). **Lexemes** are the vocabulary used by speakers of a language. They are unstructured within the linguistic realm, but are by definition meaningful. That is the stuff from which vocabularies are made. Finally, the nonlinguistic world has a bearing on the language, just as the language has a bearing on the speakers' perception of the world. This is the topic of a host of disciplines derived from descriptive linguistics: **historical linguistics**, **sociolinguistics**, and **ethnolinguistics**, to name but three. These topics are discussed in chapter 5.

Phonetics

Articulatory Phonetics: Anatomy of the Vocal Tract

Articulatory phonetics refers to the study of the articulation of speech sound using the physical mechanisms of speech. There is much that could be studied that won't be covered here. We have already mentioned **Broca's area**, **Wernicke's area**, the **arcuate fasciculus** that connects the two areas, and the **angular gyrus** that coordinates the modes of hearing, speech, vision, and smell. We have already mentioned the **hypoglossal nerve** that leads from the brain directly to the tongue. For now, however, we will only address the speech mechanisms that are directly related to speech articulation itself.

To begin at the beginning. When we speak, we **articulate**. That is, we move our tongues from one position to the next, move our lips together or round them, and perform other functions in our

TABLE 4.1 Language Design by Level

Level No.	Level of Language	Linguistics Subdivision	Meaningful/Nonmeaningful/ Significant/Nonsignificant**	Structured or Unstructured*
1	Nonlinguistic World	Language and Culture Disciplines	Meaningful	Unstructured
2	Vocabulary	Leximics	Meaningful	Unstructured
3	Sentence Structure	Syntax	Meaningful	Structured
4	Morphemes	Morphology	Meaningful	Structured
5	Phonemes	Phonology/Phonemics	Nonmeaningful/Significant	Structured
6	Phones (Speech Sounds)	Phonetics	Nonmeaningful/Nonsignificant	Unstructured
7	Speech Mechanism	Speech Anatomy/Physiology	N/A	N/A

*Refers to linguistic structure or lack thereof. In linguistics there are two kinds of structure: the nonmeaningful phonemes and the meaningful morphemes and syntax.

**Nonmeaningful refers to structure that has nothing to do with meaning; significant refers to a nonmeaningful element that affects the structure of a language, but has no meaning in its own right. Phonemes are significant but nonmeaningful.

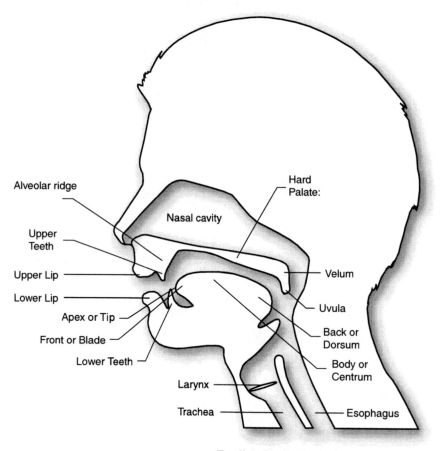

English Stops			
	Bilabial	**Apico-Alveolar**	**Dorso-Velar**
Voiced	[b]	[d]	[g]
Unvoiced (Voiceless)	[p]	[t]	[k]

FIGURE 4.1
The vocal tract
O'Grady et al. 2001. *Contemporary Linguistics.* Boston and New York: Bedford/St. Martin's, p. 23.

mouths that we are barely aware of doing. There is no mystery to what we do. When it comes to analyzing what we do, we have to slow down. That's the difficult part.

In following this discussion, you should refer to Figure 4.1 often, especially as each part of the speech mechanism is described.

There are two broad categories of speech mechanisms in the mouth itself. The first category is the **articulators**, which are the movable parts in the lower mouth (the lower lip, the lower teeth, and several parts of the tongue). The second category comprises the **points of articulation**, the immovable parts (except for one, the upper lip) that are located in the upper mouth (the upper lip, the upper teeth, the alveolar or gum ridge behind the upper teeth, the hard palate or roof of the mouth,

and the velum or soft palate). Three other parts fall outside this two-fold category: the uvula, or the bit of hanging flesh just in back of the soft palate, the nasal cavity, and the vocal cords that form part of the larynx.

The **articulators** play the active role when the speaker articulates; refer to Figure 4.1 as this discussion proceeds. At the front is the **lower lip** (or to go Latin on us, the lower **labium**, meaning "lip"). It helps in the formation of **consonants** and, together with the upper lip, is important for forming **vowels**. Next come the **lower teeth** (of which the Latinate adjective is *dental*, which you should know from all those years you've visited dentists). Thanks to the **mandible** (lower jaw), the lower teeth are movable.

Then come the four major parts of the tongue, which plays the main part in articulating both consonants and vowel and so is clearly a set of articulators. The foremost part of the tongue is the tip or **apex**. Behind the apex is the **front** part of the tongue (go figure; but see Figure 4.1). The center of the tongue is called, not surprisingly, the **centrum**. Finally, the back part of the tongue is called the **dorsum**. (Think dorsal fin of the shark if you have trouble remembering the last.)

The **points of articulation** are the parts of the upper mouth and, except for the upper lip, are stationary. The **upper lip** (upper **labium** to go Latin about it) usually works with the lower lip in articulating consonants and vowels and, obviously, is movable. The **upper teeth** are immovable, and so is the gum ridge located in the back of these teeth. The gum ridge is known as the **alveolar ridge**, and is important for English speakers. The roof of the mouth is known as the **hard palate** and forms a part of the phonetic description of those languages (like Russian) that use it. Finally, there is the **soft palate** or **velum** in the back of the hard palate. The **uvula** is the rounded piece of membraneous flesh at the far end of the velum.

To round out this description, the **larynx** contains a pair of **vocal cords** that, when taut, vibrate and so give us **voicing** in our utterances. The **nasal cavity** also plays a role in the formation of phones.

Articulatory Phonetics: Describing the Sounds of Speech

Having reviewed the anatomy of speech, we now shift to the study of the production, transmission, and reception of speech sounds; mostly, this discipline is concerned with how the physical sounds of speech are articulated, as the forthcoming exercise will show. No one really knows how many phones exist in the world's languages. Henry Sweet, a 19th-century English linguist who was the model for Henry Higgins in Bernard Shaw's *Pygmalion*, from which *My Fair Lady* was adapted, could distinguish some 120 vowels (of which a, e, i, o, and u are examples).

Consonants and vowels are the most common phones. Consonants are a class of phones characterized by constriction or closure at one or more points in the breath channel. Vowels comprise a class of phones in which the breath channel is not closed or constricted, but which do resonate in the mouth by level of front, middle, or back of tongue combined with rounding or unrounding of lips. There are other phones; they may vary by tone (as in the two major Chinese languages) or by emphasis of vowel ("accents"). Clicks, or phones made by enclosing air between two stop articulations of the tongue, enlarging the enclosure to rarify the air, characterize some southern African languages (including the Xhosa and the !Kung or Ju'/hoansi).

We examine **consonants**, which are formed by a **position of articulation**, when an **articulator** (lower lip, lower teeth, or part of tongue) moves to a position relative to a **point of articulation** (upper lip or teeth, alveolar ridge, or velum) to close or constrict the flow of air through the mouth. Those that halt the air stream momentarily are known as **stops**. Others that constrict the flow of air are known as **fricatives**, **laterals**, or **nasals**, depending on how the constriction takes place. Such stops are called **voiced** when the **vocal cords** in the **larynx** are vibrating, and **unvoiced** or **voiceless** when they are not.

The next exercise describes the positions of articulation in voiced and voiceless stops. In following this exercise, you should (1) refer to Figure 4.1 frequently as the positions are named and described, (2) make the positions of articulation yourself while reading the descriptions, and (3) compare the vibration or lack of vibration in your throat as each voiced stop is compared with its voiceless or unvoiced counterpart.

The first set of stops involves the two lips of your mouth. Utter the words *bin* ([bɪn] in IPA orthography) and *pin* ([pɪn] in IPA) in turn while placing your fingers against your throat. Notice what when you utter *bin* ([bɪn] in IPA), your throat vibrates, starting with [b]. However, when you utter *pin* ([pɪn]), the throat does not vibrate until you reach [-ɪn]. You have just uttered two common English stops, both known as **labio-labial stops**. The [b] is a **voiced labio-labial stop** and the [p] is a **voiceless labio-labial stop**, or, if you prefer, an **unvoiced labio-labial stop**.

Notice the principle behind this naming. The **articulator** plays the active role, and that happens to be the lower lip, or the lower **labium** (we're going Latin all over the place). For that reason, the **labio-** portion of this stop refers to the articulator. The **point of articulation** plays the passive role, so even though the upper lip (oops—**labium**) moves (the only point of articulation to do so), most points of articulation are immovable; that's why they play the passive role in articulation. In formal identification, it is the upper lip that is identified by the **-labial** part of the identification of the **labio-labial stop**.

One last fact before we move on: Since **labio-labial** will become an eternal tongue twister, why not make it easier for ourselves? After all, the linguists do the same thing. So we shall call this **position of articulation** the **bilabial stop**. Simple, eh?

Now we move on to the next **stop**. Again, utter the word *din* (you know—the noise you hear at the stroke of midnight on New Year's Eve or at some football game), whose IPA version is [dɪn], then utter the word *tin* ([tɪn]). Notice, first, that in both instances the tip of your tongue touches the gum ridge behind the back of your upper teeth. This gum ridge is known as the **alveolar ridge**. The part of the tongue touching it is known as the **apex**. Remembering again that for all positions of articulation for consonants are identified first by the articulator, then the point of articulation, this position is identified as an **apico-alveolar stop.**

Now put your fingers on your throat again and repeat in turn *din* [dɪn] and *tin* [dɪn]. Notice that the throat (vocal cords) vibrate when you utter [d] of [dɪn], but that, when you utter [tɪn], your vocal cords do not vibrate until you utter the [–ɪn] portion of the word. You have now uttered two phones: the **voiced alveolar stop** [d] and the **voiceless alveolar stop** or **unvoiced alveolar stop** [t].

Finally, we look at the last of the three pairs of stops. Pronounce the words *gin* [gɪn] and *kin* [kɪn]. If you are watching your tongue (so to speak), you may find that it is not positioned the same when you pronounce the two words. When you pronounce *kin*, the back of your tongue (the **dorsum**) may be touching the soft palate, your **velum**. This position is known as the **dorso-velar stop**. The dorsum is the articulator, and the velum is the point of articulation, and in that order. So far so good.

But if you pronounce *gin* the way most people pronounce "gin," the distilled liquor, you may notice the tip of your tongue touching the alveolar ridge, and also a puff of air being expelled. In other words, the IPA expression of this kind of gin is actually spelled [džɪn] in IPA script. Correctly pronounced, [gɪn] is the pronunciation of a proper noun, Ginn, that also identifies an educational publishing company.

This time, pronounce [gɪn] and [kɪn] interchangeably, and again put your fingers against your throat. Notice once again that your vocal cords vibrate when you pronounce [g] but remain still when you pronounce [k], vibrating only when you reach [-ɪn]. You now have the final pair of phones,

namely a **voiced dorso-velar stop** and a **voiceless dorso-velar stop** or **unvoiced dorso-velar stop**.

The exercise you just completed is essentially the task that the linguist faces in the field when describing a previously unknown language. She or he asks an **informant**, or actual speaker of the language, how to pronounce a phone, string of phones, or a word (more on refining that concept later). By trial and much error, the linguist finally makes the correct pronunciation and writes it down. It is a long involved process, and the exercise you actually went through is an oversimplification. You will get some idea of how oversimplified the procedure is under the next section.

There are, of course, other phones. **Stops** are not the only **consonants**. There are **nasals**, or sounds produced by lowering the velum, allowing air to pass through the nasal passages, of which the phones bilabial [m], apico-alveolar [n], and dorso-velar [ŋ] are examples. There are **fricatives** or **spirants**, or sounds produced with a continuous airflow through the mouth, accompanied by a continuous audible noise. These sounds include the voiced apico-alveolar [z] and the unvoiced apico-alveolar [s]. There are **laterals**, sounds made with the sides of the tongue lowered in which the air passes in two streams around either side of the tongue; [n] is an example.

There are also **vowels**, or sounds not produced by any audible blockage or constriction of the air stream, but differing by the resonance created by the interior shape or form of the mouth. The main factors in the type of resonance are the position of the tongue in its part (front, middle, or back), the height of the tongue part (low, mid, or high), and the rounding or rounding of the lips. In English, the letters *a*, *e*, *i*, *o*, and *u* are familiar examples, but they mask many more phones than five. For example, *a* could be pronounced as [a], [æ], [e], or other phonetic vowel. Finally, **semivowels** or **glides** refer to vowels that are shorter in duration than most vowels and function as consonants; examples include *w* [w] and *y* [j].

Nor do the distinctions stop there, and this is where the foregoing examples are simplifications. As we will see momentarily, some consonants may vary by being aspirated—accompanied by a puff of air—or nonaspirated—not accompanied by a puff of air. For example, the word *pie* has an aspirated *p* [p'] in [p'aij] but the word *spy* has an unaspirated p [p=] in *spy* [sp=aij]. In Chinese, the vowels differ by rising, even, or falling tone, in addition to the changes in the sounds themselves. What defines a phone is not only its type of consonant or vowel, but also its modification. This explains in part why the number of phones is unknown and probably infinite.

Phonology

Phonemes: Definition and Identification

Therefore, it is not surprising that phones provide the material for the building blocks of a language, but are not themselves building blocks. In all languages, certain phones and clusters of phones form units that, to the speaker of a given language, sound different. This is the basis for defining **phonemes**, but as you will see, definition is no simple task.

Let's go back to the six phones we have identified. Do the utterances [b] and [p] sound different to you? Of course they do; you've been using these utterances for years. How about [d] and [t]? Again, yes. And [g] and [k]. Yes again. Of course, [b], [d], and [g] sound different, as do [p], [t], and [k].

So here we have sounds that are not only **phones**, but also **phonemes**. How do we know that they are phonemes? All we need to do is to match them in pairs, so that [bɪn] and [pɪn] differ only by the utterances [b] and [p]. The rest of the utterance, known as the speech **environment**, is one and the same ([-ɪn]). This pair of utterances is known as a **minimal pair**, which may be defined by a pair of utterances that differ by only one phone. By this standard, the utterances [dɪn] and [tɪn] are likewise minimal pairs—differing only by [d] and [t]—and so are the utterances [gɪn] and [kɪn], which differ by [g] versus [k]. Incidentally, any pair differing by position of articulation also qualifies as a minimal pair: [bɪn] versus [dɪn], [dɪn] versus [gɪn], [kɪn] versus [bɪn], and all other possible combinations. Pairs containing a stop and a nasal would also qualify as minimal pairs: [dɪn] versus [nɪn] (a surname, as the well-known author Anaïs Nin), for example. The list can go on. The bottom line: Any pair that matches except for a recognizable phone in the same position of the utterance is a minimal pair, thereby qualifying the two phones as separate phonemes.

Now we are ready for a formal definition of phoneme: A **phoneme** is the smallest significant unit of sound in a language. The significance of this definition, is that one phoneme *sounds different* from another phoneme in a language.

This means that we have to change the notation of the six stops we have been following, because as speech units, they sound different. Phonemes are identified by enclosure between two forward slashes (/). Therefore, [b] becomes the phoneme /b/, [p] becomes the phoneme /p/, and so do the others, now written as /d/, /t/, /g/ and /k/. We must emphasize that these are phonemes for one language: English. Other languages have their own phonemes.

Identifying Allophones

Now we reach another complication in defining phonemes. Note we said that a phoneme is the smallest significant *unit* of sound in a language, not a significant *phone* in a language. This is because many phonemes may incorporate two or more phones; therefore, we have to call them units, not phones. We foreshadowed this problem when we identified the problem for [p] in *pie* versus *spy* in a preceding section (see "Articulatory Phonetics: Describing the Sounds of Speech").

Let's take another unvoiced utterance, [k]. Put your hand in front of your mouth and pronounce the two words *key* and *ski*. Focus on the consonant *k* in the two examples. Which *k* is accompanied by a puff of air and which one is not?

If you peeked ahead, or if you carried out the experiment above, you now know that the *k* in *key* is accompanied by a puff of air—in other words, it is **aspirated** (IPA; [kʼ] in [kʼij]). You also know that the *k* in *ski* is **unaspirated** (IPA, [k=] in [sk=ij]). Try as you may, you will never match the speech environment of a [kʼ] with the speech environment of [k=] in the English language; nor, for that matter, will you match the speech environment of an aspirated *p* ([pʼ]) with the environment of an unaspirated *p* ([p=]). (In my classes, I promise an A for the course if any student can find [kʼ] and [k=] in a minimal pair. No one has won yet!)

Nevertheless, the two phonetic variants that are unvoiced dorso-velar stops play their own roles in the phoneme we identify now as /k/. We call them **allophones** of one phoneme; the different-sounding variants of the unit we know as /k/. One is aspirated under certain conditions (initial [k]) and unaspirated under others ([k] after [s]). It's something like a B-grade mystery. The suspect and the butler never appear together, so we are led to believe that the suspect and the butler are one and the same person. Likewise, [kʼ] and [k=] never appear together, so we suspect that [k'] and [k=] are one and the same phoneme /k/. (Where is Sherlock Holmes when we need him?)

One Language's Allophone Is Another's Phoneme

All the information we've provided so far refers to the English language, and only the English language. In Old Sanskrit (from which Urdu and Hindi are derived), there are two phones similar to [k'] and [k=]. Unlike English, they can be matched in a minimal pair: [k'il] means "parched grain" and [k= il] means "small nail." So, unless you have an iron deficiency, if you are looking for grain, be sure to aspirate your *k* at an East Indian food market. In this instance, [k'] and [k=] do form a minimal pair, and so are separate phonemes /k'/ and /k=/—in Old Sanskrit, not in English.

On the other hand, Chipewyan, a language spoken among native Indians in the western sub-arctic regions of Canada, makes no distinction between [b] and [p], between voiced and voiceless bilabial stops. We can hear the distinction, mostly because they are phonemes in English; the Chipewyan cannot, because the phones [b] and [p] are not phonemes.

Three points arise from these examples. First, two sounds that are allophones in English may be separate and distinct phonemes in another language, as Old Sanskrit illustrates. Second, no phone is exactly the same across cultures. There are many aspects by which a [k'] and a [k=] in English are not exactly the same as a [k'] and [k=] in Old Sanskrit. Although exacting techniques are demanded in linguistics, linguistics is not an exact science, because the language corpi are so diverse. Finally, no language exhausts all the possible sounds, phones, or even classes of phones and phonemes, that it has. We have only something in the order of four dozen phonemes, but we haven't exhausted all their possible combinations, nor will we ever.

Phonemes: Structural Duality I

Recall that we said that language contains a dual structure. The first structure involves phonemes. When we say that a sound unit we call a phoneme sounds different from another unit called a phoneme, we are also saying that one phoneme is defined relative to another. There is no such thing as a one-phoneme language—you need at least two,

and most languages have many—any more than there is music with only one note.

That means that phonemes *contrast* with one another, and there is a structure, or arrangement, in that contrast. You can readily see this when we draw a diagram whereby the IPA symbols represent the six stops we've been analyzing, and the lines represent the contrasts between the six:

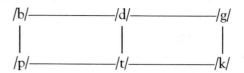

Here, the phoneme /b/ is shown to contrast with /d/. The horizontal line indicates the phonetically closest units that comprise a phone: a bilabial versus apico-alveolar stop. Likewise, /b/ contrasts with /p/; the vertical line indicates that the phonetically closest units are a voiced bilabial stop /b/ and an unvoiced/voiceless bilabial stop /p/.

You would not draw such a diagram for Chipewyan, which makes no such phonemic distinction between [b] and [p] (note the square brackets rather than slashes). As for Old Sanskrit, you would need to draw a line between /k'/ and /k=/ because, as the slashes indicate, they are phonemes for that language:

$$/k'/\text{———————}/k=/$$

This diagram also puts into visual form the structural basis of phonemes. When a linguist has completed the phonetic analysis of his/her informants' utterances and determines which ones they use in creating their actual language, he or she draws a diagram to show graphically the phonemes of that language, and how they contrast.

To conclude, language is built on sound; by definition, linguistics is primarily the study of language as it is spoken. Orthography is used in writing down an unwritten language. Contrast how a deliberate misspelling of a common everyday word

ghoti

is known to speakers of English as

fish

How so? The letter combination *gh* is often expressed as an *f* (*cough*, *rough*), although other pronunciations occur (*bough* with an *–ow* sound). The *ti* combination is often pronounced as an *sh* sound (*motion, locomotion*); indeed, an enterprising boat builder named Ted Jones designed and built a hydroplane that he dubbed *Slo-Mo-Shun* back in 1950, and it won the national Gold Cup Race and the international Harmsworth Race—but no spelling contest.

Oh, yes, and the *o*? Well, pronounce the plural for *woman*, which we spell *women*. Do we pronounce it the way it's spelled? Well, if you're like me and millions of other English speakers, you pronounce it *wimmin*. Good spelling does not guarantee good pronunciation.

That is why linguistics focuses on spoken, not written, language. That's why we need the IPA to record our phones and phonemes. And, when sounds of speech are analyzed on paper, we see that phones do not form structures; phonemes do.

Morphology and Syntax

Morphemes and Morphology

Once the significant elements of a language, the phonemes, have been identified, the next task for the linguist is to develop the meaningful utterances for that language. This is where morphology and syntax come in.

The smallest unit of meaning is known as a **morpheme.** Morphemes may be words, or a string of speech sounds, that together form a meaningful utterance that stands alone, just as words do. Alternatively, the string may not stand alone, yet form a meaningful utterance. Morphemes that stand alone are known as **free morphemes.** They may be nouns (*cat*) or verbs (*run*) or any other so-called part of speech, such as adjectives, adverbs, conjunctions—all that you learned from grade 3 or 4 onward.

Not all morphemes stand alone as words, however. Some may be prefixes, such as *pre-* in *predawn* or *prehistory*. Others may be suffixes, such as the plural *-s* as in *cats*. Morphemes that cannot stand alone but rely on a free morpheme to give it meaning are known as **bound morphemes.** This is where the analogy between word and morpheme breaks down. The expression *cats* is one word, but contains two morphemes—one free, one bound.

In addition, just as there are **allophones,** or phonetic variants, in **phonemes,** so there are phonetic variants in **morphemes.** These variants are known as **allomorphs.** For example, there are several variants in the bound morphemes that form plurals. The most common are the bound morphemes /-s/, /-z/, and /- z/ as in the utterances *cats* (/kæts/, *dogs* (/dogz/), and *horses* (/horsez/). Other plural allomorphs include **infixes** (changes within the free morpheme itself), such as *teeth* (/tiΘ/ for *tooth*, and *zero allomorphs*, such as *sheep* for *sheep* (no change).

Finally, here's a trick question. *Cats* is plural for *cat*, right? Well, yes, if it is part of the utterance for *two cats*. However, what about *cat's meow*? Clearly, the *–s* in this context is a possessive. But doesn't this *–s* have an apostrophe? Yes it does, in writing. Do you pronounce an apostrophe in your utterance? I doubt it. So, the IPA spelling for both the plural *cats* and possessive *cat's* is identical: /kæts/ and /kæts/. Isn't that just too cool for words?

What differentiates the two bound morphemes is the context in which they occur. If /kæts/ is preceded by a number or other element indicating plural, then it is the plural *cats*. If /kæts/ modifies some noun like *meow*, then it becomes the possessive *cat's*. **Morphology,** or the study of morphemes and their formation, takes into account not only the lexical (dictionary) definition of any meaningful utterance, but also its context. All morphemes are part of a larger string of utterances, be they phrases or be they sentences, and morphology has to take this fact into account.

Phrases, Sentences, and Syntax

Syntax means both the process whereby strings of morphemes are put together to form a phrase or sentence, and the study of this process. Syntax involves the principles—rules—whereby morphemes are placed within a structure, involving phrases and sentence—to form progressively more complex meaningful utterances. However, how morphemes—both free and bound—are placed affects the meaning of the morpheme itself. For example, whether *author* is a noun or verb depends on its position in the sentence. If it starts at the beginning of the sentence, as follows

This *author* wrote Silence on the Mountain

author becomes the subject. If it follows a noun

Daniel Wilkinson *authored* Silence on the Mountain,

author(ed) becomes a verb. Finally, if author is repositioned as follows,

> Daniel Wilkinson is the *author* of Silence on the Mountain.

then *author* becomes the object.

Given the complexity of sentence structure in any and all languages, and given that most of us have had some exposure to English grammar and sentence structure (most readers of this text will not have had previous experience with phonetics and phonology), we will only give a few suggesting examples of how syntax works.

Generally speaking, all languages have nouns and verbs, but different languages have different subclasses of nouns and verbs. For example, Romance languages (Spanish, French, Italian) divide nouns into masculine and gender subclasses; Latin, from which the Romance languages are derived, has an additional subclass, the neuter. German, not derived from Latin, also has a threefold division of nouns by gender. Yet the relationship between noun and gender role is tenuous at best. In Spanish, for example, what is masculine about *día* (day) or feminine about *noche* (night)? One might argue that night is associated with darkness and the feminine mystique, but then how about the association with Satan or the Devil (translated into Spanish as the masculine *diablo*)?

Other languages divide their nouns under other categories. Kivunjo, an East African language, has 16 classes (Pinker 1994:27). Papago, a Native American language spoken by people along the banks of the lower Colorado River, divides its nouns into "living things," such as people and animals, and "growing things," or inanimate objects such as rocks and plants (Nanda and Warms 2004:104).

There are other issues in syntax; one involves procedure. One such procedure involves **frame substitution**, which serves to identify syntactic units of language. Nouns comprise one frame, verbs another, adjectives yet another—the list goes on. They involve **form classes**, which identify parts of speech or categories that work the same way in each language. For example, the noun *cat* in *the cat died* and the noun *dog* in *the dog died* are mutually substitutable as noun forms. However, *house* in some contexts is not substitutable for *cat* or *dog*. The utterance *the house died* bears this out

(although one does hear, facetiously, *the car died*). So there can be many forms of noun phrases, just as there are many forms of verb phrases and so on. In other words, there are nouns and nouns, and verbs and verbs, and each set has to be given separate treatment—and that is within a language.

To conclude, all languages require their own analysis of the rules governing the strings of sounds we call meaningful utterances. Nouns, verbs, adjectives, adverbs, and other parts of speech can be analyzed only by the principles peculiar to a language; the same applies to nouns as subject, objects, and other categories not applicable to English or to other Western languages. In other words, every language has its own **grammar**, or the sum total of all rules governing that language.

Morphemes and Syntax: Structural Duality II

Both morphemes and syntax have two elements in common. First, they govern meaning. In their structure, they bear messages for the speaker to send and the listener to hear. What the speaker has to say depends on the speaker; how he or she says it depends on the language. Second, the meaning depends on the structure of the language. Structure generates the rules by which morphemes are formed and by which the parts of speech—its syntax—are arranged. We have already seen how phrases affect the meaning of a bound morpheme *–s: two cats* versus *cat's meow*.

In English, word order also affects meaning. "Dog bites man" is different from "man bites dog." In the first sentence, *dog* is the subject, *man* the object. Reverse the nouns, and *man* is the subject, and *dog* is the object.

For that reason, morphemes and syntax treated synergistically comprise the second structure of language's **structural duality**. This is the structure that renders language a meaningful system. You cannot have meaning in a language, however, without having the first structure, the sound units that contrast, or **phonemes**.

Lexemes and Meaning

Having said this, to say that morphemes and syntax convey meaning is not to guarantee that utterances in perfect English will be understandable to all speakers, or to any at all. Take Noam Chomsky's renowned utterance "Colorless green ideas sleep furiously" (1965; cited in Nanda and Warms

2004:104). The adjectives, subject, verb, and adjectives are in correct order; any speaker of English would recognize that the utterance should make sense. (They would not recognize "Furiously sleep ideas green colorless" as potentially making sense.)

But does the first utterance make sense? For most of us, probably not. Nor would many of the words from "Jabberwocky" in Lewis Carroll's *Through the Looking Glass:*

'Twas brillig and the slithy toves
Did gimble and gyre in the wabe.

We know that a *wabe* or a *tove* is a noun, but we don't know what else it is. (How do we know they are nouns?) *Gimble* and *gyre* are verbs. (Again, how do we know? For answers, see chapter 5.) But they lack meaning in English. They are **nonsense words**, which are perfectly acceptable strings of sound in English, but which carry no meaning. We need content, and this is where lexemes come in. **Lexemes** represent the words that provide meaning in the everyday sense of the term; we might even call them terms with dictionary definitions (though most languages lack dictionaries). Lexemes represent the border between descriptive linguistics and the culture in which a language is used.

Universal and Generative Grammar

Are the phonemic, morphemic, and syntactical structures in a language unique to that language? Is the attempt to compare one language with another a useless enterprise because of this uniqueness? For decades, this was thought to be the case, but in recent years, some linguists and linguistic anthropologists have made this very attempt. Noam Chomsky, usually known (if at all) for his work in radical political studies, is the foremost linguist advocating just such an attempt.

To Chomsky, all languages seem diverse because of their **surface structures**, or rules governing the grammar of specific languages: English, Spanish, Japanese, !Kung, and so on. Nevertheless, all languages can be reduced to a common structure that he calls **deep structure** and comprise a common set of rules he calls **universal grammar**. In other words, all languages are essentially the same; as Scupin put it, a hypothetical Martian visiting the earth might decide that all humans speak a dialect of the same language.

Chomsky's model is known as **generative grammar**. In other words, he argues that speakers of a language **generate** their sentences from a set of rules we have covered under **syntax**. Many sentences can be generated with a relatively small number of rules operating on the **lexicon,** or vocabulary, of a language. The following examples draw upon Scupin's (2003:104–105) review of Chomsky' model (1980, 1995). Take English for example.

Let the following symbols be used:

S—Sentence	N—Noun
V—Verb	P—Phrase
Art—Article (a, the)	NP—Noun phrase
VP—Verb Phrase	

For those who forgot their grade-school English, a noun is a person, place, or thing; a verb expresses action of some sort, an article refers to *a* (an indefinite article) or *the* (a definite article); and a phrase is a group of two words or more. A preposition is a word that indicates location (*in, above, below, of, under,* and so on). A sentence is a string of words containing at least a noun (subject) and verb plus object (predicate).

Now let the following expressions be made from those symbols.

S → NP VP (a sentence consisting of a noun phrase plus a verb phrase)

VP → V (NP) (a verb phrase consisting of a verb plus an optional noun phrase

NP → Art N (a noun phrase consisting of an article plus a noun)

Now let's bring in some examples:

N → girl, dog
Art → the, a
V → sees

From this set of rules (simple, in case you are unconvinced), we can generate such sentences as *the girl sees the dog* or *a girl sees a dog* or *the girl sees* and any of several combinations that you might experiment with yourself.

Since he first proposed this scheme, Chomsky and others have simplified this approach even further, leading to the **principles** and **parameters** approach. In English, one example is the **head parameter**, which determines whether the **head** of a phrase precedes or follows its **complement**. Here are a few examples

Phrase	Head	Complement
Verb + Object	sees	the dog
Preposition + Object	over	the rainbow
Noun + complement	President	of Mexico
Adjective + complement	afraid	of spiders

In other languages (Japanese and Aymara [an indigenous language in Bolivia], for example), heads follow their complement: *the rainbow over* or *the dog sees* (*dog* is object, not subject).

As this example suggests, the multiplicity of rules characteristic of surface grammar in a language is reduced to a few, and languages can be compared on that basis. If Chomsky's model is confirmed, then it may be true that linguistics may be added to the list of elements among cultures to be compared.

Conclusion

The preceding section provides the nuts and bolts of linguistic analysis: how phones are articulated, how phonemes are contrasted, how meaningful utterances are structured from strings of speech sounds. Other species of animal are not creatures of culture, with the limited exception of chimpanzees and related nonhuman primates. There remain three questions: How does language compare with the communication systems of other animals? How does language articulate with culture? How do languages diversify? These are covered in the next chapter. Language acquisition is covered in chapter 14.

Chapter 5

ANTHROPOLOGICAL LINGUISTICS: LANGUAGE AND CULTURE

In chapter 3, we discussed some of the physical bases of language in the context of human evolution. The brain structure, including **Broca's area**, **Wernicke's area**, the **arcuate fasciculus** that links them, and the **angular gyrus** were all discussed. We also mentioned the importance of the **hypoglossal nerve** linking the brain to the tongue, and we continue discussion with the physical mechanisms of speech in chapter 4.

Also in chapter 4, we spelled out in some detail the principles of **articulatory phonetics**, which involve the study of speech mechanisms and their role in forming **positions of articulation** that involve **articulators** and **points of articulation** and thereby produce **phones**.

In chapter 4, we also defined **phonemes** and their relationship to phones, then went on to examine **morphemes** and **syntax**. We showed that the contrastive features of phonemes combined with the rules governing the flow and structure of meaningful utterances to form the **structural duality** of a language. Language as a structure, cannot alone generate a vocabulary, or **lexemes**, and so we discuss the process in this chapter.

Thus, we reserve for this chapter three matters: comparing other features of human language with nonhuman communication, and how **signs** and **signals** serve to amplify language, which comprises **symbols**; delineating the relationship between language and **culture**; and tracing the course of language diversification through the techniques subsumed under **historical linguistics**.

In chapter 3, we traced the probable course of language evolution. In chapter 14, we will discuss **language acquisition** as a part of child development from a cross-cultural perspective.

Communication Systems: Cross-Species Comparison

Defining Communication

Derived from Latin, *communicare*, which means "to share" or to "impart that which is (in) common," **communication** may be broadly defined as the ability of one organism, or living thing, to trigger—produce a response in—another.

Let's take an example and counterexample from the street. Suppose a doorman (OK, a bouncer) has to eject an unruly patron in the local pub. If the bouncer asks the miscreant to leave, he/she triggers a response if the miscreant leaves, and so communication has occurred. Alternatively, if the miscreant throws a punch and the bouncer gives him/her the old heave-ho, he/she has used a direct application of force to get the drunk out the door. In that case, two organisms are involved, but communication has not occurred.

Here's another counterexample. If the rising sun wakes you up, it has triggered a response—you get up—but the sun is not an organism, a living thing. Therefore, communication has not occurred. Hurricanes, volcanoes, and earthquakes may force people to flee their homes—but nonliving phenomena, not living organisms, have triggered this response.

Communication, therefore, involves two living lifeforms, one triggering a response in the other.

Three Types of Animal Communication

All members of the animal kingdom engage in communication of some form. Let's take three examples of animal communication: stickleback courtship, bee dances, and gibbon calls. Then let's compare them with that human communication mode known as language, using six common characteristics.

Stickleback Courtship.   A stickleback is any of a variety of small fish (family *Gasterosteidae*, for those of you in biology) having two or more spines in front of the dorsal, or back, fin. In courtship, the male first builds a nest at the bottom of a lake or stream, then swims about to find a female with a distended belly, which contains the eggs.

To lure her to the nest, the male swims in zigzag fashion around the female; this, together with his red belly, induces her to follow him to the nest. On arrival, the male stickleback moves to a vertical position, "pointing" at the nest with his nose aimed downward. The female swims into the nest. Now swimming down, the male rubs the female's abdomen with his nose. The courtship ends when the female deposits her eggs in the nest, the male discharges his sperm on the eggs, and the two swim their separate ways. (So much for family values!)

Bee Dance.   Worker bees, as you know from grade school, produce the honey for each hive, obtaining nectar from plants flowers and blossoms, and process it into honey. You probably know that it's the females who do all the work; males are the drones, whose only value is to impregnate the queen bee. Rather than being allowed to sit around, the drones are killed off. I leave to you its implications for feminist theory.

Here is how bees communicate. When a worker bee discovers a source of nectar, she flies back to the hive and performs a dance in the midst of the other workers. The dance conveys three essential messages: (1) The distance of the nectar source is indicated by the type of dance: A figure "8" dance indicates distance of 5 meters from the hive or fewer; a sickle dance indicates a distance of 5 to 20 meters from the hive; and tail wagging indicates a distance of 20 or more meters. (2) The direction of the nectar source is indicated by the open side of the figure "8" relative to the sun; where the bee performs a tail-wagging dance, the angle of the wagging path relative to the hive's vertical angle indicates the direction of flight toward the nectar source relative to the sun. (3) The quantity of pollen available is indicated by the intensity of the dance; the more pollen, the more intense (O'Grady et al. 2001:635–637).

Gibbon Calls.   Gibbons, any of various species of small ape (genus *Hylobates*) found in the tropical rainforests of southeast Asia and Indonesia, have some nine calls; we'll use only two here. One call, composed of clatters and clicks, is used when a group of gibbons is widely dispersed; it means, roughly, "come together," or "close in." Another call is a series of high-pitched shouts, denoting "danger." There is no way to specify the danger: a predatory cat, a human hunter with a gun, or a forest fire.

These calls are clearly signals. They are each "married" to a generalized meaning. More important, they cannot be combined to form more meaningful utterances. Clatters and clicks cannot be combined with a high-pitched shout to mean something else.

Human and Nonhuman Communication

However different, there are six features of language that are comparable with stickleback courtship, bee dances, and gibbon calls. These features are arbitrariness, productivity, displacement, interchangeability, cultural transmission, and specialization.

Arbitrariness.   **Arbitrariness** is the absence of an intrinsic, or obvious, or natural relationship between the sound or structure, or any feature of the communication element and the thing or event to which it refers. This is the defining feature of **symbol**. The presence of such an inherent relationship between sound or gesture and the thing referred to is called **iconic**, from "icon," not unlike the pictorial icons that you find on your computer desktop. (This comes from *eikon*, or "to resemble" in classical Greek). *Iconic* is the adjective form of **sign** or **signal**.

What is important about an arbitrary expression or symbol is that it is not "married" to a particular meaning—that means two or more elements can be rearranged to yield a different meaning. For example, take three common English words, "cat," "act," and "tack." They are made up of identical sounds, but arrange them differently. To illustrate this point, we need to use the International Phonetic Alphabet, or IPA. In IPA, they are spelled [kæt], [ækt], and [tæk]. (Phonetic letters and "words" are enclosed in the square brackets [and]; see chapter 4 for more details.)

Notice that none of the three elements—[k], [æ], and [t]—means anything in the English language. Because they are not "burdened" with meaning, they can be freely combined to form a new utterance. Therefore, a "cat" or [kæt] is a common household feline animal; an "act" or [ækt] is what you polish up on before you go on a stage; and a "tack" or [tæk] is what you use to put up your flyer on a bulletin board. When these "meaningless" elements (phonetic letters) are combined, they mean something; if they are rearranged, they mean something else. That is the power of arbitrariness in a language.

How about the three animal communication systems we just reviewed? First, they are **iconic**. Their expression cannot be separated from their meaning or their context. The behaviors of stickleback fish—the male's zigzag dance and the female's swimming toward and then into the nest—are all tied in with their courtship and reproduction. As for the bee dance, none of the behavior—speed of dance, angle of body, amount of pollen carried to the hive—is separated from the business of gathering pollen to be processed into nectar. Gibbons' clatters and clicks forever mean "come together," and high-pitched shouts mean nothing but "danger."

Second, they are **closed systems**. They cannot be combined with anything else to create a new meaning. The courtship behavior of stickleback cannot be combined with any other behavior for that purpose, nor can the clatters and clicks of gibbons be combined with their high-pitched shouts to mean something else. The bee dance retains the same function: location of nectar sources.

Nevertheless, some nonhuman species of animals are capable of manipulating arbitrary systems of meaning. Several experiments demonstrate that chimpanzees can use American Sign Language, an arbitrary system of communication designed for the deaf; other experiments show similar results with other arbitrary communication systems. So far, however, no chimpanzee, bonobo, gorilla, orangutan, or gibbon has been observed using arbitrary communication in the wild.

Productivity. Another major attribute of language, **productivity**, refers to the capacity for elements of a communication system, including language, to be combined to form new meanings, which neither the speaker nor the listener may have heard before, yet understands perfectly. For example, suppose I say a word you never heard before: *wug, or [wəg] in the IPA form (the asterisk * denotes a nonexistent or nonsense word or phrase). Then I ask you to say two of them. Would you not automatically pronounce it as "wugs" ([wəgz] in IPA), as if the *s* were a *z*? This automatic assignment of a –*z* to a plural for this word illustrates productivity.

Or take a second look at two lines from "Jabberwocky," the classic poem already mentioned in chapter 4, from Lewis Carroll's *Through the Looking Glass*, a sequel to *Alice in Wonderland*:

'Twas brillig, and the slithy toves
Did gyre and gimble in the wabe.

Here we find the conjunction *and*, the article *the*, the preposition *in*, and even two verbs (*was*—as part of the poetic 'twas—and *did*) and the pronoun *it* (in the poetic 'twas) intermixed with such **nonsense words** as *brillig*, *toves*, and *gimble*.

Before reading on, see if you can identify the nouns, verbs, and adjectives among the nonsense words in this verse.

You can tell that *toves* and *wabe* are readily identified by *the*, which precedes them, and that *gyre* and *gimble* had to be verbs from the auxiliary verb *did*. As for *slithy*, its –*y* ending combined with its position preceding *toves* betrays the word as an adjective—no different from *rainy*, *sunny*, or *windy*.

The fact that any of these nonsense nouns, verbs, and adjectives could be substituted by any other noun, verb, or adjective—nonsense or with meaning in English—renders the utterance a productive one. There is a structure to all language, any of whose elements could be substituted for another. There is little wonder, then, that second-language drills involve the use of productivity.

Do the communication systems of other animals involve productivity? Some do; for example, the bee dance involves variations in its signals for direction and distance of the nectar source and the amount of pollen available. On the other hand, neither the courtship behavior of sticklebacks nor the calls of gibbons vary, so do not entail productivity.

Displacement. Language also involves the ability to refer to things and events that are not immediately present, that are abstract, or that may not even exist. If you do not live in Washington, you can still visualize and talk about the Washington Monument, the Lincoln Memorial, the White House, and Capitol Hill. We can conceive of square roots and numbers (even absent their symbols) without difficulty, though our proficiency may be another matter. We can conceive of unicorns, though they do not exist and never have.

Animal communication systems usually do not include displacement, though there are notable exceptions. Bees perform their dance away from the blossoms and flowers that elicited their response. Gibbon calls refer to the presence of unseen dangers. Chimpanzees' ability to make and use tools—twigs or sticks to fish for termites from their hills, or chewed leaves to sponge for rainwater in tree hollows—involves displacement. Twigs are not obviously useful for termite "fishing" until their leaves are stripped, nor do leaves have an apparent use for retrieving water until they are chewed. (Goodall 1986).

Unlike chimpanzees, baboons are unaware that termites are present when their hills are sealed, and so lack displacement in this context. Likewise, stickleback fish show no sign of displacement outside the context of their mating.

Interchangeability. The term *interchangeability* refers to the capacity for the sender and receiver to use the same communication system. Clearly, language is interchangeable. You are reading this passage in English, the same system I am using to write the same passage. The speaker and the listener use the same language.

Interchangeability characterizes both the bee dance and the gibbon calls. The bees watching the dance are using the same system to receive the messages as the dancing bee is in sending it. Likewise, gibbons hear the high-pitched shout used by the one giving the call, and react accordingly.

A counterexample to interchangeability is the courtship behavior of stickleback fish. The male can perform the zigzag dance, and the female can receive it. However, the female cannot perform the zigzag dance, nor can the male receive it in any meaningful way. The male, not the female, directs his partner to the nest. The female, not the male, enters the nest to trigger the partner's next response—to rub the abdomen.

Cultural Transmission. Cultural transmission entails behavior that is acquired by learning within the context of a group. As developed in chapter 1 of this text, humans learn the skills and values of their society; only the capacity for language and culture is inherited genetically.

Do other animal species acquire behavior through learning as part of a group? There is evidence that some do. Chimpanzees, for example, show the same trial-and-error behavior in such activities as carrying their young, learning to fish for termites, or chewing leaves to sponge for rainwater, and threatening their rivals with bared canines and bodily displays. Moreover, such behavior varies by population. Unlike their counterparts at the Gombe National Preserve in Tanzania, the chimpanzees in West Africa do not fish for termites; rather, they plant sticks in the paths of ants and lick off the ants that climb up the sticks.

Specialization. *Specialization* refers to the degree to which complex messages are conveyed by relatively short utterances, such as language. Generally speaking, the greater the physical effort, the less specialized the communication system. Generally, specialization can be put in a continuum.

For example, the threat display of male chimpanzees involves a great deal of physical activity. They may tear branches of nearby trees and bushes, vocalize, charge at their adversaries, and bare their teeth. Contrast this with a simple threat at a darkened office: "Your signature or your brains will be on this agreement." Although a pistol may help, the message is profound, the utterance short and unobtrusive.

Stickleback communication in their mating behavior is clearly unspecialized, as is the bee dance. Gibbon calls are more specialized than either, inasmuch as vocalization alone is enough to issue the warning or suggestion. In this category, however, the prize clearly goes to language.

However, this is not to say that language is purely without physical expression. Few if any languages lack tone of voice or physical gesture. Indeed, such modifications reflect the communication systems of nonhuman primates and our own probable ancestors. Two prelinguistic elements, **paralanguage**, or the extralinguistic noises that accompany language, such as sobbing or laughing, and **kinesics**, or gestures, facial expressions, and body motions, are still with us. For that reason, the study of these two areas forms an integral part of anthropological linguistics, and is discussed below.

Structural Duality.   As we've seen from the prior chapter, language involves **structural duality**, that quality whereby a system of speech units we call **phonemes** forming a set of contrastive arrangements constitute one structure, and the arrangement governing the strings of meaningful utterances—**morphemes** and **syntax**—constitute the second structure.

Of all animal communication systems, human language alone is known to involve structural duality. The cry of chimpanzees, the high-pitched shout of gibbons, the dance of worker bees—none has this attribute. Chimpanzees may be able to learn American Sign Language, but ASL is not dual in structure. It involves sequences of meaningful gestures, but gestures themselves cannot be recombined to create new utterances in the way that phonemes can be so recombined. ASL is structural in one dimension only.

Kinesics, Paralanguage, and Other Signals

Although language comprises **symbols**, we also use **signs** or **signals** to amplify what we are saying. When wanting to drive home a point, you may gesticulate—use gestures. When amused, you may laugh; when sad, you may cry; or when angry, you may raise your voice. None of these expressions substitutes for language—it is not true that how you say something is more important than what you say—but how we gesture, how close we stand relative to our listener, or how we use our tone of voice does amplify what we say.

Kinesics and Related Motions

Smiles, gestures, winks, twitches—all of these movements exemplify **kinesics**, or the study of body position and movement, facial expressions, and gaze. In the United States, we are trained to trust anyone who looks you in the eye, and to distrust those who look away with shifty eyes or body language. Smiles are universal, although their meaning may differ by culture: happiness in the United States, desire to make another person comfortable in Japan, or a sociable gesture in all societies (Lewis 1996:267; Matsumoto and Kodoh 1993). Birdwhistell identifies eight parts of the human body usually involved in kinesics: total head, face, neck, trunk, shoulder-arm-wrist, hand, hip-joint-leg-ankle, and foot (1955). Not all body movements have significance. A wink may carry a message ("Trust me!"); an involuntary tic may not.

Related to kinesics are several other forms of body motions. **Proxemics** is the study of personal space. Middle Easterners, for example, stand closer to each other in conversation than do Americans. Within the United States, social roles determine space; lovers stand closer together than friends, friends stand closer together than acquaintances, and acquaintances stand closer together than strangers (Hall 1968). Proxemics also covers spatial studies not closely related to communication, such as architecture, interior design, and placement of furniture or equipment. **Haptics** is the study of social touching, which again varies with culture and situations within cultures. **Chrometrics** is the study of time, the ways time is understood, and how it is used to communicate. For example, Americans and northern Europeans tend to be more precise in measuring time than a wide range of peoples elsewhere—much to the chagrin of Americans and northern Europeans.

Paralanguage

The tones of voice and pitch are examples of **paralanguage**, which refers to the sounds, noises, and other arts of speech that work together with language to facilitate communication. **Vocalization** is one category, referring to identifiable noises turned on and off at short intervals. They include **vocal qualifiers**, such as laughing to indicate happiness or amusement, or breaking voice to indicate sadness or fear; they include pitch, such as anger accompanying the expression "Get out!" They may also indicate tone, such as a steady level of voicing expressing anger or determination. There are also **segregates**, which involve expression not involving words. Examples are "Shh!" to demand silence or "Oh oh" to indicate fear of something gone wrong. Voice qualities may betray speakers' mental states. For example, tones of voice may indicate the emotional state of the speaker; a steady tone may indicate determination or anger; a quaking tone may suggest fear. Other forms of paralanguage involve **voice qualities**, examples of which are slurs indicating tiredness or intoxication, or other background noises (Haviland 2002).

Language and Culture

There are several channels whereby a language acquires its **lexicon**, or vocabulary, from the culture or cultures in which it occurs. They may be subsumed under two broad categories: **ethnolinguistics**, or the relationship between language and its structure and content, and the *culture* in which it occurs, and **sociolinguistics**, or language and its structure and content, and the *society* in which it occurs.

Ethnolinguistics

This field is underlain with a chicken-and-egg question: Is it language that structures the culture through which the speaker perceives the world, or is it the speaker's culture that structures the language's structure and its content? This is the question that the Sapir-Whorf Hypothesis (1956) brings up (Scupin 2003).

Named after Edward Sapir and his student Benjamin Lee Whorf, the **Sapir-Whorf Hypothesis** posits that perceptions of time, space, and matter are conditioned by the structure of a language. If I place into the category "cousin" all my aunts' and uncles' children, I perceive all these relatives in a different category. As an English speaker, the sex of the couple is less important to me than my French counterpart, who inflects *cousin* and *cousine* by gender. Nor do we distinguish between children of different-sex and same-sex siblings, as the Yanomamö or Iroquois do. This distinction has an importance to the Yanomamö and the Iroquois that we do not find among Americans (or, for that matter, the Inuit or so-called Eskimo).

To cite another example, Sapir and Whorf themselves contended that the linguistic structure of Hopi does not divide time into chunks known to us as minutes, hours, days, and weeks, as the structures of English and most other western European languages do. In their conception, the language is the causal factor of Hopi versus American time perception, not the reverse.

Primarily, critiques of this hypothesis have centered around two issues. First, other ethnographers have reported that Hopi divide time into chunks as Americans and Europeans do. For example, the anthropological linguist Ekkehart Malotki found that in fact the Hopi calculate time in units similar to native English speakers. The dissimilarity lies in tense: Hopi divide time into future and nonfuture tenses, rather than in future, present, and past tenses (1983). Hoyt Alverson, comparing 150 different languages, finds that each language essentially divides time into partible and divisible categories, and that both linear and circular metaphors are used (1994). Scupin suggests that such findings may offer implications for humankind's genetic heritage, cognitive evolution universal in scope, and a common identity for the human species (2003:108–109). This may confirm the Sapir-Whorf Hypothesis in a backhanded way—language structure may predispose the formation of categories—but it also suggests intraspecies and intercultural commonalities in time categorization. Contrary to this thesis, Sapir and Whorf had hoped to explain variation by language structure.

More important is the direction of causality. Cross-cultural comparisons show that the environment actually influences language. The Inuit, for example, have far more categories for snow—powder, corn, solid ice, and numerous others—than we do. So do English-speaking skiers in North America. The cattle herders of East Africa like the Nuer or Masai also have elaborate vocabularies for their animals. They have detailed categories for cattle—by color, temperament, personality; they even name individual bulls or cows, and compose long oral poems about them. Nuer boys are named after individual cattle. A violence-prone culture like our own uses extensive vocabulary and metaphors drawn from the military—we make a *killing* on Wall Street, we *bomb* our exams, we *slaughter* our opponents in football games, the boss *goes ballistic* over our mistakes, the government conducts a *war* on drugs, Congress *battles* over the budget—the list goes on (Haviland 2002).

In other words, when a human group encounters a new environment—migrates to snow country, discovers grasslands suitable for cattle, develops a militaristic culture—language is perfectly adaptable to fit into the new conditions. Balinese adopt foreign words—communication, tape recorder—to run the radio and television stations they just bought. It seems that culture influences language no less than language influences culture.

Sociolinguistics

Language also reflects society: gender relations, social stratification, political power, and all other aspects of social relations. The term *sociolinguistics* refers to the relationships that structure society. Examples include gender, kinship, and power in various guises.

Kinship.   Variations in **kinship terminology** are important to most preindustrialized societies, and involve the categorization of one's kin based on the terms one uses toward another relative. For example, we do not distinguish our cousins by whether they are linked to us through mother's brother or father's sister versus father's brother or mother's sister. To the Yanomamö, the distinction is all-important; cross-cousin marriage is expected, if not mandatory. The fact is reflected by the term that Yanomamö men apply to their female cross-cousin and wives: *suaböya*. For us to do the same might land us in jail for incest.

This important topic will be reserved for chapter 10, on marriage alliance. For the present, it is important to know that terminology is an important indicator of kinship relations, which form the core of almost all non-Western societies. As we shall see in chapter 8, the economic, political, legal, and even religious societies do not function outside marital and family relations, together with the rules of descent that structure them.

Gender.   Used in anthropology and sociology, **sex** refers to the biological differences between women and men; **gender** refers to the cultural and social attributes derived from the biological differences of sex. Each gender has its own vocabulary, its own interpretation of what words mean. Tannen, for example (1990), points out that women prefer a language of interpersonal connection and intimacy, whereas men prefer a language of status and independence. Each woman or man learns their respective "language" from childhood. Girls play in small groups or pairs; best friends are their preferred relations. In contrast, boys prefer to play outside in large groups that are hierarchically structured. Words reflect this distinction: "I'm sorry" to men

means acceptance of responsibility for a mistake; to women, it means regret for the situation created by the mistake.

Gender stereotypes pervade language. During the 1980 election, vice presidential candidate Geraldine Ferraro was perceived in the news media as "needling" Ronald Reagan, the successful presidential candidate. Male candidates might be cited as "lambasting" Reagan (Haviland 2002).

Dialects.   In every language, there are variations in syntax, pronunciation, word usage, and other parts of speech that nevertheless are intelligible to all the speakers of that language. Such variations are known as **dialects**. They vary by region. In Boston, you may hear the word "bahgain," yet you understand it no matter where you are from. They vary by ethnicity. In African-American communities, a dialect known as Ebonics ("Black English"; the word is derived from *ebony*, a kind of wood whose color is black).

Code Switching.   We all vary our conversation from informal talk to formal presentation. Who we are and with whom we are talking vary with social situation. We speak in slang or colloquialism at a pub, use standard informal English at a class discussion, and use formal English at a conference presentation. When applied to blacks, individuals may speak in Ebonics to each other or in front of an African-American audience; speaking to a non-black audience, he or she may use formal English. This process is known as **code switching**, for which Martin Luther King was famous. This is not so much a dialectical phenomenon as a situational one that applies to us all (Haviland 2002).

Historical Linguistics

Languages change: some estimates suggest that languages become mutually unintelligible at 1500 years, if not before. **Historical linguistics** is the study of relationships between earlier and later forms of a language, antecedents in older languages of developments in modern languages, and relationships among older languages.

Concepts of Historical Linguistics

Those who take another western European language often recognize words from their own; in German, *Haus* and even *Katze* may correspond to *house* or *cat*. From Spanish we may find *profundo* or *comprendar*, even if we translate them to *deep* or *understand*. They also mean *profound* or to *comprehend*.

Known as *cognates*, these words reflect the common roots between English and German, and suggest that English is not far removed from Latin, from which Spanish is derived. These put them all into a common **language family**, or a group of languages that are ultimately descended from a common language (Haviland 2002).

Our language family is known as **Indo-European**, which includes not only English, German, and Latin languages such as French and Spanish, but also Persian and Hindi. Paradoxically, the Scandinavian languages Swedish, Danish, and Norwegian are Indo-European, but Finnish is not. Finnish, together with Hungarian, belong to the **Finno-Ugric** language family, which also includes Estonian, Samoyed (a Siberian language and culture), and 12 other languages. In the Americas, the **Uto-Aztecan** link the foraging peoples of the Canadian Yukon and Northwest Territories with the Utes of the Nevada Basin (who give their name to Utah), and the Nahuatl spoken by the Aztecs (Mexica) and their descendants in central Mexico.

Language subgroup refers to a group of languages that are closer to each other than to other groups within a language family. English and its antecedents (e.g., Old English) have closer roots with German than with Spanish. As a Romance language, Spanish has closer roots with French, Italian, and even Romanian than it does with English. Scottish (scotch is what you drink) and Irish Gaelic belong to the Celtic subgroup, along with Welsh of Wales in southwestern England and Bretagne of the Brittany coast of northwestern France. And so it goes: Hindi and Farsi (Persian) are part of the Indo-Iranian group.

Glottochronology

When languages actually split apart, the process is known as **linguistic divergence**. This may occur when two **dialects** become mutually unintelligible. Spanish and Portuguese were dialects at one point; now they are two separate languages. Catalan is another language that split off from Spanish (whose actual name is Castilian or *castellano*, a fact often noted throughout the Spanish-speaking world). In

Cantel, Guatemala, the school specializing in teaching Spanish to Quiche-speaking children is known as the *Instituto de Castellanización*).

How do we know when languages diverge, even unwritten ones? This task represents the science of **glottochronology** (from the Greek *glotta*, meaning *tongue*, and *chronos*, meaning time), or the statistical study of linguistic divergence. Morris Swadesh developed a **core vocabulary**, or list of words for any language that were likely resistant to change even with contact with other languages or cultures. The vocabulary comprises a list of words that every culture has: body parts (nose, mouth, finger), natural objects (rock, tree, earth, wood), numbers, and pronouns. If a people moved, say from the Canadian Shield to the Nevada basin, their name for plants and animals might change, but the body parts, sun, rain, or numbers would most likely stay the same. By Swadesh's reasoning (1964), the closer the core vocabularies of two languages, the more closely they were related (Scupin 2003).

There were faults to this reasoning. For example, the Yanomamö have only three numbers: one, two, and more than two (Chagnon 1997). The word for *hundred* that might serve for European languages (*hundert* in German, *hund* in Old English, *centum* in Latin, and *ekaton* in Greek, all progressively increasing in distance from English) would not exist in Yanomamö.

Nevertheless, the technique seems to have stood up over the years, and is still used today. Linguists use logarithmic formulas in calculating the probable divergence of related vocabularies, two at a time. Core vocabularies tend to change at a more or less constant rate: 19 percent every 1,000 years; about 81 percent would be retained. Findings have shown languages to change at different rates, swiftly in some circumstances and slowly in others. Linguists have long given up the idea of ever finding a "first language" for all the languages of the world. Even reconstructed "protolanguages" were not, in all probability, actually spoken.

Multiple borrowings also influence the rates of change, and there are few languages that have not borrowed from others. You can hear English numbers when Kawelka tribesmen of New Guinea count out the pigs and the dollars for the next major *moka*, or feast. You can hear the Balinese priest mention "tape recorder" and a fractured "communication" when explaining the role of technology in Hindu ritual in Balinese.

Conclusion

Language is the solvent by which cultures survive. Every language has its own set of phonemes, its own rules of morphology and syntax, its own grammar. In this chapter, we have seen that gestures amplify communication, though their origins are the signaling systems of animal communication.

Nevertheless, language works only because its lexicon works; gestures are but icing on the lexemic cake. For that, language depends on the culture of the speaker for its content. The Sapir-Whorf Hypothesis argues that languages affect the speaker's perception of the world and therefore his/her culture; the reverse proposition seems to be the more likely case. There are several channels between language and the culture of every speaker; we have looked at ethnolinguistics and sociolinguistics.

Finally, every language has a history. Often one language arises from another, or splits off from a related language. The task of glottochronology is to identify how it split off, and how long ago. Another benefit is to trace the probable migration of a culture or group of culture. Without linguistic evidence, who would believe that the empire of the Mexica (Aztecs) in the Valley of Mexico might have some distant link to the foraging Athabaskan groups of the Canadian north?

Chapter 6

SUBSISTENCE SYSTEMS AND MATERIAL CULTURE

Making a Living Cross-Culturally: An Introduction

When Christ preached "man cannot live by bread alone," He did not add that man cannot live without bread. Indeed, He did not ignore the use of fishes and loaves to attract his flock, however miraculously He multiplied them. In this section, we examine subsistence, or food-getting systems, and the role they play in forming and structuring cultures.

Because our cells do not contain chlorophyll, we, as members of the animal kingdom, cannot produce food with photosynthesis; plants with this capacity do this. Like other species, we ultimately rely on plant foods, even though we also depend on other animals for subsistence. The pork bellies futures are safe on Wall Street.

Why are many anthropologists so oriented toward subsistence techniques of various sorts? The tradition of **cultural materialism** takes the view that cultures are what its members eat—or at least work for. This is the notion that focuses primarily on technoenvironmental and economic factors that constrain culture, and the primary sector involves the transfer of energy by technological means from the environment to members of a culture. This orientation reflects an academic Marxist tradition,

and indeed might represent what C. Wright Mills called vulgar Marxism (1962).

The basic model entails a technoenvironmental base, combining an environmental base—grasslands, northern forest, desert, tropical rain forest—with the tools that a human population has at its disposal. In grasslands, for example, a society with a gasoline-driven tractor and plow has an advantage over one with a horse and plow—so long as the oil doesn't run out. In turn, the society with a horse and plow enjoys an advantage over one with nothing but a hoe or digging stick in the same grassland environment; in fact, the hoe-bearing farmer cannot penetrate the sod at all. Then there are the herders, with another adaptive advantage; with cattle or sheep, who needs plows or tractors?

Then who does the work? Who assigns the tasks? Who owns the property on which the cattle graze or the crops are grown? Who owns the cattle and the crops? How are the workers compensated for their labor? In short, how is the **economy** organized? To answer these questions takes another chapter, and these matters are discussed in chapter 11.

Like other species, our forebears were **foragers**, or **hunters and gatherers**, or, to use a term used by some, **food collectors**. Whatever term is used, they relied strictly on what nature could yield; a few populations in the world may still be foraging, and others, such as !Kung or Eskimo (Inuit) did so until recently.

The constraints of foraging were evident: Laws of nature governed human populations as it governed nonhuman populations; population had to be within carrying capacity of environment, for example, or some member would die out.

Some human measure of control over the food supply came with the domestication of animals and plants, probably about 9,000 to 11,000 years ago. Even then, domestication did not free our forebears from ecological forces, nor (even with industrial agriculture providing almost all our food) is this the case today. Indeed, we may be running out of oil needed to do the job (see chapter 16).

This is where cultural materialism makes its strongest case: the genre of anthropological thought that links cultures to their respective subsistence systems. To survive, every culture must adapt to its physical environment through the use of whatever food-getting or food-producing technology is at its disposal.

Therefore, this chapter first examines five main types of subsistence systems:

1. **foraging** (hunting and gathering, food collection, and in some instances fishing);
2. **horticulture**, or hoe cultivation, some of which involves **slash-and-burn**, or swidden cultivation;
3. **pastoralism**, or herding of animals of various sizes from goats and sheep to cattle and horses;
4. **equestrian hunting**, which, although it involves hunting, involves the use of a domesticated animal (horse or reindeer) to hunt other animals; and
5. **intensive agriculture**, which involves the use of the plow or other means of making high agricultural yields, some using fossil fuels.

Foraging or Hunting and Gathering

Often known as **hunting and gathering**, the term **foraging** refers to the hunting of animals (including fish) and the gathering of vegetation (including nuts, fruits, edible leaves, roots, tubers, and everything else borne by plants). As omnivores, we rely on both animals and plants. As we saw in chapter 3, we make and use tools—spears and arrows to hunt animals, baskets and digging sticks to gather plant foods—to forage. With minor exceptions, tool manufacturing and use separates us from other animal species.

Once upon a time, our ancestors were all foragers. Until the Mesolithic period, they practiced **simple foraging**, which involved all the attributes that will take up most of this section; low yield technology, nomadism, reliance on sharing. Then, in a few areas of the world, some of our ancestors took on **complex foraging**. Here, the people could rely on large animals to feast on, or could rely on several sources of food at one place; at that point, they abandoned nomadism and could develop fairly complex societies. The only contemporary example we have of this are the Indians of the Northwest Coast, who relied on rich salmon runs and abundant game in the forests, and other cultures, such as the simple chiefdoms of the Chumash along the Santa Barbara Channel (Feder 2004; Fagen 2004).

Simple Foraging

The foragers of today—or more accurately, of the recent past—have several common attributes. First, they are found in **marginal environments**, those unsuited for most forms of intensive cultivation (cattle ranching may be a relatively recent exception). The environments include deserts like the Kalahari of southern Africa and most of the interior in Australia; tropical rain forests in inaccessible places, such as central Congo, the outliers of the Thai and Malay Peninsulas, and parts of Amazonia in South America; and the arctic regions of Canada, Alaska, Greenland, and northern Russia. The deserts are too dry for intensive cultivation, the tropical rain forests too moist, and the arctic too cold (Scupin 2003).

Foraging strategies are clearly environment-specific. Desert and rainforest peoples have a relatively simple hunting technology: bows and arrows tipped with a weak poison among the !Kung (also known as the Ju/'hoansi, San, and the politically correct or incorrect Bushmen); spears, bows and arrows, and nets among the Mbuti "pygmies" of the Ituri Forest in Central Congo; blowguns and harpoons among the Semang of Malaysia. The notable exception are the Inuit of Arctic Canada and Alaska; they rely on harpoons, spears, kayaks and uniaks (boats of animal skin), and a sophisticated assemblage of other tools and weaponry. Gathering is even simpler; women use digging sticks to harvest and baskets, karosses (a leather cape among the !Kung), and skin pouches. Except for the Inuit, whose climates preclude vegetation except for short seasons, plant foods form a greater portion of the forager diet than meat; percentages range between 60 percent and 80 percent. Game, especially large animals, are hard to track and harder to kill. Each !Kung is lucky to bag 10 large animals per year; the Semang stopped hunting water buffalo years ago (Lee 2993; Turnbull 1963, 1983; Balikci 1970).

Among all regions, the primary attribute for simple foragers is the overreliance on natural sources of food. Nature rules. Resources fluctuate by time and place. In the Kalahari Desert, the mongongo nut tree that is abundant one year may be stingy the next—perhaps because the rainy season was too wet. Waterholes filled to the top one year may be empty the following year. Some places may vary in the same season. Some waterholes are empty, others full, all in the same year. The same rule applies to plant foods, animals, and fish (Lee 2003).

Second, because of fluctuation in resources, the people have to move around a lot. When the tubers are exhausted, the nuts overpicked, or the game not showing up, the band must migrate to a more promising site. Nomadism means minimal possessions—all that can be carried—so it is unsurprising that the material culture is thin at best. An exception are the Inuit, who can carry a lot of material on their dog sleds and rely on kayaks and uniaks to move around when the ice is thin (Lee 2003; Balikci 1970).

Third, the environment imposes upper limits on population: the **carrying capacity**, or the upper limit of population that a specific environment— desert, rainforest, ice field—can support. Carrying capacity affects all cultures—even our own if we paid attention—but the effects are direct among foragers. Therefore, **Liebig's Law of the Minimum** is most evident. Formulated by Justus von Liebig, a German fertilizer manufacturer in the 19th century, the law states that lack of growth is limited not by the total of resources available, but by the scarcest resource. In crop science, the limit was imposed by the scarcest nutrient. In human populations, the limit is imposed by the scarcest resource: food supply in all three environments, and water supply in desert environments. The leanest year imposes the upper limit under this law, regardless of the abundance in other years (Wynne-Edwards 1986; Scupin 2003:152; Bodley 2001:71).

Fourth, again with the exception of the Inuit, foragers lack means of storage, particularly of meat. This provides an incentive to consume meat, soft fruits, tender leaves, and other perishable foods as quickly as possible. Less perishable foods can be stored and consumed at leisure. One example is the mongongo nut among the !Kung; it can be stored for up to 18 months. Root crops also take longer to decay (Lee 2003; Balikci 1970).

Fifth, partly because of the relative absence of storage means, foragers are known for their propensity to share; in other words, their primary mode of transaction is **generalized reciprocity** (see chapter 11). Among the !Kung, for example, if a party of hunters bags a wildebeest (an ungulate resembling an ox) or a giraffe, they own the meat—but it is theirs only to distribute. Whoever owned the arrow that first entered the beast—the owner may be a child, a woman, an old man who is not at the kill site—is also part owner of the meat, but again only to give away. This mode of exchange provides security for the less successful hunter, or one who may be down on his luck. Making gifts of meat also strengthens kinship ties, and there are rules as to who receives priority (Lee 2004).

Sixth, the foregoing description suggests that foragers are ever on the edge of starvation, but studies show that they may be nowhere near that level. Lee, for example, finds that although preferred foods may be exhausted before the next harvest season, not all food is. The !Kung of Dobe simply had to settle for the food they least desired, once the preferred mongongo nuts were exhausted (Lee 2003). Sahlins (1972) argues for a "Zen road to influence," or **affluence hypothesis**. Foragers, not knowing about all the amenities of civilization—television, cars, or cell phones to update the examples—do not miss them; in the meantime, they are gathering enough to live comfortably. Forager needs are few, the hypothesis runs, and they do not need to spend time pursuing the means of satisfaction.

There is documentation, however, that foraging peoples are at the brink of starvation. Some are: the Inuit may have fit this description, if Balikci's portrayal on film is to be believed. Among San (Bushmen), the Nyae Nyae !Kung San are described as being in a less productive environment than the Dobe !Kung San (Marshall 1965). In any case, it is true that foragers' diets are much more varied than that of many food producers, particularly intensive agriculturalists. Whether there is more then enough to eat appears to depend on the location (Scupin 2003).

Seventh, a corollary to the affluence hypothesis suggests that foragers do not spend much time working for a living. Lee (2003) calculates that the Dobe !Kung spend fewer than 20 hours of week in nonintensive labor hunting game or gathering vegetation, and Sahlins reports the same results on a comparative sample of other cultures (Sahlins 1972).

Eighth, there are suggestions that foragers are relatively egalitarian in both property and power. Among the !Kung, property notions are minimal. Game is owned only to be given away. Plant foods are owned by women who harvest them, and their family. Waterholes are freely available to all and to visitors, who need only request permission from the headman, who freely gives it (Marshall 1965). Indeed, Lee denies that there is any such thing as a headman among the Dobe !Kung (2003).

Finally, there is the longstanding debate as to whether foragers are our "contemporary ancestors." In other words, are foragers of today or the recent past similar to foragers of the Paleolithic? Although at first an appealing notion, there are several shortcomings of this view. First, the undisturbed foragers (if there are any) have existed in the same past 10,000 years as the nonforagers (including ourselves). Much can happen in the meantime, including culture change among the foragers themselves. Second, most foragers live in marginal areas; they cannot necessarily resemble the foragers who hunted game in the richer plains of East Africa, the moderate climates of Italy or Spain, or the rich floodplains of the Indus or Yangtze rivers. Third, their very presence in marginal areas suggests they were forced to the margins by the stronger, more technologically sophisticated populations who took the best lands and other resources (Carneiro 1967, 1970; Scupin 2003). A possible exception are the Australian Aborigines—some 500 bands—who had lived in isolation since they migrated to the continent 40,000 years ago. Even then, there is reason to believe that inhabitants of the richer coastal regions forced weaker populations into the vast, arid lands of the Outback. Archaeological evidence suggests exactly this pattern; the coasts were populated first, then the inland (Feder 2004).

Complex Foraging

By definition, **complex foraging** refers to the hunting and gathering of food whose energy yield approaches that of the food-producing systems that involve domestication. Complex foraging was more commonplace in the Upper Paleolithic and Mesolithic than it is in the recent past. For exam-

ple, the Japanese site of Nittano, known for the Jomon tradition in pottery, showed signs of a permanent village. Fish was caught in the summer, game, in the winter, and a wide variety of wild vegetation was available in all seasons but winter. Other sites, such as Monte Verde in Chile and Dolni Vestonice in the Czech Republic, relied on megafauna—big game—such as mammoths, mastodon, giant bison, and wild cattle (Sanders and Price 2004).

The best known contemporary examples are the villages strung along the Northwest Coast of the United States and the west coast of Canada. (Ozette, Washington, contains archaeological characteristics that fit in with the Northwest Coast complex.). The Northwest Coast consists of moderate climate rainforest, mostly comprising cedar and several varieties of pine: ponderosa, fir, and balsam. The communities relied heavily on salmon, which were harvested every salmon run in the hundreds. Salmon was preserved by smoking, rendering it edible for several months. Game was also plentiful, from small game such as rabbits up to deer and elk. Flora was in abundance as well, with several varieties of berries and other wild plants. They did not cultivate crops, nor did they domesticate animals, which in any case were not amenable to domestication (Drucker 1955; Sanders and Price 2004).

Given a plentiful supply of wood, the Northwest Coast natives were known for their longhouses, seagoing canoes, totem poles, boxes, and other objects, beautifully carved and painted. The high-yield subsistence base rendered a nomadic existence unnecessary. Although war often occurred, the villages maintained a complex ranked society headed by a chief, whose validation was secured by a major feast known by the Chinook name potlatch. Unlike most simple foraging societies, the Northwest Coast native people recognized property ownership of not only salmon streams but also houses, canoes, and even intangible rights such as particular dances (Drucker 1955).

Thus, complex foraging societies are highly different from simple ones. The energy yield is much greater, whether because of megafauna or because of a rich and diverse food source. Sources do stand the risk of yearly fluctuation but, at least in the case of salmon, were unlikely to vary much from one year to the next. The environmental carrying capacity is much higher than that of simple foragers, as is the limit specified in Liebig's Law of the Minimum. Thus, settled communities are more likely to develop from complex foraging, although humans do not exercise control over their crops that domestication would bring. The institutions associated with simple foraging—communal control over resources, minimal power of headmen where they exist, sharing and generalized reciprocity—are nonexistent. Societies may be characterized by extended families, perhaps lineages and clans; ranking is likely to occur, and property is important, though more clan-based than individual-based (Sanders and Price 2004).

Food Production

We now take up the four major **food-producing** subsistence systems, which may be defined as all forms of subsistence technology whereby a population obtains its food through domestication of plants, animals, or both. These modes of technology consist of **horticulture, pastoralism, equestrian hunting**, and **intensive agriculture**. We discuss these modes in technology in turn.

All four systems share common characteristics. First, compared with food collection, food production is steady from year to year, with the exception of drought, soil exhaustion, plant disease, and plant decimation by insects or other pests. Second, storage facilities are made or constructed. Often, the food itself is nonperishable, such as maize, wheat, barley, or other seeds. Preservation techniques have been devised for other foods, such as a freeze-drying technique the Inca developed for preserving potatoes and duck, then storing them in ceramic containers. Third, permanent or semipermanent settlements accompany domestication. They may be villages, such as the communal *shabono* or corral among the Yanomamö; cities that are familiar to us all; or semipermanent camps, such as the herding peoples who, unlike simple foragers, move seasonally rather than opportunistically. Fourth, part-time or full-time artisans arise to pursue their craft. As energy production rises, more and more specialists outside the primary sector (hunters, gatherers, fishers, or cultivators) come into existence.

Finally, one should bear in mind that each of the food-collection systems does not necessarily exist in isolation. Some do; the cattle-herding Masai do not hunt, nor do they plant and harvest crops. Others combine two or more food-production systems. Yanomamö combine hunting with garden cultivation. Some central Asian herders plant gardens before moving their herds to their summer quarters, and harvest any crops that survive weeds, insects, and weather.

Horticulture

Horticulture entails the growing of crops of all kinds with relatively simple tools: digging stick and hoes for turning the soil, and axes or machetes to clear the brush and to weed. Two types of horticulture predominate: cultivation of long-growing tree crops, such as coconuts and breadfruit in Samoa and other Pacific islands; and **slash-and-burn** (also known as *swidden, extensive*, and *shifting*) cultivation. Secondary characteristics include higher productivity compared with simple foragers, small permanent (sometimes semipermanent) settlements; incipient part-time craft specialization; and, in some instances, status differences among kin groups.

Tree Cultivation

A classic example of tree cultivation is represented by Samoa, a chain of islands formed by volcanic action, whose porous soils prevent overwatering from the frequent heavy showers that range up to 200 inches per year. The combination of heavy rain and warm, sunny weather fosters a lush plant cover. The main sources of crops are three fruit-bearing trees: breadfruit, coconut, and banana, none of which requires much maintenance. Taro is also another source of starch, and these are planted on sloping land; when the soil is exhausted, Samoans clear other sites for cultivation. Weeding is nonexistent; the leaves and combined shallow-root and deep-root structures of taro plants and weeds prevent the erosion of a loose volcanic soil from the torrential rains. Samoans obtain their protein primarily from fishing, though they also keep chickens and pigs.

As this brief discussion indicates, tree cultivation may be interspersed with slash-and-burn cultivation, as we see for taro in Samoa. The Yanomamö, while relying primarily on slash-and-burn cultivation, also harvest the fruit, a highly prized delicacy, of peach palms, hearts of palm, Brazil nuts, and cashews (Ember and Ember 2002:73–74).

Slash-and-Burn Cultivation

Of all systems of horticulture, **slash-and-burn cultivation** is the best known and most widely practiced. The commonalities are evidence enough.

The process begins with cutting brush and trees at the beginning of the dry season in tropical regions. Once dried toward the end of this season, the slash (brush and felled trees) is burned, and around the start of the rainy season, seeds, cuttings, or both are planted. Once the garden is planted, it is usually typical for harvests to take place on an as-needed basis, and often the actual planting may be staggered so that the crops mature at different times of the year. When the soil is exhausted, anywhere between two to three years, the plot is abandoned, a new site is cleared, and a garden is planted. Inasmuch as 12 to 24 years are needed for the soil to regenerate, extensive territory is required and so this type is also called extensive cultivation.

Tropical Cultivation in Amazonia

Rain forest cultivation in Brazil's riverine basin known as Amazonia has been extensively studied, so it is perhaps worth one's while to bring it to closer scrutiny. A systematic comparison of five Amazonian tribes has been made in Betty Meggers' appropriately titled book *Amazonia: Man and Culture in a Counterfeit Paradise* (1996). Meggers describes the general features of the Amazonian rain forest, its adaptive features to an extremely hot and wet climate, and how the slash-and-burn cultivation of tropical rain forest Indians is an unconscious imitation of the real tropical rain forest. We'll go through this here.

Amazonia is divided into two ecological zones: the Várzea, or the riverside silt that accumulates every spring when the banks of the Amazon and its tributaries are flooded; and the Terre Firme, or the Amazonian basin away from the rivers. Lands in the Várzea are replenished by silt deposited by the floods, and so are extremely rich and capable of cultivation. The description that follows refers to the Terra Firme, which is a plain, lush with trees but with thin and poor soil; "counterfeit paradise" is an appropriate part of the book's subtitle.

Ecology of Tropical Rainforests. The combination of intense heat and torrential rains is destructive to any exposed soil in the tropics. For Amazonia, Meggers describes three absolutes that affect the soil. The first is high atmospheric temperature, which affects several biological and chemical processes crucial to soil maintenance. For example, humus, the topsoil essential to all agriculture, cannot form if the soil temperature is above 77 degrees Fahrenheit. Below that temperature, humic materials, formed from the decay of animal droppings combined with plant and animal remains, can build up. Above 77 degrees, the rate of decomposition of humus exceeds its rate of formation, because much of the carbon and nitrogen in the compounds escape as gasses into the air.

A second constant is rainfall, which acts on the surface of the ground in two ways: erosion and leaching. As the water scours the surface of the soil, particles are carried off. The erosion rate increases exponentially, meaning that if the rate of flow is doubled, the scouring capacity quadruples, the carrying capacity of water increases 32 times, and the size of the particles transported increases 64 times. Leaching acts on the composition of the soil, so that soluble nutrients such as nitrogen are removed to levels below the reach of plant and tree roots. The higher the temperature of the moisture, the more the soluble nutrients that are lost.

The first two constants—high solar temperature and torrential rainfall—combine to induce a chemical reaction in the terrain. All tropical soils contain trace amounts of iron and other minerals. The intense heat and extensive moisture serve as catalysts in the oxidation of these minerals in a process that converts the minerals, and the soil itself, into **laterite**. Called **laterization**, the process also removes phosphorus, another nutrient essential to plant growth. The soil also loses its permeability and so is unable to retain other essential nutrients, such as ammonia, lime, potash, and magnesia. Once initiated, laterization is irreversible. It is worth noting that most mining in the tropics involves separating the ore from its oxides with a process that involves intense heat, which requires high fossil-fuel intake. The process becomes unprofitable if the price of petroleum increases.

The age of soil is the third constant. The terrain in Amazonia is one of the oldest geological formations in the world. The processes already described have been going on for millions of years, so that the soil is so devoid of nutrients that they would be barren in a temperate climate. Soils are acidic, some moderately and others extremely so. Soils consist primarily of sand and clay. The soil is perennially short of calcium, an essential nutrient for plants with high protein content.

Features of Tropical Rainforests. The main features of tropical rainforest serve as an adaptive means to minimize the effects of sunlight and tropical rains. These consist of a protective canopy, diversity of species, and high rates of growth. We discuss these in turn.

First, the forest canopy is so thick that the forest floor is dark; it lacks foliage for that reason, and, indeed, requires an explorer to carry a flashlight to make his or her way through the forest base. The canopy contains not only the leaves of the trees, but also several species of **epiphytic plants**, which anchor themselves on the treetops and derive their nutrients from the atmosphere-borne moisture and minerals. Their vines are trailed like streamers from the treetops.

This canopy has several functions that protect the soil. First, it provides a shade keeping the soil temperature below the 77 degrees necessary to ensure topsoil formation and minimize loss through gasification of nitrogen and carbon compounds. Second, it breaks the heavy rainfall. Some— 25 percent—of the rainfall is absorbed by the leaves and epiphytic plants; the remainder falls to the ground in a fine spray. Thus, reduction of water flow minimizes erosion, and the reduced water volume also minimizes leaching.

Also preserving the soil is the juxtaposition of species with differing nutrient requirements in the same space. As Meggers puts it, such vegetation is "consequently characterized by a great proliferation of species but low concentration of individuals of the same species" (1996:17). Estimates are that the number of species of trees is more than 20 times the number in European forests; nevertheless, they look the same to the untrained eye. The interplanting ensures that all nutrients will be used; what one tree does not use, another tree does. An added bonus are the different root characteristics and penetration, so that the resultant root mat improves the structure of the soil during the life of the plants, whose death contributes to the organic matter to be processed into humus (Meggers 1996:18). Their dispersal also lessens the spread of disease and pests.

Even the spectacular growth rate observed for tropical forests have a function. Because of their volatility, nutrients have to be processed at a high rate. The intense heat and high rainfall make for this acceleration. Not surprising, then, is that the rate of litter fall (animal remains and waste, combined with dead vegetation) is four times the rate of New York woodlands; the nutrients range in proportion from double in phosphorus to tenfold in nitrogen. Adding to the rapid processing are the nutrients captured from the atmosphere through rainwater, which contributes 75 percent of the potassium, 40 percent of the magnesium, and 25 percent of the phosphorus absorbed by the topsoil (Meggers 1996:17).

Meggers summarizes two major conservation functions of the primary tropical rainforest: (1) It sets up and maintains a closed cycle of nutrients, so that the same ingredients are kept in continuous circulation and loss is reduced to a minimum, and (2) it mitigates the detrimental effects of the climate to the extent that soil impoverishment by erosion or leaching is either arrested or reduced to a very slow rate (1996:18).

Slash-and-Burn Cultivation Primary Forest in Microcosm? In lesser respects, tropical horticulture performs adaptive functions not unlike the mature tropical rain forest. To some extent, tropical gardens maintain a continuous circulation of the same nutrients and reduce the rate of soil impoverishment.

The Mundurucú provide a representative illustration of slash-and-burn cultivation as practiced throughout Amazonia. At the beginning of the dry season, they first clear brush and small trees. Then they fell the larger trees systematically, by partially cutting all trees in the path of a "keystone" tree, which knocks the others down. Trees left standing are felled individually. After two months, the slash is burned on a day a slight breeze serves to fan the flames, but not strong enough to leave behind unburned slash. The burning must be completed by the end of the dry season.

Planting begins at the onset of the rainy season, with cuttings interplanted. A hole is made with a digging stick, cuttings or seeds are inserted, and the soil is moved over them with a foot. Usually, twelve or so food plants are raised, with sweet potato and manioc (a root cultigen highly prized throughout Amazonia and known in Spanish as *yuca*) interplanted at the center and other crops planted at the edges. Planting is staggered, so that when one crop (especially manioc) is harvested, a cutting is immediately planted. Weeding is done usually twice annually. Decline in productivity leads to abandonment of the field, usually by the third year (Meggers 1996).

Yanomamös' cultivation is similar, but varies in certain details. First, once a site is planted, the Yanomamö clear and plant a new plot every year. This makes it unnecessary to do all the work of clearing a new plot, and the site shifts as new plots are cleared and the old ones abandoned. Their crops include a nonnative plantain tree, which produces a high energy yield for a tropical plant, and the tree may be harvested years after its site has gone back to brush and forest (Chagnon 1997).

The two sites share common characteristics. First, the larger plants provide shade for the smaller ones and the soil itself. Ground cover is additionally maintained by harvesting a few plants at a time and staggering the planting, so that the soil is rarely exposed to the sun and rain. Interplanting ensures maximal utilization of nutrients by plants whose requirements differ, and discourages the spread of pests and diseases that attack specific plants. Weeding is of mixed value; although gardeners remove weeds competing with crops for space and nutrients, they also hasten soil deterioration by removing shade and protection from erosion. Finally, burning the slash returns some nutrients to the soil, as do decomposing trunks and large branches; they also divert certain pests and diseases from crop plants (Meggers 1996).

Finally, the genuine poverty of the Amazonian environment is evident when one considers the scarcity and dispersal of wild foods, coupled with their low nutritional value. Amazonia contains the most varied plants in the world, yet they are not concentrated. Furthermore, protein sources are scarce. With the exception of the Brazil nut and other nuts, seed-bearing plants are scarce. A great deal of protein is required for seed reproduction. Therefore, most plants reproduce by vegetative means, whereby new plants grow from the shoots of their parent. Most animals are thin, isolated, and often nocturnal. Monkeys and peccaries (wild pigs), which are large and move in groups, are the exceptions. The primary factor of this poverty of protein in the environment is the age of the soil, dated back to the Tertiary, whereas most soils of Europe and North America date back only to the Pleistocene of the Quaternary. Thus, most Terra Firme soils consist of clay and sand, and are highly acidic which, to Meggers, would render them barren in moderate climates. Low calcium content in tropical soils is one primary factor in this poverty of protein (1996:35–37).

It is not surprising, therefore, that most peoples of Amazonia supplement a diet, consisting mostly of starch and of plant foods that reproduced by vegetative means rather than by seed, and seek their protein by hunting and fishing. "Over the millennia," Meggers contends, "each aboriginal group suc-

ceeded in developing a seasonal cycle that combines hunting, fishing, gathering, and agricultural of various intensities, but which in every case assures the availability of nutrients indefinitely without endangering the equilibrium of the ecosystem" (1996:37).

We cannot conclude without recalling the so-called "Protein Debate" between Marvin Harris, who never set foot in Yanomamö territory, and Napoleon Chagnon, who spent at least 66 months over several years with them. In his *Cows, Pigs, Wars, and Witches*, Harris explains Yanomamö warfare in terms of protein scarcity; when two tribes converge at the same hunting ground, they start fighting over game animals. Chagnon counters with the argument that the abduction of women, not game, sparks off the war. The argument went on for decades until Harris's death in 2001, and involved Kenneth Good, a student of Chagnon's who nonetheless supported Harris's protein scarcity theory. Harris sees the evolutionary significance of the Protein Debate in light of competition for resources; Chagnon sees the significance of the Abduction-of-Women theory in light of reproductive success. For a review of the arguments—and the infighting—see Harris (1974, 1979), Chagnon (1997:91–97) and Good (1997). The student should be cautioned against the kind of futile—or feudlike—arguments such as this one.

Pastoralism

Some cultures domesticate animals, but not plants. In other words, they practice **pastoralism**, or the primary dependence on the products of domesticated herd animals. They range in size from goats and sheep to cattle, horses, and camels. They occur primarily in grassland regions, whose soil is too impenetrable for horticulture or preindustrial agriculture. The climate may also be too hilly, too arid, or too cold to support intensive cultivation. So long as there is grass or like vegetation, pastoralism is a feasible strategy of subsistence (Sahlins 1968).

Pastoralists move their animals as the seasons change. They may be transhumant or nomadic. **Transhumant pastoralism** occurs when men and boys move their herds from one region or elevation to the next and back again, while their families stay in one place. East African herdsmen are transhumant pastoralists. **Nomadic pastoralism** occurs when entire families move with the herds throughout the year and there are no permanent villages. Central Asian peoples, who live in transportable yurts, are examples.

Animals vary with the climate, region, and purpose. The Bedouins of Arabia, for example, use camels primarily for transportation, and rarely consume the meat; other Middle Eastern peoples, such as the Basseri of southern Iran, raise sheep, goats, horses, and donkeys. East Africans are particularly famous for their cattle, which they value in the way we value money.

Because they can produce only animal consumer products—milk, hides, meat, and in East Africa blood—some anthropologists refer to pastoralists as **incomplete food producers**, because they do not also grow crops. Therefore, they often depend on settled communities for plant food products—nuts, fruits, root crops—and for crafted goods. Sahlins argues that there develops a hostile symbiosis between herders and community folk— symbiotic because each depends on the other, but hostile because herders may find it more profitable to raid the communities than to trade with them. Indeed, warfare is often associated with pastoralists. As we shall see in chapter 13, an entire age grade is devoted to defending the tribes' own herds or raiding their neighbors' (Sahlins 1968; Sangree 1965).

Because of the need to move, valuables are small and portable; they include coins, jewelry, ornaments of gold or other precious metal, and so on. Generally speaking, property is limited in amount and size by the need to be carried in carts or on the backs of animals.

Because males often (though not always) raise animals and defend their herds, male cooperation is usually important among pastoralists. Therefore, residence tends to be patrilocal (where the wife moves in with her husband and husband's kin), households tend to center around a core of related males, and descent tends to be patrilineal. These concepts are discussed in chapters 7 and 9.

Because pastoralism is an incomplete food-producing system—animals but not plants are domesticated—it was early thought that animal husbandry was a transitional phase between hunting and gathering and agriculture. However, most archaeological evidence suggests that pastoralism arose during, or even after, the domestication of plants and animals both; this suggests that some populations may have left settled communities, by choice or by force, to develop this complex (Sahlins 1968).

In recent years, governments have encouraged or forced nomadic pastoralists to move into settled communities, in the interest of maintaining control over them. Called *villageization* in Kenya and by other names elsewhere, the effect has been a marked reduction of nomadic peoples as they take up agriculture or wage work.

Equestrian Hunting

As you may know, the classical stereotype of "The Indian" is one who hunts buffalo while riding on a horse, wearing a war bonnet, brandishing bow and arrows or lance, and who lives in a tipi—in short, everything you see in this or that cowboys and Indians movie or the over-romanticized *Dances with Wolves*. **Equestrian hunting** refers using draft animals—horses—to hunt other animals (Sahlins 1968).

In anthropological fact, this practice is rare. In North America, this kind of hunting was not an aboriginal trait in North America, even in the Great Plains. Before the horse was introduced in the Great Plains in the 17th century, plainsmen either hunted on foot—the Comanches for one— or practiced horticulture along the major rivers, as did the Cheyenne. Horses indigenous to North America died out in pre-Columbian times; the horse population domesticated by the Plains Indians were probably introduced by Spaniard colonists who settled northern Mexico and what is now New Mexico between the 16th and 19th century. The greatest known period of diffusion of horses was from 1740 to 1800.

The use of the horse in hunting spread quickly as horses became more plentiful. It may be that settled peoples took to the horse because of its economic superiority to river-bottom agriculture, but a more likely explanation was the importance of the horse in warfare—higher mobility and speed of mounted warriors as compared to foot warriors—so that village-dwelling peoples had no choice but to defend themselves.

Trade with whites may have also contributed to the spread of equestrian hunting, as individual tribes hunted even more buffalo—or stole horses for trade—and fought each other to gain trading advantages. Guns, which gave even greater military advantages to their owners, were also prized.

In many respects, equestrian hunting was similar to pastoralism. Buffalo moved wherever there was good pasture, and this changed with the seasons; Native Americans moved with the buffalo. Buffalo moved in huge herds during late spring and early summer (when the grass was tallest—and it was also rutting season), then dispersed in late summer through winter, when grass was sparser and in winter under snow. Accordingly, the Cheyenne and other Plains Indians massed during the spring and summer, and dispersed in smaller bands in the fall (Sahlins 1968).

Communal hunting was the most common and the most productive. Unlike the environmentalist image that *Dances with Wolves* projects, the real Cheyennes' aim was to kill off the entire herd if they could. Mounted men stampeded the herd into an ever tighter circle, picked off any buffalo they could, and repeated the process. Then the skinning and butchering began, with women doing the greatest amount of work in preparing the meat and dressing the skins. Meat was dried into jerky (derived from the Spanish word *charqui*), then pounded with berries to make pemmican, which was stored in rawhide sacks. In this case, large amounts of meat could be made to keep the winter, and it was no advantage to consume it immediately, as it would be among the !Kung.

Intensive Cultivation

Known also in the anthropological literature as intensive agriculture, **intensive cultivation** refers to food production that is characterized by the permanent cultivation of fields, high levels of productivity, and sometimes sophisticated technology such as irrigation canals or terraces, plows drawn by draft animals, and varieties of farm machinery. However accomplished, all forms of intensive cultivation share the following attributes.

Intensive Cultivation: Common Attributes. Intensive cultivation provides a high yield per unit of land as compared with horticulture, but it can vary. For the peasants in the Chinese village of Kaihsienkung, who rely on terraced irrigated fields, 186 work-hours are required to produce 1 million calories (yearly requirement for one person); in the United States back in 1947, 2.2 work-hours were required to produce the same amount.

Generally, most land is devoted to a single crop. In the case of Kaihsienkung, 90 percent of land was devoted to rice, with wheat, beans, cotton, and soybeans accounting for the remainder. Elsewhere, the staple crop(s) consisted of maize in Mesoamerica; potatoes in Andean America; grain, predominately wheat, in the Near East and, later, Europe; millet in northern China; and rice in southern China and southeast Asia (Service 1978).

Intensive cultivation involves risk of famine. Drought, insect pests, or disease could wipe out a single crop, the major disadvantage that is not found in horticulture. In many high civilizations, grain was stored against this contingency. The intercropping practices found in many horticultural systems minimize this risk (Sahlins 1968).

Most staples can be stored. Grain, unless moist, is slow to decay, and can be stored for several years. Means have been found to store such perishable root crops as potatoes; for example, the Inca of Andean America froze their potatoes (among other foods, such as duck) at night and dried them during the day—an originator of the freeze-dry technique of food preservation (Steward and Faron 1959).

Formation of Intensive Cultivation: Some Explanations. Did our ancestors take up agriculture because it was obviously superior to foraging when it comes to yield? Most anthropologists, including especially archaeologists, reject this explanation. This is because farming is an arduous task. One has to plan each season—for that matter, each day—carefully. Seeds must be planted; then there is watering to be done, frequent weeding, protection against predators, harvesting, storage, and selection of seeds for next year's crop. Add animals to the equation, and there is more work to be done, from helping cows or mares birth their young through maintenance while the animals are in their nonproductive periods to milking, slaughtering, butchering, and meat preservation. Foraging is a much simpler life, and not much less productive per capita per year.

Why take up farming then? Perhaps a partial answer to this question may lie in the fact that, whereas foraging, horticulture, and pastoralism all are *extensive* strategies—they take up a great deal of territory—intensive cultivation, by definition, takes up relatively small areas of land and makes efficient use of it. Perhaps the reason lies in population increases relative to usable land.

Most of the explanations for the **Neolithic Revolution**, defined by plant and animal domestication, center around the theme of population density relative to land and water availability, although occurrence of plants and animals that can be domesticated play a part. The **oasis hypothesis**, formulated by Vere Gordon Childe (1951), posits that agriculture emerged where there was water in an increasingly water-scarce environment; communities developed along the Tigris, Euphrates, Nile, Indus, Huang Ho, and other rivers, all in regions where land was fertile but water was otherwise scarce. Lewis Binford's **edge hypothesis** (1983) suggests that land use became intensified at the edge of natural hunting and gathering habitats by populations that otherwise might have been forced out. Arguing from a similar premise, Cohen (1979) suggests that intensification occurred everywhere because population densities increased everywhere, beyond the region's carrying capacity. Each explanation has its problems. Some point out, for example, that agriculture developed in places where water was not particularly scarce, nor the population dense.

Other explanations are more complex. For example, Braidwood offers a **natural habitat hypothesis** (1960), which proposes that agriculture emerged where domesticated plants developed at the site of their natural ancestors. Jarmo, for example, developed at the edge of the Fertile Crescent, which extended from the eastern shores of the Mediterranean, eastward through southern Turkey, Syria, and northern Iraq, and thence into Iran. Most archaeologists would argue for a multivariate theory, one that posits several contributing factors—population, habitat ideal for cultivation, domesticable plants, and so on. The relative importance of these variables also varies by location and by cultivation techniques employed.

Intensive Cultivation Technologies. Although preindustrial civilizations are often identified with irrigation canal systems (Mesopotamia) or flood plain irrigation (Egypt), the term covers a large variety of techniques. This can be accomplished by a combination of the following factors:

One of the most common forms of intensive cultivation is **irrigation**. The simplest known technique involves **flood plain irrigation**, in which fields are abandoned to flooding during the rainy season and planted when the flood recedes. This form was best known in Egypt during the Old and Middle Kingdoms, but was supplemented with the **shaduf**, a lever with a bucket that was dipped into the Nile and the water transferred to a sluice and

thence to the field (Price and Sanders 2004). Other irrigation systems involved the construction of canals from the river (as was the case for the Tigris and Euphrates Rivers in Mesopotamia), and the construction of **terraces** in Meso-America, China, and southeast Asia. One unique system was the construction of **chinampas**, or raised fields constructed from alternate layers of earth and decayed vegetation to form a rich—and relatively dry—platform for the crops. This was characteristic of the swamps around the Aztec capital of Tenochtitlán, but Mayan city states may also have been sustained by these platforms (Schele and Miller 1986; Berdan 1982).

Many agricultural systems rely on draft animals, such as the horse or ox, and plow. Plows with wooden shares (some tipped with metal) were common throughout the Near East, where the soil is mostly silt, which is light and pliable. In Europe, where much of the soil is heavy, a metal share was a necessity.

Much of the civilizational world, however, relied on what Scupin (2004) calls **intensive horticulture**, whereby most of the cultivation, including canal construction, is or was done by hand. Except for the llama in the Andes, the New World lacked draft animals of any kind, and practically all work was done by human power.

At the opposite end of the scale, modern agriculture has replaced draft animals with the tractor, but the plow has been refined rather than replaced; it has many rather than one share, so a wide swath of soil can be turned on one trip; harrows, with spikes to smooth and pulverize the soil; and other devices. More important is the question of energy consumption. In a comparative study of energy consumption, Earl Cook (1971:136) finds that the daily per capita consumption in kilocalories (kc) was 5,000 kc among hunters and gatherers (foragers), 12,000 kc among horticulturalists, and 26,000 among agrarian (preindustrial intensive cultivators); in contrast, modern industrial societies shot up to 230,000 kc (Scupin 2003:272).

Although industrial agriculture is highly productive in comparison with preindustrial agriculture and other subsistence systems, there is substantial evidence to indicate that when calculated as a ratio-to-energy input, food energy output is much lower in comparison with nonindustrial subsistence systems. Nor is the input confined to the cost in gas and oil for running farm equipment.

First, there are the energy costs to manufacture this equipment in the first place. Second, as Heinberg points out,

> nitrogen fertilizers are produced from natural gas; pesticides and herbicides are synthesized from oil; seeds, chemicals, and crops are transported long distances by truck; and foods are often cooked with natural gas and packaged in oil-derived plastics before reaching the consumer. [Therefore] from farm to plate, depending on the degree to which it is processed, a typical food item may embody input energy between four and several time its food energy. This energy deficit can only be maintained because of the availability of cheap fossil fuels, a temporary gift from the earth's geologic past (2003:175).

There are secondary effects. With the advent of intensive cultivation, a large number of workers are freed to pursue other, nonagricultural crafts. Thus, a high degree of craft specialization is likely to emerge, and trade develops not only among specialty craftspersons within but also between communities or cities. Settled communities not only accompany the intensification of agriculture (indeed, the complex foragers of the Upper Paleolithic and the Mesolithic were able to found settled communities) but sooner or later develop into cities.

Conclusion

We have presented five basic subsistence strategies as ideal types—as if each culture employed only one of these strategies. In fact, most cultures employ two or more strategies. The complexities were hinted at for Amazonia, where most cultivators also hunt animals and gather wild fruits and other plant foods. A reason was also suggested: Amazonia is a protein-poor environment. Nor are they all of one type: pastoralists may herd cattle, horses, sheep, goats, or some combination thereof. Cultivation techniques vary as well. Some involve flood plains, others canals from rivers, still others in terraces, and yet others in raised fields in swamps.

There are also other questions. How is the work organized? Who owns what? These are issues taken up in chapter 11, on economic anthropology. Many of these questions, though, are predicated on the question of who is related to whom and who marries whom. We take up these questions in the next four chapters on marriage, family, and kinship.

Chapter 7

PRINCIPLES OF KINSHIP AND DESCENT

Introduction

Most preindustrial societies, except those with large populations (mostly states, but with a few exceptions), are based on primary, or face-to-face, relations. Of these, the most important is kinship, or human relations based on the facts of birth, marriage, and death. It is perhaps the first organization known to humankind, because it is closest to the biological functions affecting all human groups: copulation, reproduction, maturation, and death.

Why Kinship?

Kin groups, or groups based on marriage and family, are often the unit of property ownership; you cannot know anything about property ownership until you know who is included and is excluded from the property-owning group, and to know that, you need to know the principles of descent. Kin groups are often the unit of economic cooperation. They also govern the political units of a culture and society; for example, in **chiefdoms** or **states**, descent determines who will be chief or king, and it may rank nobles to each other, as is the case among Northwest Coast native peoples. Certainly, with the widely reported practice of ancestor worship, kinship has some bearing on supernatural beliefs, as we will see in chapter 15. Finally, kinship affiliation

may even determine whom one fights, as is the case among the pastoralist Nuer of Ethiopia and the Sudan.

Constants of Kinship

Based in part on Robin Fox's *Kinship and Marriage* (1967), one might identify six constants—four biological and two sociopsychological—that underlie kinship affiliation and its uses. They are as follows:

Biological Constants:

a. Women bear the children.
b. Men impregnate the women.
c. Children are dependent on adults for a long period (15 years more or less).
d. Death comes to all and demands a replacement.

Psychological and Social Constants:

a. Primary kin may not mate with each other (the incest tabu).
b. Men exercise the authority in households and wider social groups.

Biological Constants.   No human population is free from sex, reproduction, child rearing, or death, so these four qualify as constants, functions that kinship must fulfill. The first two constants—male procreation and female childbearing—involve at least minimum cooperation between the sexes. The third constant recognizes the long period of the mother's nurturance of her child, followed by a long period of **enculturation**, or child rearing, whereby the child acquires the skills, values, and norms of the society necessary to become a full participant in the affair of the band, village, or other society. Finally, death takes away a member and demands a replacement. The member's property must be inherited or otherwise disposed of, the household headship must be filled by a survivor, and the vacated kingship demands a successor. As we shall see, each of these constants generates a role that kinship must play.

Psychological and Social Constants. Although neither the incest tabu nor male dominance is entirely universal, they are statistical equivalents of constants. Almost all cultures, according to prevailing assumptions in anthropology, prohibit sexual behavior among **primary kin**: father–daughter, mother–son, brother–sister. (A few find, however, that not all, or even most, cultures prohibit this act; see next chapter). Others prohibit sexual behavior among **secondary kin** as well, those who are related by **consanguineal** or blood ties. They may range from cousins to any two persons related by a distant ancestor whose identity may not even be known. Only the royal lineages of Egypt, the Inca, and the Hawaiian allow brother–sister marriage (and therefore mating). The exigencies of kinship take incest strongly into account.

As for male dominance, the question is less certain from a statistical standpoint. Many households are female dominated. Among the Iroquois, women owned the longhouses and the gardens, and had enough influence to initiate a divorce by placing their husbands' belongings outside the doorway. We look at this issue in the next chapter. Women's status varies from complete subordination among the Masai and Chinese, to equal partnership among the !Kung, to strong influence among the Iroquois and Hopi. Nevertheless, some kinship roles assume male dominance in many societies, if not all.

Overview of Sex, Marriage, Family, and Kinship

The importance of kinship requires that we devote the next four chapters to the topic. We begin with the all-important topic: **rules of descent**, or the

rules whereby kin are reckoned (recognized) as such, regardless of their actual biological relationship. We do so because much of what follows will not make sense without understanding these rules.

Chapter 8 begins by drawing a distinction between **sex** and **gender**, issues of sexual behavior, why incest tabus exist, and **gender roles** including the **gender division of labor**. Chapter 9 examines marriage, its definitions, what may pass as marriage (such as the **sambandham** practices among the Nayar of India), the functions of marriage, and how alternative arrangements, such as the **consanguineal family** and households created by **woman marriage**, may fulfill them. **Postmarital residence** and the extended families created are covered, and the chapter concludes with a discussion of divorce.

Chapter 10 covers wider kinship groups, known as **lineages** and **clans**, defined respectively in terms of **demonstrated** and **stipulated** descent. Also introduced are **ambilineal** or **nonunilineal descent groups**, **kindreds**, and the differences between **sociocentric** and **egocentric** descent groups. Marriage is also reintroduced, this time as alliances between kin groups; they include **bridewealth** and **bride labor** and **cousin marriage**, involving both **parallel cousins** and **cross-cousins**. (Chapters 12 and 13 will discuss the role of cousin marriage in political alliances.)The chapter concludes with a section on **kinship terminology**, or the patterns of terms individuals use to categorize their relatives.

Rules of Descent

Kinship as a Social Reckoning of Biological Fact

It must be remembered that biology alone does not determine kinship. If this were true, the Romans would not have to write into family law, as they in fact wrote, that "the father of the child is the husband of the mother"; that would have been understood. As we will soon see, the father is not always the husband of the mother, nor in some societies does it matter.

We could also point out that our own system of **reckoning** kin, or recognizing persons as one's relatives, goes along the lines of biology. We do recognize kin on our father's side as equal to those on our mother's side. This assumption, however, overlooks our forgetfulness. Let's do a few exercises to see how this works. To start, take a sheet of paper and list the first names of your siblings, then your parents, then your parents' siblings (your aunts and uncles), then all four of your grandparents. Presumably, you have no trouble in naming them all.

Now here is where the fun begins. On a separate sheet, list the first names of all the **siblings**, or brothers and sisters, of all four of your grandparent. My bet is that you will forget at least some of them. (My paternal grandfather had ten siblings; I can remember only one.) Now list the first names of all eight of your great grandparents. Again, if you can do so, you are unusual in this society. For fun, list the first names of your great grandparents' siblings. Now list the first names of all sixteen of your great great grandparents. For fun, list *their* siblings. This should drive home the point that we eliminate most of our biological relatives from our memory.

This exercise also shows that rules of descent are as *exclusionary* as they are inclusionary. In the world's culture, most mechanisms of exclusion are not so arbitrary as a poor memory. Some involve choices, as occurs when a couple chooses whether to reside with the groom's or the bride's kin. Other mechanisms are automatic. How these work is the focus of this chapter and also of chapters 9 and 10.

Mechanics of Kinship Analysis

In the next several pages, we will examine the nuts and bolts of kinship analysis. In preparation for learning how to trace the rules of descent, you may want to copy the diagrams on pages 70 and 71, expand the images to standard paper size, and make several copies of each one.

The symbols for the diagram are as follows:

1. Triangles (Δ) represent males.
2. Circles (O) represent females.
3. Squares (□) represent persons of either sex.
4. Horizontal lines above the shapes (Δ̅ ̅ ̅O̅) represent sibling, or brother–sister, links. These are known as **sibling** links. This is one type of **consanguineal** link, or link between relatives "by blood."
5. Vertical lines linking two shapes link persons of different generations (|). These are known as **generational** links. This is the other type of **consanguineal** link, or link between relatives "by blood."

6. Equal signs represent an **affinal**, or marriage, link between two persons (usually but not always of the opposite sex). Sometimes, kinship diagrams require that the marital couple be placed at a distance from each other; in this case a vertical line is drawn below the two figures (Δ̲ ̲ ̲ ̲ ̲O̲)

This discussion will revolve around the diagrams on pages 70 and 71. Again, you may want to copy them, expand them to standard paper size, and make multiple copies to follow the discussion below. While you're at it, you might want to copy the images from pages 70 and 71 on overhead transparencies. (Diagrams are also available in the glossary.) You'll see why when we discuss **double unilineal descent**.

For the present, make at least two copies, but I suggest you make more.

Also in the discussion that follows, the term **ego** is used throughout to emphasize the relationship of a chosen individual with other individuals on these diagrams. Ego is No. 25 (male) on one diagram and No. 26 (female) on the other.

For the latter, make at least one copy, but I suggest you make more.

Defining Rules of Descent

The term **descent** refers to the rules that affiliate individuals with particular sets of kin because of known or presumed common ancestry. More prosaically, descent concerns those rules by which individuals are placed into the category "kin" or "relative" because of known or presumed ancestry. Descent implies rights and obligations. They may involve certain rights, such as inheritance, or access to use of cattle or land, or rights of political succession. They also involve duties, such as hospitality, or cattle herding, or defense of the homestead against invaders.

Taken at a broad perspective, there are two major kinds of descent: **bilateral** and **unilineal**. Note the etymology, or Latin, origins of the two words. "Bilateral" comes from *bi-* or "both" and *-lateral*, which means "side"; that means that bilateral descent emphasizes both sides of a person's descent affiliation. "Unilineal" comes from *uni-* or "one" (more precisely, "one, and only one") and *-lineal*, which means "line." Therefore, the term emphasizes a line of males or females that links a person to his or her ancestor. The meanings of

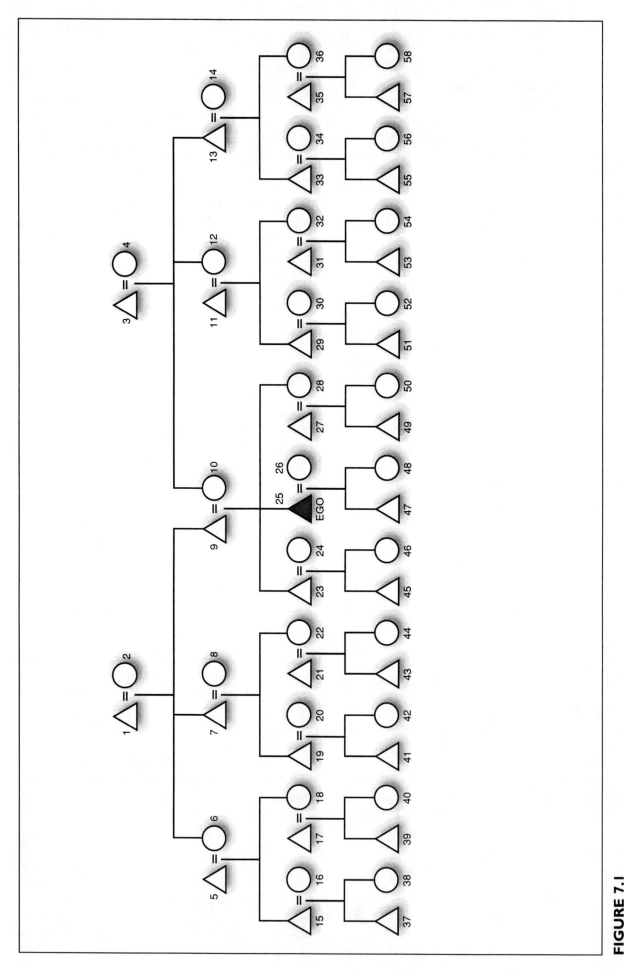

FIGURE 7.1
Bilateral and patrilineal kinship diagram. Make several copies of this diagram and use them to follow the discussion.

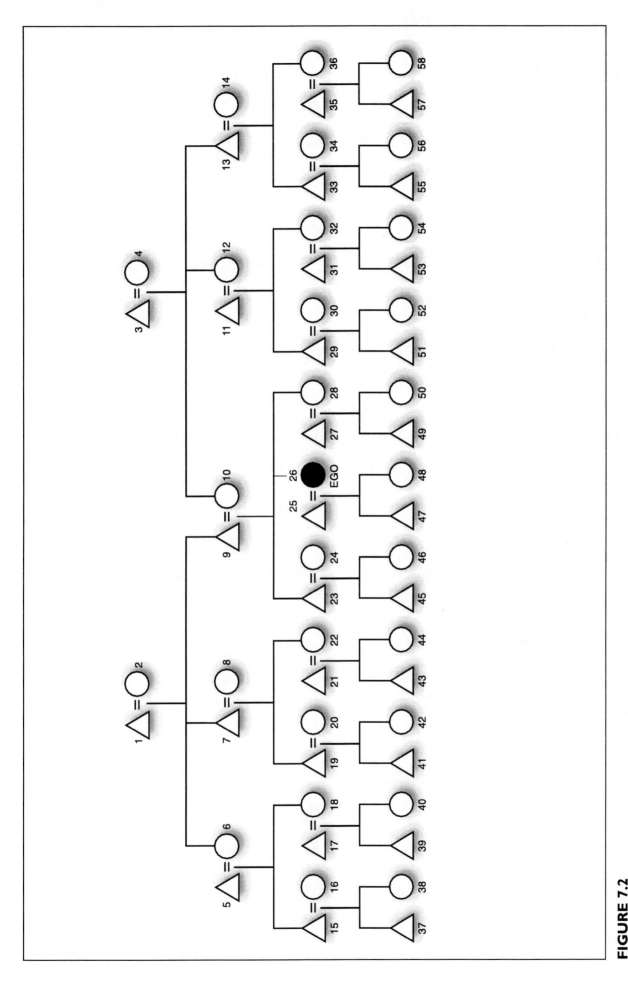

FIGURE 7.2
Matrilineal kinship diagram. Make several copies of this diagram and use them to follow the discussion.

bilateral and unilineal involve two referents—*two versus one* and *side versus line*—and not just one referent (*two versus one*). This point is important and will be repeated throughout our discussion; kinship will not make sense without this understanding.

Bilateral Descent.   **Bilateral descent** refers to the rule of descent whereby kinsmen are reckoned (recognized) through both male and female kin equally; distance between kin is used to mark off different kinds of kin. Emphasized here are the sides, or lateral aspect, as well as the two sides of one's family (namely, the "father's side" and the "mother's side").

One example of bilateral descent is our own. First, as you may see from the diagram in Figure 7.3, we consider that our mother's family and relatives are no less related to ourselves than those of our father's family and relatives. Furthermore, under the laws of most states and provinces, sons and daughters whose parents die intestate (without a will) have equal inheritance rights, legally and often in practice. If we mention our "grandmother," others might ask "which one?" since she could be our father's mother or mother's mother or, to express it in common language, my "grandmother on my father's side" or our "grandmother on my mother's side."

So far, then, we cannot really speak of ancestors. Which ancestor would you choose two generations back? Your father's father? Your mother's mother? How about your father's mother, or mother's father? As you can see, bilateral descent means that you could have four ancestors two generations back, eight ancestors three generations back, sixteen ancestors four generations back—the possibilities are endless and in the end useless. (Actually, cultures with a bilateral rule of descent do reckon ancestors, but only by rules of exclusion that make their relationships manageable. To understand this, we first need to discuss unilineal descent and then sample one rule of exclusion, residential rights to land.)

Therefore, it is not surprising that everyone on the diagram is related to everyone else. All the **consanguineal** kin are related to each other, and all the **affinal** kin are tied together by their children. By definition, affiliation through bilateral reckoning is limited only by biological ties, and only socially derived rules can limit these ties.

Unilineal Descent.   **Unilineal descent** refers to the descent rule whereby kin is **reckoned** (recognized) through one line of descent only, either

through males or females, but not both. Here, the lineal, not lateral, aspect is emphasized. **Patrilineal descent** is the rule of affiliation through descent lines of males only. **Matrilineal descent** is the rule of affiliation through descent lines of females only. Put some woman in the male line, and you break that line of descent. Put some dude in the female line, and you break that line of descent. If you observed a unilineal rule of descent, you would be unrelated to many people on the three diagrams.

Patrilineal Descent.   It's one thing to rattle off definitions of new and exotic words; you could probably get them all correct in tomorrow's quiz. It's another thing to understand them. Fortunately, we have in our midst a way of illustrating patrilineal descent; our system of assigning last names, or surnames. For this exercise, you will need to refer to the diagram in Figure 7.1. on page 70. (You did make some copies, didn't you?)

1. Let's say that Ego on the diagram is a man called P—pick a name that starts with P. (As a former chess fan, I chose Petrosian, after the late grandmaster of the game Tigran Petrosian, but any surname beginning with P will do. Note that P also stands for "patrilineal. Yes, I'm being cutesy. Now let's get back to work.). Now look at Ego, who is No. 25 on the diagram.

2. Before following this procedure, cover the text under (3) below and the diagram on Figure 7.4 until you figure out the answers. You could peek, but why blow the opportunity to learn this on your own? Now, on this diagram, who else besides No. 25 meets the following criteria for retaining the name Petrosian (or any P): the person is born with this name, retains this name upon marriage, and passes the name to the kids in the next generation? Mark them with a P or, better yet, fill in the symbol entirely with blue pen, pencil, or marker. Before looking at the next paragraph, labeled (3) and Figure 7.4, ask yourself what they have in common. For one thing, they're all Petrosians or whatever surname you selected. Why?

3. Now you can look. Shaded in black Ego, No. 25, is included by definition. So is 25's father, No. 9. So also is his father's father, No. 1. So is his father's brother, No. 7, not to mention his offspring, No. 19 (that's ego's cousin—what kind of cousin?), and *his* offspring, No. 41. And look here: No. 23, ego's brother, is black, and so is his

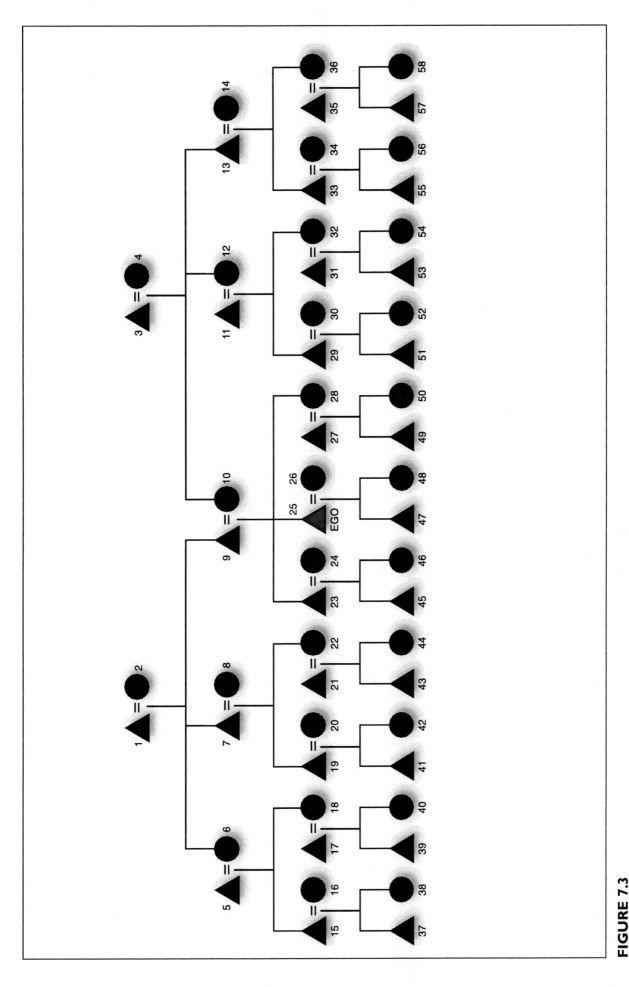

FIGURE 7.3
Bilateral descent: All persons represented here are Ego's bilateral kin.

offspring, No. 45. And there's No. 47, Ego's own offspring. What do they all have in common, you ask? They are all males and they are all direct descendants of No. 1. Not a single female is to be found in those lines (see for yourself). By the way, if you marked a symbol whose number is other than the above, then either look for the errant female or check the symbol to see which sex it represents. (That's what learning is all about; you make errors, then correct them.)

4. To make your exercise less than boring, try this. Which of the folks represented on the diagram are born as Petrosian (or any old name with a P), but lose the name upon marriage, and whose offspring carry the spouse's name? Use Ego No. 25 as the reference point, and you might have a look at his sibling, No. 28. Identify them by shading the left of each figure with your blue writing device. (They call it a pen, pencil, or marker, don't they?) Again, don't peek; cover item (5) and Figure 7.4.

5. If you guessed right or figured it out, the left-shaded figures include Ego's sibling, No. 28; No. 22 (his cousin—but which cousin? How are they linked?); No. 6 (No. 9's sibling or Ego's aunt—again, what kind?); No. 42, No. 19's offspring; No. 46, Ego's brother's (No. 19) offspring; and No. 48, Ego's own offspring. What do they all have in common? If you haven't figured it out by now, they are all females. They are also someone's (the someone being male) sister or daughter. They were born Petrosian, then changed their names when they married someone with another name. This assumes that they practice *patrilocal postmarital residence,* in which the women leave their residence of birth upon marriage. Women's kinship status varies widely; in China, they are completely absorbed into the patrilineage into which they marry; among the Tallensi of Ghana, they retain strong ties with the patrilineage of their birth and at death are buried with their natal kin (Fox 1967). In both extreme cases, however, they do not pass their patrilineal affiliation on to their children.

6. Now let's turn to the last of this set of exercises: Who on this diagram is not a Petrosian (or your P-name) at birth (again use Ego, No. 25, as the reference point), assumes the name Petrosian upon marriage, and has offspring named Petrosian? Identify them by shading the right side of each figure with your blue writing machine called a pen or marker. What do they have in common?

Again, take a crack at this question before looking at item (7) and Figure 7.1.

7. If you guessed they were female (how can you not figure it out?), you are correct. If you notice that they all are linked to a male listed in item (3) above by an equal sign, right again. (Sorry, no cigar.) They each have married a male named Petrosian (or your P-choice). They include No. 26 (Ego's wife), No. 24 (brother's wife), No. 10 (No. 25's own mother), No. 2 (the paternal grandmother, No. 8 (Ego's paternal uncle's wife) and No. 20 (the wife of Ego's cousin on his father's side—but what kind of cousin?).

A completed diagram showing all patrilineally based relatives appears below (on p. 75). Compare it against your own completed diagram, and study it while reading the following discussion.

You now know many things you didn't know before starting this exercise. You know, first, that the male Petrosians are linked in an unbroken line to the first known Petrosian. If (actually when) a female enters the picture, her offspring have a surname other than Petrosian, or else she is married to one. Patrilineal descent operates exactly the same way. Even though we reckon our kin bilaterally, this principle does not extend to our system of surnames; our naming system is patrilineal.

You might also notice that referring to, say No. 1, as Ego's grandfather on Ego's father's side doesn't make sense. His wife—Ego's grandmother—is on Ego's father's side, yet she is not a member of Ego's patrilineage (or named Petrosian) except for marriage. Ego's grandfather (father's father) *is* a member of Ego's patrilineage (indeed, thanks to him, Ego is in that patrilineage).

Finally, notice how Ego's relatives not named Petrosian are linked to Ego. For example, No. 15 isn't a Petrosian because No. 6, a female, lost her name upon marrying No. 5. No. 43 is not a Petrosian because his mother, No. 22, lost that name upon marriage. Of course, none of the persons on Ego's mother's side of the family is a Petrosian, because she is not male.

Try this experiment on your own family. See if you can trace everyone with your surname on the diagram you just reproduced (you might want to copy another one) and determine for yourself if you can trace unbroken male links back to your father's father, or father's father's father. Now find out from your paternal relative not bearing your surname how they are "disconnected" from that person.

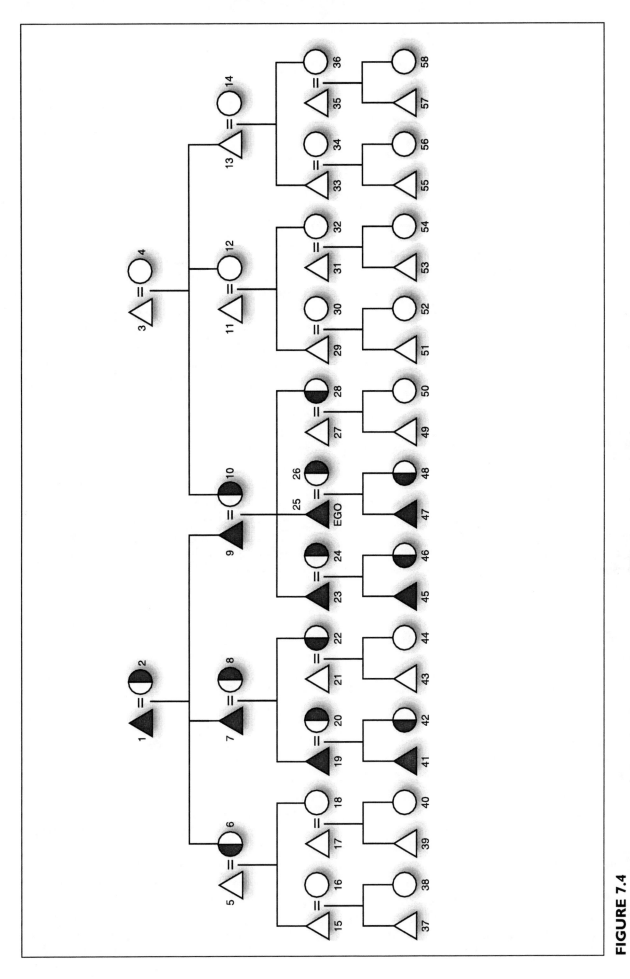

FIGURE 7.4
Patrilineal kin: All persons fully shaded are Ego's patrilineal kin; all persons shaded to the left are Ego's out-marrying kin upon marriage; all persons shaded to the right are in-marrying affines.

This exercise illustrates the advantages of unilineal versus bilateral descent. Exclusion is automatic: if a female links you to another "relative," that person is excluded from your own group. He or she belongs to some other group—but one to which you do not belong. Second, there are relatively few kin to keep track of. The number of possible ancestors go down from infinity to one.

This explains why the Bible could list so many "begats." Let's go through some, taken from Matthew, I:2-16: "Abraham begat Isaac; and Isaac begat Jacob; and Jacob begat Judas and his brethren; and Judas begat Phares and Zara of Thamar; and Phares begat Esrom" and so the list goes on to David the King, Solomon his son, and eventually arrives at Joseph, whose son Jesus is conceived by the Holy Ghost (so Matthew I:16, 18 tells us). By mentioning only the males, and the eldest ones at that, this genealogy is simplified. This is why many cultures can keep genealogies without benefit of writing; this may have been the case of the Hebrews as well. Polynesians kept long genealogies, as did Mongol tribes of the Asian Steppes, and others.

Matrilineal Descent.   In contrast with **patrilineal descent**, the term **matrilineal descent** refers to the rule of descent whereby kin affiliation is through the line of females only. The principles that govern patrilineal descent apply, in reverse, to matrilineal descent. For this exercise, we will construct a "what if" scenario. What if it were the women who retained their surnames on marriage and the men who gave theirs up? For this exercise, refer to the diagram in Figure 7.2 on p. 71 above, in which Ego, this time, is No. 26. As before, copy this diagram, expand it to standard paper size, and make several copies.

1. Now Let's say that ego on the diagram is a woman called M—pick a name that starts with M. (For no particular reason, I choose Miller, but any name begun with M will do. Note that M also stands for "matrilineal," just as P stood for "patrilineal. Cutesy, you call it? I call it a learning device. Now let's get on with the job.) First, look at Ego, who is for this purpose No. 26 on the diagram.

2. As before, cover the text under (3) and Figure 7.5 below, until you figure out the answers. Now, on this diagram, who else besides No. 26 meets the new criteria as follows for retaining the name Miller (or any M): The person is born with this name, retains this name upon marriage, and passes the name to the kids in the next generation? Mark them with a M or, better yet, fill in the symbol entirely with a red pen, pencil, or marker. Before looking at the next paragraph, labeled (3), ask yourself what they have in common. For one thing, they're all Millers or whatever surname you selected. Why?

3. Now you can look. Shaded in gray, Ego, No. 26, is included by definition. So is 26's mother, No. 10. So also is her mother's mother, No. 4. So is her mother's sister, No. 12, not to mention her offspring, No. 32 (that's Ego's cousin—what kind of cousin?), and *her* offspring, No. 50. Next, No. 28, Ego's sister, is gray, and so is her offspring, No. 50. And there's No. 48, Ego's own offspring. What do they all have in common, you ask? They are all females and they are all direct descendants of No. 4. Not a single male is to be found in those lines (see for yourself). By the way, if you marked a symbol whose number is other than the above, then either look for the errant male or check the symbol to see which sex it represents. (That's what learning is all about; you make errors, then correct them.)

4. To make your exercise less than boring, try this. Which of the folks represented on the diagram are born as Miller (or any old name with a M), but lose the name upon marriage under the new "what if" rule, and whose offspring carry the spouse's name? Use Ego, No. 26, as the reference point, and you might have a look at her (male) sibling, No. 23. Identify them by shading the left of each figure with your red writing device. (They call it a pen, pencil, or marker, don't they?) Again, don't peek; cover item (5).

5. If you guessed right or figured it out, the left-shaded figures include Ego's sibling, No. 23; No. 29 (her cousin—but which cousin? How are they linked?); No. 13 (No. 10's sibling or Ego's uncle—again, what kind?); No. 53, No. 32's offspring; No. 50, Ego's sister's (No. 28) offspring; and No. 47, Ego's own offspring. What do they all have in common? If you haven't figured it out by now, they are all males. They are also someone's (the someone being female) brother or son. They were born Miller, then changed their names when they married someone with another name. This assumes that they practice *matrilocal postmarital residence,* in which the boys leave their residence of birth upon marriage.

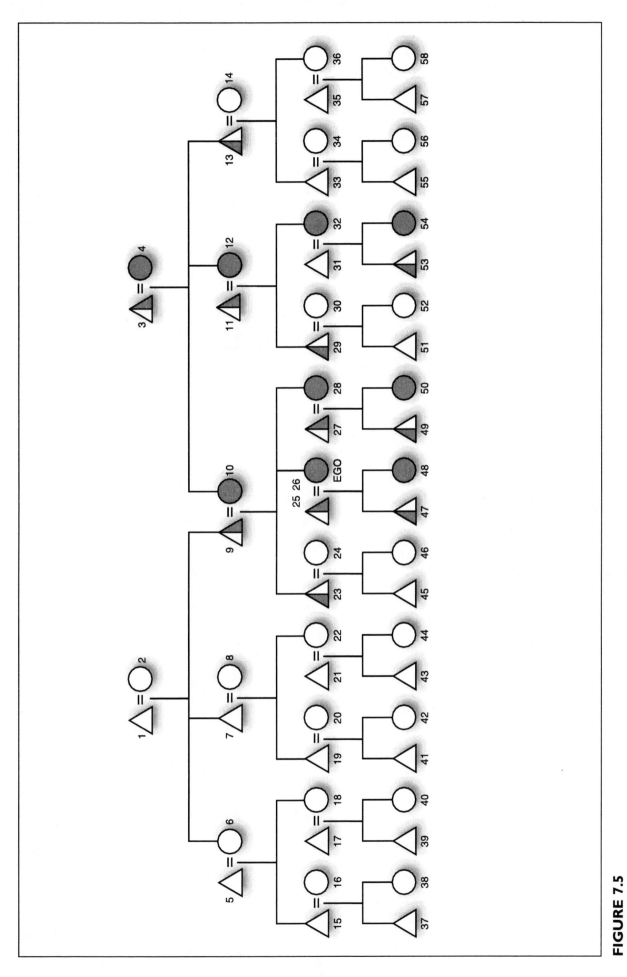

FIGURE 7.5
Matrilineal kin: All persons fully shaded in gray are Ego's matrilineal kin; all persons shaded to the left are Ego's out-marrying kin upon marriage; all persons shaded to the right are in-marrying affines.

Groups like the Navajo and Iroquois practice this form of residence; there are other forms of postmarital residence as well within matrilineal descent. We examine this in chapter 10.

6. Now let's turn to the last of this set of exercises: Who on this diagram is not a Miller (or your M-name) at birth (again use Ego, No. 26, as the reference point), but assumes the name Miller upon marriage and has offspring named Miller? Identify them by shading the right side of each figure with your red writing device. What do they have in common? Again, take a crack at this question before looking at item (7).

7. If you guessed they were male (again, how can you not figure it out?), you are correct. If you notice that they all are linked to a male listed in item (3) above by an equal sign, right again. (Sorry, no cigar this time, either.) They each have married a male named Miller (or your M-choice). They include No. 25 (Ego's husband), No. 27 (sister's husband), No. 9 (No. 26's own father), No. 3 (the maternal grandfather), No. 11 (Ego's maternal aunt's husband) and No. 29 (the husband of Ego's cousin on her mother's side—but what kind of cousin?).

Again, notice the following: First, exclusion is automatic; this time, it is the males who cut off affiliation of any female to her ancestor. Second, it is as easy to discern the line of females to their female ancestor as it was to discern the line of males in the patrilineal case. Third, matrilineal descent is a virtual mirror image of patrilineal descent, and if you put your diagrams side by side, they are indeed mirror images.

There is one caveat, however, As we will see in chapter 9, male dominance, the last constant we listed at the beginning of this chapter, plays a role in at least in some of the matrilineal societies around the world. Remember that according to this constant, men are responsible for making the key decisions that affect both the household and the larger matrilineal group. So long as matrilineal units are just that—descent units that has no control over property, or a role in the common defense, or similar functions—matrilineal units are mirror images of patrilineal units. This would be so in surnames, or in such obligations as hospitality among the Navajo. But if matrilineal groups are units of inheritance of, say, "male" property, or do have some estate it owns or defends, they are not mirror

images of patrilineal groups. We discuss this issue further in chapter 9.

Double Unilineal Descent. In kinship analysis, there is a concept that is easily confused with **bilateral descent**, already defined above. This is **double descent** or, more precisely, **double unilineal descent**. This is a system that affiliates an individual with a group of patrilineal kin for some purposes and with a group of matrilineal kin for other purposes. No rule says that two forms of descent cannot coexist in the same society. We have seen this for our own society, with bilateral descent governing inheritance, kin reckoning, and other functions, and with patrilineal descent governing the assignment of surnames.

Like **bilateral descent**, **double descent** involves both genders; unlike bilateral descent, double descent does not involve both sides of Ego's family equally. Rather, it combines the unbroken male line with the unbroken female line. Both lines can even govern rules of inheritance equally, so long as they do not overlap.

To illustrate this point, we take up the case of the Yakö, located in the state of Cross River in southeastern Nigeria. This group lived in a densely populated city called Umor (population 11,000) and relied on a mixed complex of orchard cultivation and cattle herding for its subsistence. The city comprised patrilineal residential units, and the city was surrounded by cattle grazing grounds and orchards. Residence was patrilocal—the couple moved in with the groom's kin—so it is the men who stay and the women who move (Fox 1967:137).

Given this brief sketch, the Yakô had a unique system of ownership and inheritance. First, patrilineal groups were the units of ownership of all immovable property: agricultural land, fruit trees, and houses. These passed from fathers to sons. This fit in with the pattern that men did not move upon marriage; women did. However, matrilineal groups were units of ownership of all movable property: cattle, money, even the fruits from the trees owned by the patrilineal groups. It should be emphasized that men, not women, owned movable property. Movable property, in other words, was passed from male to male matrilineally (Fox 1967:136).

This leads us to the next exercise. If you made transparencies, slip one over the other so that both patrilineal and matrilineal kin are visible from the top; this will give you a better feel for how these

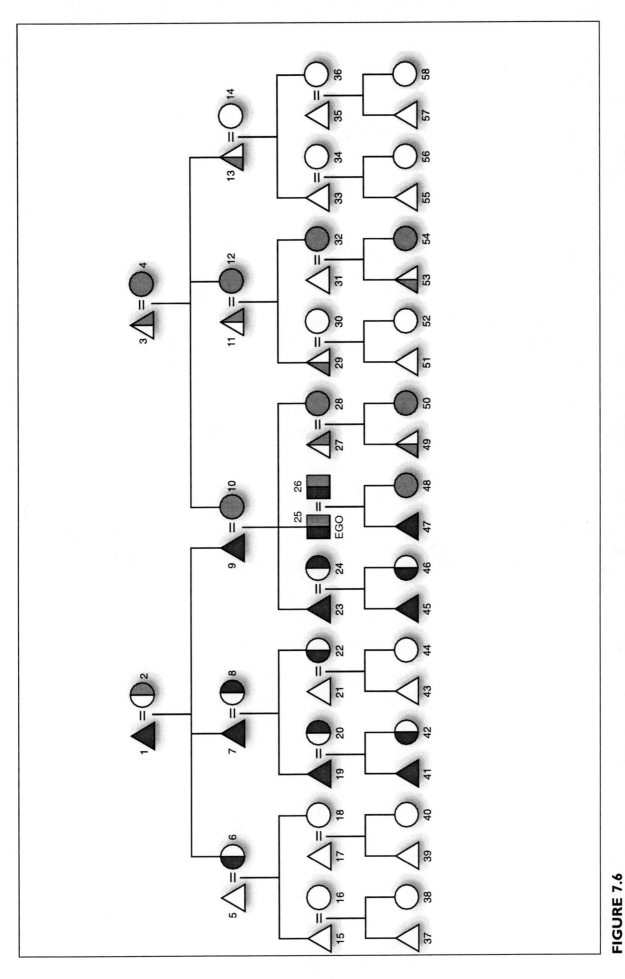

FIGURE 7.6
Double unilineal descent. All kin on Ego's father's side are shaded black as (male) Ego's patrilineal kin and those on Ego's mother's side are shaded gray as (female) Ego's matrilineal kin. Why are some people still excluded from both groups?

rules work. If not, use Figure 7.6. Identify No. 13, who is male Ego's (No. 25) mother's brother. Next, answer the following question: When No. 13 dies, who gets the movable property? (To paraphrase Bart Simpson, who has the cow, man?). Remember that we are dealing with **consanguineal** kin, so no husband or wife of anyone gets the property. Cover the next paragraph and Figure 7.6 until you figure out the puzzle.

Here's the answer: the sister's sons would get the movable booty. On the diagram, they are Nos. 23, 25 (male Ego on the patrilineal diagram), and 29. Nos. 26 (female Ego on the matrilineal diagram), 28, and 32 are out because they are female, and Nos. 25 (female ego's husband on the matrilineal diagram), 27, and 31 are out because they are the husbands, respectively, of these three women and, as we said, these are **affines**, not **consanguineals**.

Therefore, movable property, being male-owned, went from mother's brother to sister's son. This had several ramifications. For example, when a man married, he had to provide bridewealth, usually in the form of cattle, to his bride's group. He would ask his mother's brother for cattle, not his father; likewise, he gave his cattle to his sister's son when he married. Receiving the cattle was not the bride's patrilineal group, but her matrilineal one.

Let us emphasize that **double descent** is not the same as **bilateral descent**. In double descent, kin who are not directly descended from an ancestor (that is, through an unbroken male line for patrilineal, through an unbroken female line for matrilineal) are not included in the two groups (those are the folks whose symbols you did not fully color with blue and red, or did not color at all.

In bilateral descent, no one is left out at all. This is because both sexes are equally involved in the reckoning process, with no one excluded because of sex of linking relative. Male and female lines play no role in reckoning kin. Therefore, emphasis is on lateral relations, and this is why in our own society, we allude to grandparents, aunts and uncles, or cousins as being on "the father's side" or "the mother's side."

Conclusion

We have introduced the topic of kinship, its relevance, and two major types of descent: bilateral and unilineal. We have also reviewed, and run exercises on, the two subtypes—patrilineal and matrilineal—of unilineal descent, and have shown that both types can coexist in one culture. One cannot overemphasize the importance of learning these descent rules to understand the other aspects of kinship studies, namely sex and gender, marriage, larger kin-based groups, and indeed other sectors of societies and cultures: their economies, their relations of political power, their law or functional equivalents of law, and even their supernatural beliefs.

We have reserved for later discussion (in chapter 10) groups that arise from these rules of descent, such as unilineal corporate descent groups, ambilineal descent groups (which are based on bilateral reckoning), and nonpermanent groups such as kindreds. For all these, we need to discuss marriage (chapter 9), family types arising from postmarital residence (also chapter 9), and larger descent units (chapter 10). Before discussing all these, **gender roles**, the topic of the next chapter, needs to be covered.

Understanding kinship is also important to comparing nonindustrial with industrial societies. Industrial society downplays or dispenses entirely any kin group larger than the family. Yet, although corporate globalization has involved an ever tighter integration of the economies throughout the world (as we will see in chapter 16), the affected cultures have used their kin relations to adapt to these new realities.

Chapter 8

SEX AND GENDER

Introduction

Along with money, **sex** is the most popular topic in contemporary society. As advertisers are quick to point out, sex sells. Purveyors of so-called pornographic videos, films, magazines, and websites do well, though many might question whether they do good. No doubt many (mostly males) would like to follow Nike's dictum and just do it.

Nevertheless, sex involves much more than the act itself. All societies of the world place some restriction on sexual behavior. Although all but 5 percent of the world's cultures permit or tolerate copulation outside marriage, the incest tabu applies to all of them. Beyond primary kin, sexual relations among other individuals—some kin, some not—may be forbidden or restricted. Some villages prevent sexual behavior in backhanded ways; for example, the village may contain no one other than members ineligible for marriage. Many African and Middle Eastern cultures also practice clitoridectomy, which reduces or eliminates the pleasures of sexuality in women.

Beyond sexuality is the question of a related topic, **gender**, or the culturally derived attributes from the sex differences between women and men. They involve **gender roles**, or expected behaviors expected of each of the two sexes as culturally defined. Especially prominent is the **gender division of labor**.

Defining Sex and Gender

To begin with, we need to examine two concepts that are often confused with each other: sex and gender. **Sex**, in its broadest sense, denotes the physical characteristics of men and women. These include **primary sex characteristics**, or the reproductive systems of the two sexes: the penis, testicles, and associated genital parts of men; and the vagina, fallopian tubes, and uterus of women.

They also include **secondary characteristics** that comprise the **sexual dimorphism**, or marked differences in size and appearance of men and women. Several attributes contribute to sexual dimorphism. There are average differentials in physical size. Some women may be heavier or taller than some men, but overall, men are heavier and taller than women. Men also have greater average grip strength than women, proportionately larger hearts and lungs, and greater maximum uptake of oxygen. Turning to females, women have the pendulous breasts that men lack. Women also have greater portions of body fat than men, and wider pelvises to accommodate childbirth.

To what extent any of these characteristics are products of the genes or of natural selection is unknown. This question is important because other species (for example, gibbons) do not show significant sexual dimorphism; females and males look essentially alike, apart from the primary characteristics. The other extreme is found in gorillas, whose males are nearly twice the size of females.

Derivative of sex in the physical sense, **gender** comprises the elaborations and meanings assigned by cultures to the biological differentiations of the sexes. In other words, **sex** refers to the biology of differences; whereas **gender** refers to the cultural facts that arise from sex differences.

The notion that men (until recently) were the breadwinners and women the homemakers reflects gender, the roles that society assigned to the sexes. Now this is changed, but other gender characteristics haven't changed: that men should shave and women should put on make-up is gender-based; that men are supposed to be the assertive partner in a sexual encounter is gender-based; that emotion should be openly expressed in women but not in men is gender-based. We have already discussed gender differences in language; men tend to be individualistic, competitive, and hierarchical; women tend to value interpersonal relations, exercise diplomacy, and value close friendships (Tannen 1994).

Sexual Behavior and Control

As stated in the introduction, all societies regulate sexual behavior to a greater or lesser extent. Among nonhuman species, females tend to be receptive only during restricted periods of estrus. Female chimpanzees, for example, confine their sexual behavior to periods of estrus, when the sexual skin surrounding their genitalia swells, indicating receptivity. Bonobo females have more extended periods of estrus—being receptive 50 percent of their adult lives as compared to the chimpanzees' 5 percent—but their mating periods are limited (de Waal and Lanting 1997:107).

In contrast, human females are receptive whenever they wish, and this is where cultural restrictions step in. The extent and characteristics of these controls vary considerably. For example, in Anglo-American and Euro-American society, official law and ideology put a tabu on all sexual activity outside wedlock. Only about 5 percent of known societies place this severe a restriction, and even ours has become less restrictive; "living together"

has less a stigma than it did 25 years ago, and law has recognized cohabitation rights of partners equivalent to marriage. At the same time, the spread of acquired immunodeficiency syndrome (AIDS) has dampened unrestricted copulation.

At the other end of the scale, Trobriand Islanders actually encourage sexuality among their young. Children who have reached age seven or eight begin playing erotic games with one another; by ages 11 or 12, they experiment sexually with one partner after another. With advancing age, they spend more and more time with one partner, rejecting the advances of others, and one day appear at the entrance of the young man's house announcing their intent to be married (Weiner 1988:71).

Sexual strategies of women differ from those of men, and this difference is partly cultural and partly biological. Men are interested in spreading their genes around among multiple partners. Women, in contrast, are more selective because of the limited number of ova (eggs) they produce and because they must invest heavily in their infants (Harris and Johnson 2003:220–221; Small 1992, 1995). Women prefer men with good genetic composition, sufficient resources, and willingness to participate in child rearing. Culture often overrides these proclivities. In a study comparing 186 cultures, Whyte finds that 77 percent consider the male and female sex drives to be equally strong; nevertheless, female sexuality is often suppressed. Such suppression is more likely in stratified societies where questions of inheritance of land and other wealth reduce women's freedom to mate as they wish (Whyte 1978).

Incest Tabu

Of the modes of control over sex, the most widespread is the prohibition of sexual relations between **primary kin**, that is, between parents and child (i.e., father–daughter and mother–son), and between siblings (brother–sister). This is one form of the **incest tabu**, which refers to cultural prohibitions against copulation between close relatives. Although this tabu has been found widely among primary kin, it often extends to **secondary kin**, or all other kin for whom the tabu applies; these vary widely across cultures.

In Anglophone North America, this tabu applies to first cousins, although one set of siblings might marry another set. Others defined as secondary kin may be extremely comprehensive. For example, among the Navajo, one cannot engage in sexual relations with anyone bearing the names of one's mother's and one's father's clan, even if the actual links of kin between the partners cannot be traced. At the opposite end of the scale, Yanomamö are expected to marry (and have sex with) their **cross-cousins**, or cousins whose respective parents are of the opposite sex. Even so, they may not mate with their primary kin nor their **parallel cousins**, or cousins with respective same-sex parents. There are opposite-sex relatives to avoid as well (Chagnon 1997).

There are, as in everything else in the social sciences, exceptions to this tabu. In state-level societies, the royal lineage may allow marriage between close relatives. The ancient Egyptian, Inca, and Hawaiian states actually prescribed brother–sister marriage (and of course mating). There is also some evidence that even among farmers in Egypt under Roman rule, brother–sister marriage was not only tolerated, but even preferred (Leavitt 1990:973). Finally, Thornhill (1993) finds that in a sample of 129 societies, only 57 have specific rules against incest among primary kin, although 114 do have explicit rules to control copulation among cousins, in-laws, or both (Haviland 1999). Both these studies have yet to be replicated, however.

Incest Tabu and Exogamy

One indication of sloppy thinking about the subject is the distinction that many anthropologists fail to make between the **incest tabu** and **exogamy**, or a rule that one must marry outside a group. The first rule forbids sexual behavior between close kin; the second forbids marriage between close kin. However, the definition Ember and Ember offer of incest conflates the two concepts: "prohibition of sexual intercourse *or marriage* between mother and son, father and daughter, and brother and sister" (2002:332). Harris and Johnson also conflate incest and marriage: "Cultural beliefs prohibiting sexual relations *or marriage* with a close relative" (2003:351; emphases added for both definitions).

There are reasons for making a sharp distinction between incest tabus and rules of exogamy. First, although one is unlikely to marry a person with whom one may not mate, it is possible—indeed common—for one to mate with a person whom one does not marry (Fox 1967:55). Indeed, the Arunta (or Aranda) of Australia illustrate that very point. A man must marry a woman who is his mother's mother's brother's son's daughter who is also his father's mother's brother's son's daughter. (Is it any wonder that kinship is jokingly considered to be the favorite pastime of anthropologists and aboriginal Australians?) This relationship was exogamous because the two belonged to different kin groups. However, the same male is free to mate with women unrelated to him in this way. As Service points out for the Arunta,

> There are many circumstances in which intercourse may occur between people not of the proper relationship categories for marriage. Incest rule relating to sexual relations prevent intercourse only between a woman and her father, brother, or son. Otherwise, sexual license is allowed or even encouraged during many of the important ceremonies. It is quite obvious that marriage is not regarded as a sexual matter at all, but rather as a social and economic alliance between two people. (1978:30–31)

Likewise, a woman could not mate with her father, brother, or son; she was otherwise free to mate anyone else.

Second, there are theoretical reasons for the distinction. Explanations for incest tabus center around biological or psychological explanations. Explanations for rules of exogamy focus on alliance formation. We focus on reasons for incest tabus in the next section, whereas we reserve explanations of exogamy in chapter 10.

Explanations of Incest Tabus

Why are incest tabus widespread, if not universal? The short answer is that no one really knows. We bring forth three explanations—inbreeding, sibling indifference, and intrafamilial jealousy—and show the inadequacies of each one.

Inbreeding.   One truism among geneticists is that most, if not all, deleterious alleles of a gene—those that are harmful to the organism—survive because they are recessive and usually are "hidden" when matched with a nonlethal allele of the same gene. When two defective alleles are matched, then the defect becomes manifest. Therefore, one common explanation is that kin who are closely related are more likely to pass defective alleles to their offspring than those who are unrelated or distantly related. In other words, inbreeding would pass parents' deleterious alleles to offspring. Children of inbreeding are likely to develop hemophilia, have intellectual or emotional defects, or show other anomalies.

Behavior among some nonhuman animal species tends to bolster this theory. Studies show that relatively large, slow-to-mature, long-lived, and intelligent species tend to avoid inbreeding. These include chimpanzees, who, despite their promiscuous sexual behavior, tend to avoid inbreeding between siblings and between females and their male offspring (Haviland 1999:236).

Nevertheless, there are counterexamples. There are societies that do allow close inbreeding, as we have seen for farmers in Roman Egypt. As suggested in the Thornhill study, there may be numerous societies that do not explicitly forbid copulation between primary kin.

A second, more fundamental, objection to the inbreeding explanation involves the assumption that the connection between copulation and childbearing is known within a given culture, and there are cultures within which the connection is not made. For example, as perceived among the Trobriand Islanders of Melanesia, men play no role in the procreation of children. Rather, the father is merely the "opener of the way" (through copulation) for the child. It is the mother who conceives the child "spiritually." The matrilineal Trobrianders, "stuck with fathers, eliminate their procreative role" (Fox 1967:108).

Another misinterpretation involves the people on Rapa Island (also known as Easter Island) in the South Pacific, as reported by F. Allan Hanson. According to Rapanese ethnotheory, conception is most likely to occur in the three to four days following menstruation, when it is believed women are most fertile. In order to prevent pregnancy, Rapanese couples abstain from sex during this period (1970:1444–1446). While this practice is not an effective method for limiting family size, it can be understood as articulating with Rapanese theories of physiology and reproduction. Since intercourse does not always lead to childbirth, there is no obvious reason for Rapanese to behave any differently.

Even if we assume that peoples of a culture have their facts of life straight, birth defects may be explained by other reasons: witchcraft, or entry of some evil spirit in the womb. A defect may not show up for many generations.

Childhood-Familiarity.   According to another genre of explanations, developed by Edward

Westermarck (1894), close kin do not mate either because of instinctive revulsion over the idea or because opposite-sex kin reared together from birth are uninterested in each other—familiarity either breeds contempt or lack of interest.

Perhaps the best test of this theory comes from the work of two anthropologists: Melford Spiro, who conducted a study of Israeli collective farms or kibbutzim (singular, kibbutz) during the 1950s, and Yonina Talmon (1964), who conducted a similar study of mate selection in three kibbutzim. Both found that children growing up in the same kibbutz tended not to marry within it. Talmon particularly points out that, despite parental encouragement to do so, there "was not one instance in which both mates were reared from birth in the same peer group" (1964:492).

This prima facie evidence becomes problematic when one recognizes the existence of military conscription—the draft—of all men and women when they reach the age of 18, just about the time they are thinking of finding a mate. Thus, by the time they are discharged from the armed forces two years later, the children of the kibbutz are likely to have selected their mates from outside their own—or any—kibbutz.

Finally, there is the problem of logic. If it is indeed true that children reared together avoid sex together, then what is the rationale for the incest tabu? Why prohibit behavior that people do not engage in anyway? Therefore, even if data confirm Westermarck's hypothesis, the incest tabu remains unexplained.

Sexual Competition.   Several explanations have been advanced arguing that incest would lead to sexual competition among consanguineal kin, and so disrupt the family. One is psychoanalyst Sigmund Freud's Oedipus complex, which posits that the son, at age five, desires the mother and is willing to kill the father in order to possess her. This follows the Greek myth in which Oedipus the king unwittingly murders his father and marries his mother. Upon discovery of his deeds, he blinds himself and becomes a wanderer for the rest of his days. The Electra complex has the daughter desiring the same outcome—killing the mother and possessing the father.

Freud, who gained fame for his practice in Vienna prior to World War II, extended the Oedipus complex to hypothesize, in his *Totem and Taboo*, in which the father monopolized all the females in an undefined and undated primeval horde. In a jealous rage, the sons banded together to kill the father. So guilt-ridden were the sons over this deed that they vowed never to take women from their own horde for their wives, but rather marry women from other hordes. In the Freudian world, thereby the incest tabu was born. Even at the date the book was released (1913), many anthropologists regarded this theory as far-fetched at best; a critical review is offered in chapter 14 on psychological anthropology.

Bronislaw Malinowski, who studied the Trobriand Islands during World War I when he was exiled there as an enemy alien, offers a more down-to-earth hypothesis. If brothers were allowed to mate with sisters, fathers with daughters, or mothers with sons, rivalry would soon develop among other family members as they competed for the same person—whether sister, brother, or parent. What if, for example, two brothers competed for the same sister? Sexual jealousy would soon tear the family apart (Malinowski 1927).

Although both sexual competition hypotheses, unlike Westermarck's mode, see the need for a strong tabu, they both lack empirical support. Many cultures around the world practice **polygyny**, or the marriage of one man to two or more women. A few practice **polyandry**, or the marriage of one woman to two or more men. Brothers often marry the same wife. Yet there is little evidence that either marriage type disrupts households in which they are practiced. Nor is there evidence that the brother–sister marriage within royal lineages of the Egyptians, Inca, or Hawaiians disrupted the royal families. Indeed, where siblings marry the same person, evidence indicates the families are more stable, not less.

Gender Roles and Differences

Much has been written about roles that each society assigns to each of the two sexes; these are **gender roles**, or culturally derived expectations that are assigned to men and women on the basis of their sex. Where there are cultural attributions of differences between women and men on the basis of their sex, we speak of **gender differences**.

In this section, we first look at the tasks assigned to women and men, and find that, with few exceptions, men do not perform the same tasks across culture, and neither do women. Explanations are advanced for the observed variations, and eval-

uated. We then discuss the status of women relative to men, and find considerable variation. Women are second-class citizens in such cultures as the Masai and preindustrial China; they enjoy relatively high status among the !Kung and the Iroquois. Explanations for this variance are explored.

Gender Division of Labor

The term **gender division of labor** refers to the observed differences of tasks assigned to men and those assigned to women in the world's cultures. Some anthropologists call these task difference the sexual division of labor, but this obscures the important difference between **sex**, or the biological differences between women and men, and **gender**, or the culturally defined attributes derived from these differences.

Addressing the differences in the gender division of labor implies three basic questions:

a. *Does every society have different work for males and females?* By and large, the answer is yes.
b. *Are the work roles for males and females different from one society to the next?* Again the answer is yes, and we will take up some illustrative cases.
c. *What are the explanations for these differences?*

The answers to these questions are uncertain, and we will examine some of them.

How Tasks Are Divided.   Men usually handle the heavier tasks in subsistence activities. Therefore, they almost always hunt large animals, land and sea, and game birds, and trap animals of any size, large or small. They usually fish, herd large animals, clear land, and prepare soil for planting—but women may do these things, too.

Men also handle other heavy tasks not related to subsistence, so that they almost always work with wood, such as cutting trees, building boats, and even making musical instruments; and work with other materials, such as bone, horn, or shell. They also work with minerals and stone, including mining and smelting ore. Finally, men also construct houses or other shelters, and make rope and net. Again, women have been reported doing those tasks as well.

Men also engage in warfare and, in this connection, exercise political leadership over groups ranging from bands of 40 to 50 people, to tribes comprising up to 1000, to states that control populations in the hundreds of thousands. Only in recent years have women joined the military and held office. In preindustrial society, then, we can say that few women either engaged in warfare or assumed public leadership roles.

In contrast, women usually care for children, a task that men do not assume, with the exception of training boys to handle men's tasks. One generalization is that women usually handle tasks that can be interrupted to attend to children's needs. In foraging societies, women usually gather wild plants, tubers, nuts, and fruits, a task that men may also perform, though infrequently. Other tasks also tend to revolve around the household. Thus, women usually handle food preparation, do the laundering, fetch water, and gather firewood—but again, so do men.

Finally, worldwide, either or both genders may plant, tend, and/or harvest crops, milk animals, collect shellfish, preserve meat or fish, and prepare skins. Handicrafts also are handled by either women, men, or both. They include weaving, making baskets and mats, sewing and tailoring clothing, and making pottery, among many other crafts (Ember and Ember 2000: 125–127).

Explaining Gender Division of Labor

Because of the myriad tasks assigned by cultures around the world, it seems a daunting task to find a consistent explanation for the division of labor within and among cultures. Several tentative attempts at such explanations have been made: they may be divided under the headings relative strength, compatibility with child care, economy of effort, and male expendability

Relative Strength. Greater strength of men and superior ability to mobilize strength in quick bursts of energy have been cited as the reasons for the near-universal patterns of division of labor by sex. This explanation fits the description of most jobs done by males: lifting heavy objects (hunting, butchering, clearing land, working with heavy materials such as wood, stone, minerals), throwing weapons, and running. With the possible exception of gathering firewood and culture-specific instances, comparable strength is not required of women.

This explanation does not apply to all instances. For example, trapping small animals, collecting wild honey, or making musical instruments do not require a great deal of physical strength. Furthermore, women also handle tasks involving heavy labor, such as herding large animals (as Masai women do in herding cattle) and clearing land in many cultures. Women in Nepal carry heavy loads while doing agricultural work. Agta women in the Philippines hunt wild pig and deer, thereby contributing 30 percent of all large game animals in that society (Ember and Ember 2002:126–127; Murdock 1949).

Compatibility with Child Care. Women's tasks tend to be those that can be worked around the tasks of attending to children, especially if we remember that in most societies, women breastfeed their children for two years on average. Such tasks should be those that do not take them from home for long periods of time, do not place children in potential danger if they are taken along, and can be stopped and resumed if child-care duties interrupt these tasks.

If verified, this explanation would explain why dangerous tasks or those that cannot be interrupted are done by men: hunting, trapping, fishing, lumbering, and mining, all dangerous and not easily interrupted. A similar explanation would hold for full-time craft specialization, which requires production of large quantities without interruption.

Nevertheless, there are problems with this explanation. To begin with, men do perform tasks that could be interrupted and pose little danger, such as preparing soil for planting or working bone or shell. Second, women who spend much time in agricultural work find ways to work around the problems of interruption. For example, women may take turns watching and feeding her own and other women's children while the others carry on with their tasks (Ember and Ember 2002:126–127; Murdock 1949).

Economy of Effort. Economy of effort may serve to explain the tasks that do not fit well with the strength and compatibility-with-child-care explanations. For example, men may make optimal use of their time making musical instruments because they also fell trees, a task that does require strength. This explanation might also serve to explain that men do women's tasks that are close to their own. If women have to stay home to care for their children, they might as well do chores around the house—whether men's or women's (Ember and Ember 2002:127).

Male Expendability. Men rather than women tend to the dangerous work in a society because, according to this explanation, men are more expendable. The rationale is not hard to fathom: If some men lose their lives in hunting, deep-sea fishing, mining, quarrying—or warfare—reproduction need not suffer so long as most fertile women have sexual access to men, as in those cases where society allows two or more women to be married to the same man (Ember and Ember 2002:127).

Nevertheless, some inconvenient empirical facts get in the way of this explanation. Dangers do not prevent Atga women from hunting, nor stop Yahgan women from participating in fishing expeditions using canoes that are not particularly stable in Tierra del Fuego, whose very name (land of fire) reflects the storms that frequent the area. Indeed, Yahgan women actually own their canoes (Service 1978:37–39, 40–41), but this can be explained in part by economy of effort—both Yahgan men and women spend most of their time in the canoes.

Gender Relations

Gender relations is integral to the study of kinship. The status of women remains an ongoing concern. In addition, recent anthropological research has shown that gender is a multidimensional concept. Gender may refer to culturally determined behavior derived not only from the two sexes, biologically speaking, but also from cultures of homosexuality, transvestitism, and hormonal factors. Some women do not feel comfortable being women, nor men being men; sex-change operations have increased over the years, and transvestitism has become more visible. Enough work has been conducted on homosexuality—by professionals who are themselves homosexual—to warrant an organization called the Society for Gay and Lesbian Anthropologists. We sample some of these issues here.

The Status of Women

As previously noted, women vary in status from sociological doormats to joint decision makers equal to men. One major question is, why the variation? Martin K. Whyte contends, in his book *The Status of Women in Preindustrial Society* (1978), that if kin groups and marital residence are organized around men, women tend to be relatively low in status. This will be covered in kinship and postmarital residence.

Among his findings are the following:

1. Warfare seems to be a strong determinant of male dominance; in 88 percent of societies, women never participate in war.
2. Political dominance is generally exercised by men. According to a cross-cultural survey, in 85 percent of the societies sampled only men were leaders. Even among the matrilineal Iroquois, men, not women, hold political office; women may not speak on the council.

There are several factors underlying male political dominance. First, the warfare in which men engage is related to group survival; such questions, so the reasoning goes, should be in the hands of those who know most about war. Second, men tend to get around more often in the world outside the home or compound than do women; hence, the knowledge gained give men this advantage. Third, forced or induced settlements compromise women's former influence in the group decision-making process. Patricia Draper, studying settled !Kung communities, found that women, now no longer foraging in the field, lost much of their former influence in making decisions for the band (Draper 1975).

On the other hand, if kin groups and marital residence are organized around women, women will tend to enjoy somewhat higher status. Among the Iroquois, for example, women related by common matrilineal ancestry lived within a longhouse. They tended to have considerable authority in the longhouse, and often beyond. Men whom they found objectionable could be asked to leave; putting their belongings outside the door reinforced this request. It was also the women who controlled allocation of the food they produced; this meant they could regulate warfare, since men could not go off to war without provisions. Women also involved themselves in selecting religious leaders, half of whom were themselves women. Finally, although men rather than women held political office, the women controlled the selection of council members, and could initiate impeachment proceedings against those to whom they objected (Ember and Ember 2002:130, 134).

Even so, women could play important roles in male-dominated kin groups and residences. Among the Yahgan, women generally joined their husbands' kin after marriage. Nevertheless, women owned the canoes, which served as the main domestic unit. Women contributed most to food larders by gathering shellfish, and even in actual fishing expeditions, women managed the canoe. Finally, when new shelters were to be constructed, the couple worked together on the project. For these reasons, Yahgan women appear to have enjoyed particularly high status.

Homosexual and Transvestite Behavior

Homosexuality also is an important component in the world's cultures. Homosexuality is well known among New Guinean societies. For example, the Sambia initiate the boys at seven with fellatio involving an older adolescent for ten years, until he marries. Once married and having had intercourse, other men avoid him as unclean, and bisexuality becomes the dominant pattern throughout a man's married years. These practices describe the behavior of 5 percent of the male population, however (Herdt 1992). Another New Guinean tribe, the Etoro, are said to be so pro-homosexual that heterosexual behavior is forbidden 260 days out of the year. Indeed, they believe that homosexuality makes the crops flourish and boys grow strong (Kelly 1974). Interestingly, Papua New Guinea has outlawed homosexuality among males, but not among females; male intercourse is punishable up to 5 years imprisonment, with 14 years imprisonment for anal intercourse (International Gay and Lesbian Rights Association n.d.).

Other tribal societies practice homosexuality. Among the Siwan of North Africa, every male is expected to engage in homosexual relations, and fathers make arrangements for their unmarried sons to be given to an older man for a homosexual relationship (Abd Allah 1917; the ethnographic present is the years prior to 1909, when governmental policy forced the practice underground).

Despite the paucity of cross-cultural comparison on the topic of homosexuality, some tentative generalizations have surfaced. Statistically, societies seeking to increase populations have been intolerant of homosexuality. Conversely, overpopulation coupled with famines or the threat of famines may foster con-

ditions favorable to openly homosexual practices. All this assumes that heterosexual activity is correspondingly reduced, together with the rate of birth (Werner 1979:345–362). Indeed, the Soviet Union tolerated homosexual liaisons (along with abortions) amidst the 1917 revolution; by 1934–1936, as Soviet policy encouraged births and population increases, homosexuality was again banned, along with abortion (Werner 1979:345–362). Of course, this does not explain why individual homosexual behavior exists, but it may explain why societies view such behavior more permissively or less.

Similar to interest in homosexuality is research on transvestitism. Among the Papago, for example, there were many male transvestites who wore women's clothing, performed women's chores, and, if unmarried, were visited by men (Underhill 1938). The Cheyenne provide a classic example; men who proved unable to engage in warfare and other male acts of bravery might become **berdaches**, or transvestites. They wore women's clothing, handled women's chores, and would be "married" to Cheyenne warriors as "second wives." Whether homosexual behavior was involved is unclear from the literature, but it does appear that other Cheyenne attached no stigma to berdaches (Hoebel 1960).

Conclusion

Sex is where kinship begins, but even that act involves culture, given the multiplicity of possible gender differences. Nevertheless, kinship has to address all the phases of the life cycle, from procreation and childbirth to maturation to death. We have seen that rules vary from one society to another about restrictions or lack thereof on sexuality, on the incest tabu, and on the assignment of sociocultural roles based on one's sex. We also have seen the range in variation of sexual orientations: heterosexuality versus homosexuality, and on this topic, there is much unexplored territory. Finally, we address one channel of the sexual impulse in the next chapter, namely marriage.

Chapter 9

MARRIAGE AND FAMILY FORMATION

Introduction

Of love and marriage, Emile (Ezio Pinza), the lead male protagonist in the musical *South Pacific*, sings:

> Who can explain it?
>
> Who can tell you why?
>
> Fools give you reasons;
>
> Wise men never try.*

(One might wonder what wise *women* have to say about it.) In some ways, kinship analysts are fools. They give you reasons, or unlike the wise men, always try. Perhaps we need more of this tomfoolery. Throughout history, marriages have built or destroyed nations, as earlier they have built and destroyed tribes. Perhaps we need to know more about why marriages occur in the first place.

The old mother-in-law joke comes to mind. Exasperated husband asks wife, "Who did I marry anyway? You or your family?"

Well, guess what! With few exceptions, it's the family that each of the spouses marry, and the kin group, and the village, and maybe the whole tribe. *My Big Fat Greek Wedding* brings the point home when the groom, a proper Bostonian who doesn't know what he's getting into, marries this nice Greek girl—and marries more than thirty, forty, maybe fifty people in her family as well. If you

haven't, see the movie. It's as good an anthropological piece as one can get in popular culture.

On this note, we start the series on marriage, family formation, and ultimately, larger kin groups. First, we define the concept in at least two ways, and take into account the different types of marriage: **sambandham**, **woman marriage**, and other themes and variations which, though infrequent, have sparked interest among generations of anthropologists. Second, we examine marriages involving only two spouses and those with more than two at the same time, and we show how they play out structurally. Third, we examine **postmarital residence** and discuss the implications for various types of **extended families**. We also talk about divorce. We then reserve for the next chapter the implications they represent for larger kin units, **lineages**, **clans**, and **ambilineal descent groups**.

Marriage: Toward a Definition

The term **marriage** has been defined numerous ways, and reams have been written on the subject. Rather than review the hundreds of definitions offered over the years, we cover two definitions that reflect standard views of marriage, and one that covers all, or almost all, types of marriage, standard and nonstandard.

Notes and Queries Definition

Probably as good a starting point as any is the *Notes and Queries* definition, published in a newsletter by that name in 1951 under the auspices of the Royal Anthropological Institute of Great Britain and Northern Ireland. The definition, "A union between a man and a woman such that children born to the woman are recognized legitimate offspring of both sexes," emphasizes heterosexuality and the assumption that bearing and rearing children are important functions.

The key term in this definition is **legitimate offspring**. Children born of male–female unions that are culturally approved are allowed full membership in the culture in which they are a part, have a right to inherit, and have other rights that pertain to their birth. We must emphasize that what defines **legitimate** are the norms and mores of the culture in which the marriage takes place, not those defined in the United States or any other Western country.

Children born into a relationship that are not deemed valid have less than full birthright status. For example, those born of **concubines**, or women in liaison with a royal or aristocratic male, such as was the case in Imperial China, did not achieve the full status of their fathers. The same principle applies to children born to unmarried couples (Fox 1967).

However, children born within the context of **polygyny**, or a marriage of one man to two or more women, is deemed legitimate in these terms. So are those born within the rarer context of **polyandry**, or the marriage of one woman to two or more men. In both cases, the marriage is recognized as valid in the society in which either occurs, and the children are thereby deemed legitimate.

Sambandham and the Nayar: Stretching the Definition

For reasons soon to be obvious, the marriage practices among the Nayar of the Malabar coast, southwest India, have attracted a great deal of interest and debate among anthropologists as to just what constitutes marriage. The conjugal practice examined here is based on Kathleen Gough's description, which was the first in the literature (1959).

Nayar were organized into **matrilineages**, called *taravad*, descent groups which comprised a line of women and their brothers; brothers and sisters lived with each other, but did not mate. Each taravad was linked with other taravad for ceremonial purposes.

One of these ceremonies was the *tali* ceremony, or initiation into womanhood of girls who had not yet reached puberty. The girls were "married" to boys from the different lineages. After each boy put a gold chain, called a *tali*, around the girl's neck, the couple would be secluded for a few days; sexual intercourse may or may not have taken place. Afterward, they took a ritual bath to purify themselves from the pollution of cohabitation and tear the breechclout the girl had been wearing to signify that the cohabitation was over. No obligation was incurred, apart from the expectation that the "bride," and the children she would bear later in life, would observe the death pollution rites from the death of her so-called husband.

After the *tali* ceremony, the newly defined woman enjoyed certain privileges of womanhood; one was **sambandham**, or the right to sexually entertain men at night, after dinner, and before breakfast. A woman might have as many as 12 "affairs" going on at the same time (though not the same night!).

Despite Western perceptions of these liaisons (one female student called the women "sluts" when I described it in class—ethnocentrism dies hard), *sambandham* was a formal relationship, and the man concerned was expected to present her with gifts three times each year until the relationship was terminated. He had one other obligation: If or when the woman became pregnant, he or his fellow "husbands" were expected to offer a gift to the midwife for the delivery of the child. He was not obliged to her in any other way; financial support was not expected.

There were other restrictions, which are the points of contention as to whether the relationship constituted marriage. First, all the men had to be from outside the matrilineage with which the woman was affiliated. Second, they all had to be Hindu, not Muslims or Christians, who also resided in the Malabar Coast. Third, they had to be of the same caste as her own, which was that of the *kshatriyas*, or warriors, or the higher brahmin caste.

It was at the stages of pregnancy and birth that the legitimacy of the woman's liaisons were to be demonstrated. Upon birth of the child, a man was to step forward to present a gift to the woman and her midwife, and so acknowledge paternity. Again, this acknowledgement did not imply financial obligations. He might take interest in the child, but was not expected to provide financial support. If no man stepped forward, then it was assumed that she had violated one of the tabus. She was either killed on the spot or sold into servitude to one of the higher castes. The fate of the child is unknown, but it is believed it shared the fate of its mother (Gough 1959).

The child was reared in the household of the woman and her brothers, who functioned as the child's **pater** or social father; the role of **genitor**, or biological father, was played by the woman's lovers. Families of this type are known as **consanguine families**, of which more is discussed below.

Toward A Gender-Neutral Definition

From this description, Gough developed a definition that attempted to encompass both the Nayar case and others that were functional equivalents of marriage. Her definition: "A relationship established between a woman and one or more persons, which provides that a child born of the woman under circumstances not prohibited by the rules of the relationship, is accorded full birth-status rights common to members of its society or social stratum." This definition, particularly the phrase "circumstances not prohibited by rules of the relationship," allows for the exclusion of men who are not members of the same lineage as the women, who are non-Hindu, or who belong to a different caste (1959).

Other Marriage Arrangements

The phrase in Gough's "between a woman and one or more other persons" allows for woman–woman marriage practices among the Nuer and the Nandi, both East African cattle-herding societies. In both societies, a woman who is barren—incapable of bearing children—is undesirable in a culture that values a child, especially a son, to inherit the wealth of the father. To circumvent this limitation, the barren woman takes on a fertile woman to be her "wife," thereby becoming her "female husband." The "wife" is impregnated by a male friend (perhaps even a kinsman of the barren woman). Again, the role of **pater**, now the barren woman, is separated from the role of **genitor**, the compliant male, and the barren woman becomes the "father" of the child.

However, even this definition is restrictive. What about *male* homosexual couples, neither of whom is a woman? Take, for example, a relationship among the Kwakiutl not necessarily driven by child procreation motives. A man wishing to acquire privileges of a certain chief can marry his male heir. If the chief has no heir, he can marry the chief's left or right side, or an arm and leg. Whether or not accompanied by homosexual behavior, the primary motive of this marriage is social climbing. Noting this, in one introductory textbook, the definition reads "a relationship between one or more men (male or female) and one or more women (male or female) recognized by society as having a continuing claim to the right of sexual access to one another" (Haviland 2002:220). Here, "man" and "woman" are defined as social roles—as gender—regardless of the biological sex of persons filling either role. This would fit in with woman marriage, homosexual marriage, and the unusual arrangement among two Kwakiutl males described above. On the other hand, unlike the *Notes and Queries* definition or Gough's own, the question of child legitimacy is not addressed.

To sum up, marriages occur everywhere, yet they can never be defined precisely to fit every case. They range from a couple agreeing to live together one day to extremely elaborate affairs, attended by ceremonies that may last for days, and incurring huge expenses for the wedding. They all involve rights of sexual access, and have at least direct implications for the rights of children born from the relationship.

Functions of Marriage and the Family

What, then are the functions of marriage? Again, there is no small body of literature laying them out. Traditional answers, such as sexual gratification by controlled channels and division of labor by gender, have been questioned over the years. This section provides a critical review of these notions,

The issue goes back to George Peter Murdock, whose book, *Social Structure*, set out to demonstrate that the **nuclear family** (family of one man, one woman, and their children) is universal, or that it is found in all places at all times. Drawn from the Human Relation Area Files that he developed, the book sought to statistically compare the marriage, residential patterns, and kin groups across cultures selected as what he intended to be a **random** and **representative sample** of the world's cultures. He was not unaware of the Nayar case, but regarded these and other cases as marginal exceptions—and it is true that these are rare.

Some societies might have **extended families**, those of three or more generations of consanguineal kin (parents and children) together with their spouses, but this type of family is made up of three nuclear families. They can be **polygamous**, with either one man married to two or more women or one woman married to two or more men.

The first function involves sexual gratification through channels deemed legitimate by the culture in question. By confining sexual activity within the family, marriage thereby diminishes male sexual competition for females that could otherwise disrupt the larger society. Jealousy might arise if several males are attracted to one particular female (1949).

There are problems with this interpretation. We have shown that sexual intercourse often does take place out of wedlock. Concubinage is one such alternative, as Imperial China demonstrated, and it is not for nothing that prostitution is called "the oldest profession in the world." Nor can one ignore the frequency of extramarital sexuality, both in our own society and in others.

The second involves economic cooperation within the household. Murdock argues that the husband handles the tasks, such as hunting or tending to cattle or other herds, that require his absence from the household for a long period of time. The men also handle tasks requiring physical strength. Women, on the other hand, handle tasks that require her presence around the house or that can be interrupted to attend to the child. The difficulties of this explanation have been reviewed—women do handle strenuous tasks, and men handle tasks that either sex could perform (1949).

The third function concerns the long period of child nurturance and enculturation. Women bear infants and nurse them during their first year or two. It is up to the men to protect and provide for both mother and infant. As the child matures, the husband take up training of their sons to the tasks assigned to men, and the wife does the same for their daughters. A stabilizing factor of the nuclear family, therefore, is the long period of child dependence (1949).

Not all child-rearing functions, however, are reserved for the family. Apart from the cases we have already seen for **consanguine families** in which the mother's brother, not the father, participates in rearing children and for families formed by **woman marriage**, in which the two women likewise perform that task, there are nonfamily organizations with the same function. For example, males in New Guinean tribal societies live in men's houses whose functions not only include periodic pig feasts, religious ritual, and warfare, but also enculturating boys who join in at ages five or six (Meggitt 1964, 1977, cited in Ember and Ember 2002:187). Many East African societies have age sets that perform the same function—for one, the Nyakyusa. Boys move from their parental huts at age ten and are reared by their older age-mates and members of the next senior age set (Wilson 1951; cited in Scupin 2004). In industrial societies, schools assume the responsibility of child rearing during daytime hours.

Marriage Types and Family Formation

Types of families, of course, are contingent on the type of marriage that is contracted. **Monogamy** refers to the marriage of one man to one woman. A potential subtype, of course, is **homosexual monogamy**, comprising two men or two women, but a typology of unions involving homosexuals is yet to be worked out. Established in the anthropological lexicon, however, is **serial monogamy**, marriage with one spouse at a time, but with remarriage after death or divorce. With her seven husbands—one at a time, of course—Elizabeth Taylor set a standard. Most tabloids cover this form of marriage for the media star *du jour*.

Assuming that monogamy stands alone, and is not embedded in extended or polygamous families, families developing out of monogamy are typically **nuclear families**, or families comprising a man, a woman, and children. Again, homosexual couples are likely to find ways to create a family by nontraditional means. (Does that make copulation "traditional"?)

Polygamy refers to marriage of one person to two or more spouses at the same time. This is a generic term. Often, this term is confused with one of its subtypes, **polygyny**, which refers to the marriage of a man to two or more women at the same time. Although this practice is reported for around 80 percent of the world's cultures, most men probably cannot afford more than one wife, even where polygyny is the norm. Often, a man may marry two or more women who are sisters to each other; this is known as **sororal polygyny**. The other subtype, **polyandry**, refers to the rarer marriage of one woman to two men or more.

Correspondingly, the marriage of a woman to two or more men who are brothers to each other is known as **fraternal polyandry**. Fraternal polyandry occurs even in the classic East Indian epic poem, the *Mahabhrata*, which portrays the marriage of five sons of the deceased king Pandu to one woman, Draupadi. This practice has been described for the Toda of northern India and also for many Tibetan peoples (Goldstein 1971, 1981; cited in Ember and Ember 2002:157).

Group marriage, or the marriage of two or more men to two or more women, is extremely rare; only the Caingang of Brazil appear in Murdock's World Ethnographic Sample as consistently practicing group marriage, and it is not the dominant marriage form there. This practice has also been described for the chiefly families on the Marquesas of the South Pacific. On the assumption held by many anthropologists that group marriage develops from polygynous and polyandrous unions, the term **polygynandry** is also used (Goldstein 1971).

Postmarital Residence

When a couple marries, they need a place to stay. In most societies, the choices are already made for them. They may live in an entirely new home, move in with the groom's or bride's family, or make other arrangements. We describe six basic rules of **postmarital residence**, and each type has structural implications for **extended families**, or families with three generations of married consanguineal kin, which we discuss in the next and final section of this chapter. Throughout this discussion, the suffix *-local* for each term means "the place of."

The most common form among the world's cultures is **patrilocal residence**, in which the couple lives with or near the groom's kinsmen. **Virilocal residence** (from the Latin *vir* meaning "man") usually means the same thing, although where a distinction is made, patrilocal means to live with the groom's parents, and virilocal means to live near them. A moment's reflection will indicate that the men stay with their parents and the women leave theirs, while the daughters of the paternal household also leave when they marry.

Matrilocal residence is the pattern of residence whereby the couple lives with or near the bride's kin. **Uxorilocal residence** (from the Latin *uxor* meaning "woman") means the same thing, although a finer distinction may define as matrilocal residence with the bride's parents, and as uxorilocal residence near them. In this instance, the women are the ones who stay with their parents,

the men leave theirs, and the sons of the maternal household also leave when they marry.

Another type of residence is usually found in association with **matrilineal descent**. This is **avunculocal residence** (from the Latin *avunculus* or "maternal uncle"), in which the couple moves in with the groom's mother's brother. This reflects the practice among many societies, the Trobriand Islanders for one, in which a boy lives with his mother and father until he reaches the age of five or six. He then moves in with his mother's brother, because of his matrilineal affiliation, namely through his mother. Though his father is the **genitor**, his **pater** is his mother's brother. In other words, it is his mother's brother, not his father, who will rear the boy. Some societies stipulate that the girl also moves in with her mother's brother, whereas others stipulate that she stays with her own mother. When the boy reaches maturity, he brings his wife with him to his mother's brother's residence. As they say, this is a long story, and we take some of it up in the section on extended families below. The logical opposite, **amitilocal residence**, whereby the couple would move in with the wife's father's sister, is unknown among the world's culture and is a theoretical construct only.

Duolocal residence refers to the pattern of residence whereby the bride stays with her kin and the husband stays with his. The Nayar represent one example of this arrangement. This form of residence is the most infrequent in the world's cultures; indeed, the *World Ethnographic Sample* lists only eight out of roughly 400 cultures around the world. This would fit in well with societies in which the sister and brother stay together, but only four are matrilineal like the Nayar; the other four are patrilineal.

Ambilocal residence (sometimes known as **bilocal residence**) refers to the pattern of residence whereby the groom and bride have a choice between living with the groom's kin and the bride's kin. This form of residence is usually found in association with bilateral descent, and choice of residence is usually, if not always, the determinant whereby one chooses with which kin of the bilateral group the individual will affiliate. The implications of this choice are discussed below under "Extended Families"; we examine the Gilbertese *kainga* as an illustration.

Neolocal residence, the arrangement most familiar to North Americans, refers to the pattern of residence in which the couple forms their own household. This form is generally associated with industrialized societies, such as our own. In urban areas, there are not enough resources to support an extended family, only a nuclear one; hence it makes little sense for the couple to reside with the kin of either bride or groom on any but a temporary basis. Only 5 percent of the world's societies are neolocal; a preindustrial example is the Inuit ("Eskimo").

There are other variations. Some societies require the groom to provide **bride service** for the bride's family before he is free to take the bride to his own household. The arrangement arising from this obligation is thus known as **matri-patrilocal residence**, whereby the couple first lives with the bride's kin before moving to the household of the groom's kin.

Family and Households

Marriage types and postmarital residence gives rise to the kinds of family structures, and this is where we encounter one basic question. Are families residential units only, or can one have nonresidential families as well? In our own society, households containing nuclear families are the norm (although the presence of divorce, remarriage, homosexuality, and single parenthood has given rise to a plethora of family arrangements), but does that mean that grandparents, aunt and uncles, cousins, and nephews and nieces are not also part of one's family, though they may be hundreds of miles away?

Therefore, we may define as a **family** a group of consanguineally related and/or adopted kin consisting minimally of a parent and child who usually, but not always, share the same residence. We may define a **household** or **domestic group** as that part of a family that shares a common residence; families and households may be one and the same or they may not be. Households are classified by family type—thus, nuclear family household, extended family household, polygynous family, and so on.

It is also important to divide families and households into a twofold taxonomy. The first taxonomy concerns whether they are **monogamous** or **polygamous** and if the latter, whether they are **polygynous** or **polyandrous**. (There are too few **polygynandrous** households in the world's cultures to make much of an analysis.) The second taxonomy concerns whether families and households are **nuclear, joint,** or **extended**. If extended, then we need to determine what kind of composition

emerges from the pattern of **postmarital residence** observed: **patrilocal, matrilocal, avunculocal, duolocal,** or **ambilocal**. It should be emphasized that the two taxonomies of family type and residence can and do overlap; patrilocal residence coexists with polygynous households, for example, among the Masai and numerous others.

Monogamous and Polygamous Family Households

Monogamous families and **households** involve only husband and wife, plus any children they might have. **Polygamous families** comprise **polygynous families** and **households** centered around a man married to two or more women, and **polyandrous families** and/or **households** centered around a woman married to two or more men. The structure of families are distinct from one another.

In **monogamous family households**, there is one, and only one father, and one, and only one mother. There may be disputes of inheritance, but they do not arise from the presence of more than one parent of each sex. There may be questions of who the father is, but they address issues apart from the norm of monogamy. Rather, the issues revolve around sex outside of marriage, the norms governing such behavior, rights of the child born outside the husband–wife bond, and so on.

The situation is otherwise when we turn to **polygamous family households**. Here, more than one person of either sex is involved. In **polygynous family households**, two or more women each bear children, creating a fault line within the family. Biology is a factor in the social relations created by polygyny as compared with polyandry. In the diagram of Figure 9.1, we see that each of the two women married to one man bears her own children. It becomes readily apparent that a "fault line" appears between the offspring of the two wives, especially if descent is patrilineal. This has implications in several areas. For example, suppose a pastoralist society, such as the Masai, practice polygyny, as indeed they do. Inheritance would be divided among the sons of each co-wife of the husband. Assuming that there are two co-wives, each wife bears one son, and the herd numbers 100 head, each son would receive 50 head. Conflict could easily arise if each group wants more than 50 head. Each could justify their claim in terms of relative age of co-wives, relative number of sons borne by one co-wife compared to the other, order in which

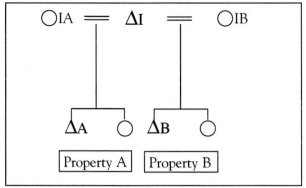

FIGURE 9.1
Polygynous family and property division. Note that the property is divided between the sons of I through co-woves IA and IB.

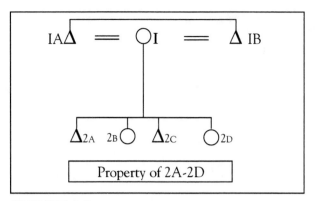

FIGURE 9.2
Fraternal polyandrous family. Note that inherited property remains undivided among the 4 offspring if I, namely 2A through 2D. Who's the father? Who knows? Often more important, who cares?

each co-wife was married to the husband, relative age of the sons, and other points of contention.

Polyandrous family households create a situation that contrasts both with monogamous and polygynous family households. First, no one really knows who the father is; this uncertainty is far greater than is the case with monogamous family households. Second, in polyandrous family households, there is one, and only one, woman who bears the children, representing an important contrast with the two or more wives who bear children in polygynous family households. Furthermore, in polyandry, we do not know who the fathers—or more accurately, the genitors—are. In some societies, especially those practicing fraternal polyandry in which the husbands are brothers, this may not matter (see Figure 9.2). Inasmuch as cultures practicing polyandry occur in the mountainous regions of northern India and Tibet, arable land is scarce, and is more effectively exploited as a unit than if it is divided among multiple heirs. The absence of a second woman and her offspring removes one source of contention among the heirs.

Joint Families

In some cultures, there are **joint families** (also known as **collateral families**), which comprise two or more families headed by siblings: two or more brothers, two or more sisters, or two or more siblings of both sexes. In India, for example, two brothers and their wives and children live in a common residence; property is held by the brothers in common. Among the Dobe !Kung, small nomadic bands are formed by any combination of siblings: two brothers, a sister and brother, even two sisters.

Here, such bands tend to be unstable and may change members from week to week. If they survive for more than a generation, we may be looking at **extended families** of various types.

Extended Families

How a family is defined hinges in part on its longevity. A **nuclear family**, defined as one comprising a man, woman, and their children, lasts no longer than the maturity and departure of the children. Sometimes, however, married children may remain with their parents temporarily until they acquire enough assets to form their own household. Therefore, we need some kind of yardstick to determine whether a household with two or more generations of married kin is extended or nuclear. Also adding to the problem of definition is the phase in the household's **domestic cycle**, or a series of phases whereby the household develops, from formation to advanced phase to termination.

One rule of thumb is the number of generations of married kin. Most definitions set the minimum number at three. Two generations could constitute a temporary arrangement. For that reason, **extended family household** refers to households containing three or more generations of co-resident married kin. By this measurement, one is reasonably sure that we are dealing with permanently, rather than temporarily, multigenerational households.

Extended families are structured by the post-marital residential patterns of newly married couples over the generations. **Patrilocal residence** generates household composition that is distinct from **matrilocal residence**, with the compositions created by both very different from **ambilocal residence**. We discuss the varieties of household composition in turn.

Patrilocal Extended Family Households.   A subtype of extended family is the **patrilocal extended family**, a group comprising at least three generations of married consanguineal males, their wives, and unmarried kin. Daughters will leave upon marriage; sons will stay. Taken over the generations, we see a core of males forming the household, together with in-marrying wives and unmarried women. If you look at the chart in chapter 7, Figure 7.4, and the one you made yourself, the shadings you made would fit the pattern of this type of household. Those triangles that are fully shaded with blue represent the males who form the core of the family. Those circles shaded to the left represent the females who will be departing from the household when they marry. Finally, those circles shaded to the right represent the in-marrying females.

What explains the presence of patrilocal extended family households? There is no completely accepted answer; for every answer advanced, there have been exceptions. Any explanation must necessary be preceded by the phrase "it is likely that . . ." One explanation is of male cooperation in subsistence activities (such as herding large animals or intensive cultivation) or in defending these assets. Other explanations center around male control of large amounts of property, particularly when it is valuable, and the practice of polygyny, which is often related to property. Thus, it is unsurprising to find patrilocal extended families among the Masai, whose *laibon* ("wise men") own hundreds of cattle, who may marry up to a dozen or so women, and who require a retinue of warriors to defend their herds.

Matrilocal Extended Family Households. Among other cultures, **matrilocal extended family households** is the norm. This time, it's the consanguineally related females who form the core group. If you look at Figure 7.5 (chapter 7, p. 77), and the one you made yourself, the red shadings you made would fit the pattern of this type of household. Those circles that are fully shaded with red represent the females who form the core of the family. Those circles shaded to the left with red represent the males who will be departing from the household when they marry. Finally, those circles shaded to the right represent the in-marrying males. This represents the mirror image of the patrilocal extended family household.

Such households seem to arise where female cooperation is important, such as in horticultural societies where women do the work, or in which political organization is relatively simple and uncentralized. Often, men do not move far from their natal homes. Ember and Ember have also suggested that matrilocal households are likely to predomininate where warfare is either nonexistent or external when women do most of the subsistence work, such as horticulture (1971:583–585).

Avunculocal Extended Family Households. When fully developed, the **avunculocal extended family household** comprises the mother's brother and his sister's son, together with their wives, sons under five years of age, and unmarried daughters (or mother's sister's daughters where they also move in with the mother's brother). It seems to be a compromise between the demands of a patrilineal society and the constraints of matrilineal descent.

This form of household seems likely by factors that favor patrilocal residence, but in which descent through women is considered crucial for transmission of rights and property. For example, in the Trobriand Islands, gardens owned and cultivated by women are valued, but cannot be inherited by a man from his father; the same is true for positions of leadership. This leaves unanswered the question of why inheritance was matrilineal in the first place. One possibility is that women were the cooperating gender in gardening at one time. Warfare and long-distance trade, both of which involve male cooperation, may explain the shift from matrilocal toward avunculocal residence and corresponding change in the type of extended family.

Ambilocal Extended Family Households. Ambilocal residence is compatible with bilateral descent, inasmuch as both sexes bear equal weight in the choice of one household or the other. **Ambilocal extended family households**, based as they are on the aggregate choices generations of couples have made, are not so predictable as the other types of extended family cooperation. We can predict with reasonable accuracy who will dwell with whom in patrilocal or matrilocal extended family households; if outcomes differ from the expected, they are the product of situational variables.

Here, the couple chooses one of two possible residences, and the problem turns on the considerations that underlie the couple's choice. The situational trumps the logical. One consideration may be the relative attractiveness of the two residences in some way. Ambilocal residence is usually found in relatively circumscribed terrain, such as mountainous regions or islands. In Scotland, the clan was actually a kin group founded on ambilocal extended families (Fox 1967:159). We find similar situations in many Pacific islands such as the Gilberts. If one household had more land than people as compared with the other, the couple would move to the first household. We will reserve for the next chapter the larger groups arising from these extended families, the land-holding *kainga*.

Neolocal Residence and Extended Families.
Neolocal residence is the one residential pattern that militates against extended family households. By definition, couples select their own residence apart from either of their parents', and when their children mature, they move away to another residence. This does not prevent the formation of extended families, however, if the term *family* is defined as nonresidential. Parents who live separately from their married children remain in the same family, as do grandparents; they simply do not live under the same roof.

Other Family Types

There are other family types. One is the **matrifocal family household**, in which the mother and her children reside. This was characteristic of many households in the Caribbean in marginal economic conditions, and has become increasingly common as the feminization of poverty becomes more widespread. A less common pattern is the **patrifocal family household**. The sexual revolution, deliberate choice to live without a spouse, and divorce have all contributed to the households of these two types. As divorce and remarriage has soared, more and more **blended families**, comprising couples and children of previous marriages, have become commonplace as well. Finally, with the removal of stigmata toward homosexuals, **homosexual households** have also developed, some legally recognized as marriage (although in the U.S. election of 2004, voters rejected the gay rights amendment in 11 states.) Children may be adopted, the offspring of

previous marriage, or, in the case of female homosexuals, reproduced through sexual relations with outside males. Though more widespread than ever in history, none of these developments is new. Homosexuality, divorce, and remarriage have gone on for centuries, perhaps millennia.

Divorce

These days, a standard commentary about marriage has it thus: "Whatever happened to 'till death do we part' "? Almost half of marriages contracted in the United States end in divorce. Nevertheless, about 40 percent of the U.S. population remarry, as if to verify Samuel Johnson's quip that "remarriage is the triumph of hope over experience." Divorce is a reality not only in the contemporary United States, but throughout the world.

The presence, extent, and procedures involved in divorce vary widely. In foraging societies, divorce appears easy to come by. Among the !Kung of southwestern Africa, divorce is usually initiated by the wife; this is a simple matter, characterized by cordiality and cooperation. The former couple might even live next to each other with their new spouses (Lee 2003). (One wonders what Johnson would say about that.) Among the Inuit, divorce was equally simple (Balikci 1970). One reason for the simplicity of divorce in both societies was the absence of formal social groups beyond the nuclear family. Another was the relative absence of strict rules regarding marriage or postmarital residence (Scupin 2003:182).

Divorce rates were variable among tribal societies. Among the East African pastoralists, the transfer of cattle that accompanied marriage had the latent, often manifest, function of marital stability; cattle was valuable and a woman's kin would be reluctant to return them if she were divorced. On the other hand, societies with matrilineal descent tend to be associated with easier divorce, because of the latent conflict among brothers and husbands over the descent group's assets. Although a man does not pass his affiliation to his own children, his primary allegiance is to his matrilineal kin, and, as we have seen for the Yakö, his assets go to his sister's son upon his death. Among the Zuñi and Hopi, the woman had only to put her husband's belongings outside her house to secure a divorce, and the man returned to his mother's households.

The situation is somewhat different in agricultural states, because, as we will see in the next chapter, marriage often involves the transfer of valuable assets—cattle, money, land—and sometimes persons in exchange marriages. Alliances among families, kin groups, and sometimes even entire villages were also highly prized. Thus, families tended to stay together, and divorce was discouraged, if not actually outlawed. India, medieval Europe, and other states legally forbade divorce, viewing marriage and the family as sacred. Inasmuch as women faced destitution if divorced, they were committed to the marriage, however much conflict existed in the bond (Scupin 2003:256).

In industrial societies, divorce rates have increased, and one factor has been the increased economic independence of women, who no longer have to tolerate a marriage gone poor. Marital dissatisfaction combined with such independence is the immediate cause of divorce. Japan has shown a reverse pattern. Prior to the Meiji period beginning in 1868, Japan had a high divorce rate; elders of a family often rejected a bride because she did not bring a large enough dowry, did not sufficiently conform to family norms, or for other reasons. The divorce rate actually decreased during industrialization, partly because women were homemakers first and thereby lacked financial independence. In recent years, the divorce rate has started to rise again but still remains one fifth the level of the United States (Kerbo and McKinstry 1998). Generally speaking, as spouses become more and more economically autonomous, the divorce rate seems to rise. Only when the stakes are high for a marriage—large bridewealth, importance of an alliance, valuable family assets—does divorce become infrequent or even outlawed.

Conclusion

In this chapter, we have surveyed the basics of marriage, marriage types, and family formation. There is no widespread agreement as to what constitutes marriage or a family, whether heterosexual unions alone should constitute either, or whether stability should be a defining characteristic of marriage. One point about which there is little debate: Conjugal arrangements vary widely, from monogamy to polygamy and from temporary liaisons—the Nayar come to mind—to lifelong bonds that last until death does the couple part. Families vary as well, from matrifocal households to the varieties of extended family households. Finally, we have looked at some of the conditions associated with divorce or its absence. The next chapter looks at suprafamily units known as lineages, clans, and ambilineal descent groups, together with the alliances that bind them. We also look at the ephemeral forms of kin groups, namely kindreds.

Chapter 10

DESCENT GROUPS, MARRIAGE ALLIANCES, AND KINSHIP TERMINOLOGY

Introduction

At the beginning of this four-chapter series on kinship and descent, we defined two broad rules of descent—bilateral and unilineal—with the latter further divided into two subtypes—patrilineal and matrilineal. We've seen the necessity of knowing the principles of descent for knowing the rules of postmarital residence, the formation of extended families, and even the distinction between sex and gender roles.

In this chapter, we discuss larger kin groups. We start with a scenario whereby a patrilocal extended family household might, because of overcrowding, split into two such units and, over time, split into four. We then ask whether there is any advantage for maintaining contact, and set forth reasons for doing so. We go on to develop a typology of descent groups based first on rule of descent, then based on whether descent from the ancestor is **demonstrated** or **stipulated**. Following this, we go on to discuss the uses to which descent groups are put, including **corporate groups**, whereby each group owns an estate with rights and obligations on the part of its members. Next, we discuss types of marriage alliances, including those involving **bride labor**, **bridewealth**, and **exchange marriages**. Discussion of **kinship terminology** arising from descent and exchange marriages concludes this discussion.

Descent Groups: An Overview

A Scenario

Imagine an extended family, say patrilocal, getting larger and larger, say by four children every generation, two boys and two girls for each man and his wife. In each scenario, the sisters leave with their husbands, while their brothers stay.

> In Generation I: The 2 men and their wives have 8 children, 4 of each sex; half of them leave for the net total addition of 4 boys.
>
> In Generation II: The wives of the 4 men bear 16 children; 8 males remain.
>
> In Generation III: The wives of the 8 men bear 32; 16 males remain.
>
> In Generation IV: The wives of the 16 men bear 64 children; 32 males remain.
>
> In Generation V: The wives of the 32 men bear 128 children; 64 males remain.

By Generation VI, the house or compound will be crowded with 128, and those are only the males; what about their wives, unmarried sisters, parents, and children? Long before we even reach Generation IV, let alone Generation VI, tempers will flare, and the time for parting of the ways will have come and passed.

After the split, there are two possible outcomes:

A. The family members may move apart and never speak to each other again.
B. They may decide to keep some ties going; after all, they were descended from a common ancestor.

Most likely, the ubiquitous Plan B will prevail. Doesn't it make sense that larger groups composed of kin may handle functions that individual households could not, or could do so with difficulty? Among intensive cultivators, for example, all the members could help with the sowing or harvest. Among pastoralists, all the kinsmen may travel together during migration or transhumance. Then there is the matter of defending the village and fields or herds against invaders. Finally, two or more families might have a falling out, leaving the elders of other families within the kin group to mediate among them.

Given this, it should be plain that larger kin groups do exist. Some may own properties, others not. Some may be concentrated in one location; others may be scattered throughout the territory. Some may have a defensive function or perform cooperative labor; others may be called upon in emergencies only, or put traveling kinsmen up for the night. Functions vary.

Descent Groups: Definitions

A **descent group** refers to a group of kin who are lineal descendents of an ancestor, extending beyond two generations. The operative term is **lineal**, or a line of kin linking the present generation to the founder. This requires some explanation.

As we have noted before, **unilineal** refers to descent involving either the male line or the female line; by implication, this is a subtype of the adjective **lineal**. Because any lines of kin in **bilateral descent** are infinite—if you trace back to your grandparental generation, you can have four lines of descent—it is unrealistic to speak of lineal descent unless there is some way to restrict affiliation. There are such rules in societies that reckon their kin bilaterally. The result is **ambilineal descent**, or a form of **bilateral descent**, whereby an individual can choose to affiliate with either the mother's or the father's group. This requires an extensive treatment, and we take up the matter in our discussion of **ambilineal descent groups**.

Unilineal Descent Groups

Some Definitions

It is simpler to start our discussion with the **unilineal descent groups**. The kind of group we have depends on how well groups of brothers and sisters know the relatives linking themselves with the **ancestor**, or founder, of the kin group If they can identify these linking relatives, say, the father, the father's father, the father's father's father, and so on to the founder, then we say that descent is **demonstrated**. The biblical "begats," true or not, are one example. Jesus Christ was begat by Joseph (unless He was begat by the Supreme Being, as claimed in the Bible), who was begat by Jacob, and so on back to Moses, Abraham, and Adam. On the other hand, if we know (or think we know) there was an ancestor way back when (only the Supreme Being knows), but can't quite put a name on each of the linking kin, let alone determine how many kin there were, then we have to **stipulate** descent. In other words, we have to assume there were links between the group and its founder, whatever the nature or number of these links.

Now we can start defining the two main unilineal descent groups, **lineages** and **clans**. A group of kin whose members trace descent from a known common ancestor is known as a **lineage**. If descent is traced through a line of males, then the group is a **patrilineage**. If it is traced through a line of females, then it is known as a **matrilineage**. In other words, lineages are based on **demonstrated descent**. In contrast, a group of kin whose members believe themselves to be descended from a common ancestor, but cannot trace this link genealogically, then this group is known as a **clan** or **sib**. If the supposed linking kin comprise a male line, then the group is known as a **patrilineal clan** or **patriclan** (sometimes **patrisib**). If the linking relatives form a female line, then the group is known as a **matrilineal clan** or **matriclan** (or **matrisib**). In either case, descent is said to be **stipulated**.

Segmentation and the Hierarchy of Unilineal Groups

At this point, we introduce the concept of **segmentation**. As a generic term, **segments** are units of anything that are alike. Worms are **segmented** because they are divided into parts that look exactly alike. The blood vessels, other tubes, and organs of one part (segment) of the worm are exactly like those of another segment; this is why you can cut a worm into halves without killing it.

In social anthropology, segments are somewhat analogous to worm segments. One patrilineage looks similar to another; each one comprises a core of males with unmarried consanguineal females (sisters and daughters) and in-marrying females. When they contain more people than they can accommodate, then they divide, or **segment**, into two virtually identical parts, which are themselves called **segments**.

However, they can do something else. The two lineages could also remain embedded as the bigger lineage into which they just divided. Not only that, these larger lineages may be embedded into still larger lineages. In other words, they form **hierarchies**, with ever-larger groups subordinating smaller ones. There is no logical reason—although there may be practical ones—for preventing them from dividing and building up into ever-larger lineages forever. **Segmentary lineages** are the result of this process; these are forms of sociopolitical organization in which multiple lineages (usually patrilineages) form at different levels and function at different contexts. We discuss these organizations under political anthropology in chapter 13.

At a more practical level, most people can remember only so many ancestors in so many lineages. It is a chore to remember who your father's father's father was who founded Lineage 1, and who your father's father' father' father's father was who founded the more comprehensive Lineage A, and your father's father nine time over who founded the even more comprehensive Lineage I. Eventually, memory fails and you have to lump all remaining kin them into one bigger mass.

This is where **clans** come in. At a certain point, there is still some value to retain affiliation with a kin group, even though you have no idea who your ancestor was (a Raven or Killer Whale, perhaps) and how you were tied to him or her. The Navajo find it useful to have members of the same clan all over the territory; one never knows when a thunderstorm or darkness overtakes one in traveling and one needs a place to stay; hospitality is obligatory among members of the same clan. So clans usually comprise several lineages, which, in turn, may comprise even more smaller lineages.

So this is the overall design. Smaller extended families usually form small, or **minimal lineages**. These, in turn, form larger **intermediate lineages**. In turn, they form larger intermediate lineages or

eventually form **maximal lineages**. Any groups comprising these lineages become **clans** and it is possible to have even larger clans.

Segmentation: Patrilineal versus Matrilineal Groups

Patrilineal and matrilineal descent units have much in common—they are unilineal, members and non-members are clearly distinguished, and they are segmentary. The similarity, however, ends there.

Patrilineal and matrilineal descent groups are not precise mirror images of each other. The main reason they are not relates to the second sociological constant we identified at the beginning of chapter 7: the tendency of males to exercise ultimate authority over both the household and the descent group. This poses no problem for patrilineages and patrilineal clans; authority is coterminous with rule of descent, both going through males (from father to eldest son, but sometimes the youngest).

Nevertheless, among matrilineal descent groups, there is a potential area of conflict between the male kinsman and the in-marrying husband: Who's the boss? The man who left his natal unit to join his wife (in matrilocal residence) would be expected to manage the affairs of a group in which he did not grow up. The men best qualified to manage the group's affairs would leave to join their wives. Therefore, there would be no continuity; male matrilineal kinsmen would not be able to train their younger counterparts to the tasks involved in managing their group's affairs. Logically, matrilocal residence would work only if the men did not live far from their household of birth. They would then participate in that household's affairs. By definition, the women would be excluded from these decision-making matters.

There is no corresponding problem of continuity in patrilineal groups. The line of descent is identical with the line of authority; the rule of succession and inheritance corresponds exactly with those individuals who will make the key decisions. In matrilineal groups, by contrast, the rules of succession and inheritance go through females, while the line of authority goes through the male kin.

Therefore, the resolution lies in the following ideal: First, the male and female siblings stay together. The husband plays a minimum role, or none at all (as we saw with the Nayar). Authority and male property are passed from mother's brother to sister's son; of course, female property goes from mother to daughter. But if the father passes property to his own son, we have the beginnings of a patrilineal system.

By contrast, in matrilocal residence, the brother of the woman might have to spend part of his time in the lineage or clan of his wife. He could do so if he doesn't live too far from his sister. The husband, who did not grow up in his wife's lineage or clans, would lack enough knowledge to make intelligent decision affecting his newly adopted household or group. Some compromise is usually arrived at. For example, authority may be divided between households for the husband and in the larger kin group for the brother.

Another difference is the process of segmentation, rooted in considerations of group placement and authority. In patrilineal descent groups, there is no logical problem: Group placement and authority are both vested in the males. The husband alone, not his wife and his (absent) sister, makes the decision, and the move is made.

In matrilineal descent groups, however, authority is vested in males but group placement occurs through female lines. Therefore, segmentation requires the decision on the part of both brother and sister. This means that both brother and sister have to agree to move from their other siblings, and the sister, adjusted to familiar surroundings, is more likely reluctant to make the break. It is not surprising, then, that the rate of segmentation in matrilineal groups is much lower than in patrilineal groups, and it is much more difficult (and takes more time) to found a new lineage. Generally speaking, households involving matrilineal descent tend to be larger than those based on the patrilineal pattern. James Deetz argued for an archaeological site among the Arikara that larger circular post hole patterns—suggesting circular dwellings—tended to reflect matrilineally based households and the smaller ones were probably patrilineal households (1967).

Finally, there is no ignoring the ethnographic data of some cultures. We have seen for both the Iroquois and the Hopi that the women run the affairs of the household. The women in both cultures own the productive property and the residential structures: longhouses among the Iroquois, adobe lodgings among the Hopi. The men are marginalized in both locations; among the Iroquois, for example, the men are usually away hunting, waging war, or sitting in councils. If these cases are considered, the issue of matrilineal brother–sister involvement in segmentation disappears.

The Uses of Unilineal Descent Groups

In point of fact, the uses of unilineal descent groups are myriad. Some are organized; others are not. Some are property-holding units, others defend the property owned by their constituent individuals or extended property, and still others have functions other than property holding or control. Unilineal descent groups may be localized or dispersed. Some are named and some are not. (**Caution:** Don't be misled by the two surname exercises in chapter 7; not all descent groups pass down names.) Whatever their uses, they perform tasks in social areas outside the familial in societies at all levels of organization, from foraging bands (particularly aboriginal Australians) to pastoral and horticultural tribes to many agricultural states. These will be discussed in their respective chapters. Here, we cite two types of unilineal descent groups as illustration.

Dispersed Descent Groups. The first are the Navajo. Originally foraging groups, the Navajo settled in the northern region of Arizona about 300 years ago and took up sheep herding. The women perform this task and combine it with some agriculture. As a result, they run the household, and residence is matrilocal. They maintain extended family households, but beyond them, there are no property-owning matrilineal descent groups.

Nevertheless, there are matrilineal clans, and the incest tabu is extremely strict. By definition, members of a clan usually have no idea exactly how they are related, but if one belongs to a Bear Clan, a Bear may not mate or marry another Bear. Members of the same clan are dispersed throughout Navajo territory.

There is one important function of this clanship: hospitality. If a Bear traveler, for example, sees a storm brewing or is overtaken by nightfall, he can repair to the nearest hogan of another Bear. Hospitality is obligatory; the Bear household must take the traveler in. The obligation is reciprocal; the now traveler will take in his current host at some future date (Fox 1967:103).

Corporate Descent Groups. At the other end of the spectrum are **corporate descent groups**, which are organized and localized, but which have attributes from other descent groups with those characteristics (e.g., Harris and Johnson 2003:145). The cultures of East Africa, know for their cattle complex, provide an apt illustration.

First, corporate groups own or control an **estate**. In East Africa, the estates comprise cattle. They may be owned outright by the corporate group, or they may be owned individually, as they are among the wealthy *laibon*, or "wise men," of the Masai of Kenya. They form the elders of the community, who have reached this status after having served as warriors in their early lives. The function of the warriors is to protect their own herds and to raid other tribes to augment them (Hodgson 2004). Other groups may control fishing grounds, as do the Kwakiutl and other Northwest Coast peoples (Rohner and Bettauer 1986). They may control land, as many peoples do in settled communities, such as the Pueblo Indians. The members of such a group have an estate, which may consist of agricultural land, or cattle herds, or even fishing or hunting grounds.

Second, corporate groups have a series of rights and obligations concerning their property. Among the Fulani of northern Nigeria and other West African states, there is an unstated but very real obligation that, if one group loses its cattle to disease such as the rindepest, other groups will replace the victim's herd with their own (Stenning 1965). Of course, all the others expect similar aid. Another example is **lobola**, a Swahili term for **bridewealth**. When a young man marries, he does not have enough cattle to meet his obligation; he must call on his brother, his parallel male cousins (male offspring of same-sex brothers) to provide him with additional cattle; they also depend on a wider network of patrilineal kin until the required bridewealth is met. Then he, in turn, must likewise provide cattle when his brother or parallel cousin is next in line for marriage.

Third, corporate groups exist in **perpetuity**. They exist beyond the lifespan of the individual. This contrasts with the life of the **kindred**, or the group of full brothers and sisters, which dies when the last full sibling dies. We discuss the kindred later in this chapter.

Fourth, in a way similar to corporations in Western society, corporate kin groups are **fictive persons**. As is true of corporations of the multinational kind—Shell, Exxon, General Motors—the corporate kin functions as a single entity, apart from its individual constituents (Haviland 2002:281). Among the Kwakiutl, who are extremely conscious of rank, murder of a noble man must be compen-

sated for by the death of a nobleman of the offending lineage (called *numaym*)—even if the murderer was actually a commoner. Even this is not unlike the corporation in our own society, where the corporation is named as the defendant of a lawsuit or a criminal charge, not necessarily the names of each and every one of the executives and staff of that corporation. Implications of that status for understanding globalization are discussed in chapter 16.

Groups Based on Bilateral Descent

Ambilineal or Cognatic Descent Groups

At first sight, it seems that for descent groups to emerge from bilateral reckoning of kin is impossible. Every generation above Ego yields new ancestors by an additive factor of four: We have four potential ancestors in the grandparental generation, eight in the great-grandparental generation, and so on *ad infinitum*. That means we have to pare down if groups are to exist. In North America, we rely on bad memory. Elsewhere, the process of exclusion is somewhat more formal.

In his classic *Kinship and Marriage*, Robin Fox conceptualizes three types of bilateral descent groups, which he names **cognatic descent groups** (1967). These are **unrestricted cognatic descent groups**, in which all the descendants of the ultimate or founding ancestor are members; **restricted cognatic descent groups**, in which all the descendants of the founders have the right of affiliation, but only exercise this right if they opt, for example, to live in the founder's territory; and **pragmatically restricted cognatic descent groups**, in which all the descendants remain members, but in practice "cannot take up membership in all the groups they belong to, since these are territorial. So they have to choose which one to affiliate with, but this is not immutable" (1967:136). For practical purposes, and in the interest of maintaining terminological consistency, I will contrast **unrestricted bilateral descent groups** (Fox's unrestricted cognatic descent groups) with **restricted bilateral descent groups** (conflating Fox's two types of restricted cognatic descent groups).

One restricted bilateral descent group has many attributes analogous to the unilineal descent groups already discussed: There is an ancestor, there are selected kin that link descendants to ancestor, and potentially at least, the links can be **demonstrated**. The principle is **ambilineal descent**, which may be defined as a form of bilateral descent in which an individual may opt to affiliate with either the father's or the mother's descent group. Groups arising from this affiliation are known variously as **ambilineal descent groups, nonunilineal descent groups,** or **ramages.**

Fox brings forth three examples, selected from the Gilbert Islands (since 1979 the nation of Kiribati): the *oo*, or an unrestricted bilateral descent landowning group; the *bwoti* (pronounced "bwo-si," like "bossy" in a New York accent), a segment of the *oo* involving seating rights to a community meeting house by virtue of land ownership; and the *kainga*, a restricted bilateral descent group involving land rights (Fox 1967:156–158). We will confine comments to the *kainga* as an example of an ambilineal descent group, and summarize the relationship among the three groups.

As mentioned in the previous chapter, **ambilocal residence** refers to the pattern whereby the couple makes a choice between the groom's and the bride's kin's residence. In the Gilbert Islands (Kiribata), the couple's choice affects the *kainga* membership of their children. *Kainga* refers to a landholding group founded by an ancestor who lived on a certain tract of land. Some of his other descendants have remained on the tract while others moved away. Those who were born on the land remained members of the *kainga* even if they moved away; however, their *children* did not inherit membership. Thus, if the couple moves to the groom's household, both the man and the woman retain their respective affiliation—the man with his family's *kainga* and the woman with hers. However, the children lose the affiliation with their mother's *kainga*, while maintaining their father's affiliation. The reverse would be true if the couple moved in the bride's household; the couple's children would inherit their mother's *kainga*, but not their father's.

Ward Hunt Goodenough, who described this system, sum up the relationship among the *oo*, the *bwoti*, and the *kainga* this way:

> All three descent groups are somehow connected with land. An ancestor having established ownership of a tract of land was the founder of all three. All of his descendents formed an *oo* (the unrestricted bilateral descent group). Those in actual possession of a share in the land are eligible to membership in a *bwoti* (a restricted bilateral descent group). Those whose parents resided on it form a *kainga*." (1963)

In Fox's words, the *oo* is concerned with *rights* in the land; the *bwoti* with actual *possession* of a piece of it; and the *kainga* with *residence* on it (1967:158).

Over time, as the ambilineal descent group develops, each generation of kin has links to the ancestor, some of whom are male, others of whom are female, on a selective basis; not all possible kin are included. In one way, they function as if they were unilineal groups, and it is true that the Gilbertese *kainga* leadership is patrilineally inherited and that most couples move in with the groom's kin; unlike patrilocal residence, however, a choice is allowed the couple.

Why do they exist? Patterns similar to the unrestricted *oo* and the restricted *bwoti* and *kainga* are found in the Philippines, the Solomon Islands, Samoa, Polynesia generally, and New Zealand. The Scottish "clan" (*clann*) was also a cognatic descent group; *clann* in Gaelic simply meant "children" or "descendants." What all these locations have in common is their location on islands, whose restricted geography and adaptability to ecological pressures are important. The couple decides which *kainga* is the best bet, by the sufficiency of land and number of people occupying it (Fox 1967:159–163).

Kindreds

There are, however, groups that do not rely on descent or orientation toward an ancestor. The group familiar to ourselves is the **bilateral kindred,** which may be defined as a group of kin related to a set of full brothers and sisters. Such groups overlap, so that your kin contains some of the same relatives as, say, your father's kindred. However, the relatives are redefined as we move from kindred to kindred. The man you call your *uncle*—from the perspective of your own kindred—is different from the kindred of your father, who calls him *brother*. Therefore, bilateral kindreds are **egocentric** groups, evidenced by the fact that when the kindred of full brothers and sisters die, the kindred dies. Of course, half-siblings belong to two separate kindreds; your half-brother and you have one common parent and one different parent.

Isn't it redundant to refer to kindred as bilateral? Not at all. Some cultures have **unilateral kindreds,** in which Ego reckons only the father's or the mother's retinue of relatives. For example, the Kalmuk Mongols have personal kindreds reckoned through Ego's father and Ego's father's father. This group is somewhat like a patrilineage, inasmuch as kin are excluded by sex: sisters and daughters' offspring are automatically excluded from the retinue of offspring. However, there is no ancestor involved; the Kalmuk also have patrilineal groups descended from an ancestor. Furthermore, the degree of kin reckoning is limited by two generations of male kin (Fox 1967:170).

Another type of kindred is the **stock**, or all the descendants of a person or of a married couple. A kindred of third-range stocks—that is, all the descendants of a couple down to the third generation of offspring—is found in the northern Philippines. This seems identical to the ambilineal descent group just defined, but with an important difference: When the couple dies, the stock disappears (Fox 1967:168–169).

Sociocentric and Egocentric Groups

Thus we come to an important distinction. When a key member of a group—bilateral or unilateral kindred or stock—dies, the group dies with him and/or her. These are known as **egocentric kin groups**, or groups that are centered around particular individuals. Their function centers around Ego's immediate relatives.

In contrast, when particular persons die in a lineage, clan, or ambilineal descent group, the group persists. Lineages last several generations; clans usually last longer. Ambilineal descent groups persist at various periods of time; they may die out, but not because particular individuals die out. Therefore, they are **sociocentric** groups, groups whose focus is on the social organization centered around the founder and his/her ancestors.

Other Descent Groups

Of course, there are descent groups that are linked in various important ways. For example, many tribal peoples are organized into two descent groups called **moieties**. Derived from the French meaning "half," they are actually derived from two lineages—one into which one is born and the other into which one marries. We will discuss this further under exchange marriage. Another group is known as the **phratry**. This is a unilineal descent group comprising two or more clans thought to be related, whether or not they in fact are.

Marriage and Exchange

Many exchange marriages—those involving transfer of wealth or **cousin marriage**—are predicated on two issues: group size and the reproductive power of women. Preindustrial societies are very small. Foragers number anywhere between 40 and 100 persons. Pastoralists and horticulturalists number up to 1,000. Therefore, the very survival of a band or tribe is dependent on women and their fertility. Viewed in this light, it is not surprising that barrenness is one frequent cause of divorce among African societies.

When marriage takes place, therefore, the bride-giving group is at risk. The incest tabu in most societies precludes brother–sister mating, and thus marriage. Therefore, it is giving up a member who could have borne members of the next generation for this kin group. In one way or another, she must be replaced with another woman capable of childbearing. It is unsurprising that we find bridewealth in many preindustrial societies, and cousin marriage in others. They form a kind of preindustrial insurance policy that the group will continue into the next generation.

It is also important that the group the daughter marries into is a good group: the daughter will not be mistreated or live in poverty, the husband and his group are good producers, and the husband's group will not attack that of the daughter and bride. Indeed, the husband's group will come to the aid of the bride's group if the latter is attacked or loses its cattle or crops to disease. Viewed in this light, mother-in-law jokes become somewhat less humorous.

We therefore discuss the logic behind marriages involving exchange. First, we examine the transfer of labor and assets: what, after all, is **bride labor** for, and how about **bridewealth** (often called, somewhat erroneously, **bride price**)? Next, we examine how transfer of persons substitutes for (or supplements) transfer of assets, and discuss main types of **parallel cousin** and **cross-cousin** marriage. We conclude with a discussion of a seemingly anomalous exchange, the **dowry**, in which the bride's group transfers some of its assets to the groom's group.

Bride Service and Bridewealth

Both bride service and bridewealth serve to consolidate the ties between groups that marriage will initiate. Both involve considerable effort on the part of the groom and his kin in payment for the loss of a daughter that her group will incur.

In **bride service**, the groom moves in with his wife's kin and works in exchange for his marital rights. Bride service is found in 19 percent of the world's cultures, mostly in societies that lack the material wealth that can be transferred (Scupin 2003:255–256). Periods of service last from several months to several years. Among the Dobe !Kung, for example, bride service can last up to ten years, and the bride and groom may not return to the husband's residence until several children are born. Another reason for bride service is that girls are married long before menarche, so that bride service often coincides with sexual maturation (Lee 2004). Most instances of **matri-patrilocal residence** are associated with bride service.

In contrast, **bridewealth** is found in societies with considerable wealth and in which women are highly valued, both for their labor and for their childbearing capacities. The term refers to the transfer of valuable goods from the groom's kin to that of the bride when the couple marries. The term **bride price** is often used for this transaction, but is misleading because it is not equivalent to the selling and buying of commodities on the market. Though the status of the bride may be extremely low, the wife-receivers do not "own" the bride in any total sense. Often if she is maltreated, her family will demand that she be returned to them (Goody, 1976; Scupin 2003:255–256).

African pastoralist societies are classic examples of bridewealth, known in Swahili as *lobola*. Cattle have traditionally been the wealth used in bridewealth, although iron tools were also transferred; today, bridewealth comes in the form of cash. The Bathonga illustrate how the process works. First, the bride-giving family receives large amounts of cattle. In turn, the family can now afford to pay with cattle for the wife of their young man. Wealth often accumulates for families with many sisters and daughters; this enhances their wealth-generating and reproductive power by attracting the reproductive and labor power of the mothers and wives whom they recruit.

In a sample of 1,267 societies conducted by Gaulin and Boster (1990:994), more than half participate in bridewealth. Their findings indicate that bridewealth is likely to occur where land is common and the labor of additional women and children contributes to the wealth and well-being of the group, especially among corporate descent groups (Goody 1976). The Bathonga fit this description.

Dowries

After having discussed the importance of bridewealth and cousin marriage to replenish the reproductive power of the family, household, and kin group, it may seem peculiar that wife-giving households would compensate the wife-receiving household in marriage, the defining characteristic of **dowry**—yet that practice is widely reported, including in European societies, as well as in China and in India.

Why the contrast? In a cross-cultural survey, Jack Goody (1976) found that bridewealth tends to occur in horticultural societies, whereas dowries tend to be found in complex agricultural societies, characterized by plows and draft animals, high population densities, and scarcity of land. One result of the dowry system, Goody hypothesizes, is the consolidation of wealth into the hands of the elite. Here, given large population size and scarcity of resources, women lose their value in their reproductive roles, and possibly their productive ones as well. This contrasts with societies practicing bridewealth, where populations are relatively low and productivity is not high, either. Bridewealth in this context is a means of circulating wealth among families through creating alliances between the groom's and bride's families, a less-than-important consideration in **stratified societies** (see chapter 12).

Cousin Marriage

On exogamy, E. B. Tylor (1888) wrote more than a century ago that "Again and again in the world's history, savage tribes [this was written in 1888] must have had plainly before their minds the simple practical alternative between marrying-out and being killed-out" (Fox 1967:176). As Fox notes, this maxim reflects not so much the negative rule of incest—"do not marry women outside the band because you cannot have sexual relations with them"—as a positive outcome of the need for survival—"enter into marriage alliances with other groups in order to live at peace with them" (Fox 1967:176). These citations emphasize the importance of marriage in forming alliances between groups—families, descent groups, villages.

Although bridewealth and bride labor also play major roles in cementing alliances among groups, the most direct means is exchange marriages. We might be reluctant to initiate hostilities against a tribe in which our sister was given in marriage. This is not to say that hostilities were indeed prevented; many tribal people have a proverb something like "We marry whom we fight," or "We marry those we fight," but they are still dependent on each other for their survival. Marriage tempers conflict, but does not eliminate it entirely.

Cousin marriage is the most widespread form of exchange marriage. In North America, we don't think very much about cousins; they are all lumped together in one term. In English, we don't even distinguish them by sex; there's no cousin term to match brother or sister. In Spanish, of course, there is an ending that distinguishes the two: *primo* and *prima*. Nevertheless, even those two terms apply equally to father's and mother's side.

But among numerous other cultures in the world, not only are the boys separated from the girls, but they are also separated by the sex of the siblings one generation up. This tendency is reflected in the kinship terminological systems, and these systems will conclude this chapter.

For the present, we concentrate on those aspects of terminology that relate to alliances among two or more lineages or clans, and these are mainly cousin terms. **Parallel cousin** refers to Ego's father's brother's or mother's sister's child. **Cross-cousin** refers to Ego's father's sister's or mother's brother's child. **Patrilateral parallel cousin** refers to Ego's father's brother's child. Of course, there is also a **matrilateral parallel cousin** (Ego's mother's sister's daughter), but it's not relevant to our discussion here. If you notice from the charts you created from Figures 7.1 and 7.2 for chapter 7, one set of parallel cousins belong to the *same* lineage as Ego's (father's brother's children in patrilineal descent, and mother's sister's children in matrilineal descent). Although the mother's sister's children in patrilineal societies and father's brother's children in matrilineal societies belong to different lineages, they are also close kin to Ego's family, and in some kinship terminology are merged with brother or sister.

Three cross-cousin terms are of particular interest because the cousins belong to different lineages. These consist of the **matrilateral cross-cousin**, or Ego's mother's brother's child, the **patrilateral cross-cousin**, or Ego's father's sister's child, and **bilateral cross-cousin**, or Ego's father's sister's child lumped with mother's brother's child. If you look

again at the charts that you created for patrilineal and matrilineal descent (Figures 7.1 and 7.2), you will see that all of Ego's cross-cousins belong to a descent group different from Ego's group.

Patrilateral Parallel-Cousin Marriage. To illustrate the workings of cousin marriage, we start with a common practice in Middle Eastern societies, of which the Rwala Bedouin are an example. This is **patrilateral parallel cousin marriage**, or marriage between a man and his father's brother's daughter (all discussion henceforth will focus on the female cousins). As you can see from your patrilineal chart, the woman's patrilineal kin group is identical with Ego's. This marriage tends to reinforce the patrilineage, and has its uses. This marriage sacrifices the benefits of alliance with another kin group, but reinforces the alliance between a man's own family and that of his cousins' (male and female). Offspring remain loyal, structurally at least, with Ego's own extended family and lineage.

Often this rule of **endogamy** (marriage within the group, from the Latin *endo-* meaning "inside," and *-gamy*, derived from the Latin meaning "marriage") serves to maintain control over valuables, such as draft animals—sheep, goats, or camels—or precious metals and stones. This is the same rationale for brother–sister marriage to which we have alluded in discussing the **incest tabu**.

Varieties of Cross-Cousin Marriage. There are two possible forms of **cross-cousin marriage**. The first, **matrilateral cross-cousin marriage**, refers to the marriage of a man to his mother's brother's daughter. The second, **patrilateral cross-cousin marriage**, refers to the marriage of a man to his father's sister's marriage. The third form of marriage arises from the combination of the first two. This is **bilateral cross-cousin marriage**, whereby a man marries either his mother's brother's daughter or his father's sister's daughter, or perhaps a woman who is both relative to the man. This will require some extended explanations.

Among societies practicing cross-cousin marriage, there are variations in the strictness of rules. Where cross-cousin marriage is but an option that is locally favored over other possible marriage choices, then we speak of one type of cousin marriage as **preferred**. However, if the cousin marriage—matrilateral, patrilateral, or bilateral—is obligatory, then we speak of that type of marriage as **prescribed**. These have implications for the pattern of alliances that are formed.

Two other qualifications should be mentioned. First, the person we define as a cross-cousin is fairly precise. Nevertheless, the term, say, matrilateral cross-cousin may be covered by a kin term that applied to a much wider field of kin than this term refers to. It could apply to, say, the father's mother's son's daughter, or the mother's mother's brother's son's daughter, or any range of kin, so long as there is some sister's brother's link in the mother's lineage. Seemingly simple, the identification of an eligible marriage partner can be a complex business.

Therefore, we are dealing with an **ideal type**. First formulated by Max Weber, a founder of sociology, this refers to an analytical construct that serves the investigator as a measuring rod to ascertain similarities as well as deviations in concrete cases. In the case of matrilateral cross-cousin marriage, the "analytical construct" is the mother's brother link; but in reality it could occur in the grandparental or the great-great grandparental generation as well as the parental. Ideal types seem to establish the *essential* link in this case—mother and brother.

The second qualification involves a careful inspection of your patrilineal diagram (your matrilineal diagram will do as well if you make appropriate changes in the numbers that follow). Let's stick with the matrilateral link—Ego's mother's brother's daughter. You can see from the link that No. 36 is Ego's mother's (No. 10) brother's (No. 13) daughter. Now trace this link backward. You will see that Ego (No. 25) is No. 36's father's (No. 13) sister's (No. 10) son. In other words, Ego is No. 36's patrilateral cross-cousin!

We have a similar result with patrilateral cross-cousin marriage. Referring to your patrilineal diagram, male Ego's father's (No. 9) sister's (No. 6) daughter (No. 18) is his potential wife—his patrilateral cross-cousin. Now from *her* perspective, Ego is her mother's (No. 6), brother's (No. 9) son (No. 25). Well now, that makes Ego her matrilateral cross-cousin. As you can see, by convention, the male Ego is the point of reference when it comes to cross-cousin marriage. By the way, patrilateral parallel cousin marriage involves no such reversal: Ego (no. 25) is her (No. 22) father's (No. 7) brother's (No. 9) son (No. 25), just as she is Ego's (No 25) father's (No. 10) brother's (No. 6) daughter (No. 22); either way, they are patrilateral cross-cousins—a world apart from cross-cousins who marry.

You may recall that kinship has strong implications for the political operations of a society. For this reason, we reserve discussion of cross-cousin marriage for political alliances in chapter 13. Marriage is one way to avoid war, or at least minimize the chance of warfare. For the Yanomamö, at least, the village that marries together stays together.

Kinship Terminology

Often the student groans when, after learning about marriage types, the family types they produce, the finer aspects of descent groups and—ye gods!—cross-cousin marriage, that there's the little matter of kinship terminology. But then, kinship terms are something that six-year-old Australian aboriginal or Masai or Yanomamö kids know already—why shouldn't we?

Generally speaking, kinship terminology has a more or less direct relationship with rules of descent and patterns of marriage. Some are easy to grasp—the Hawaiian, Eskimo (Inuit), and even the Iroquois come to mind. The Sudanese system is more difficult for the layperson, and the Crow and Omaha systems are the most difficult of all. First, however, we need to discuss some preliminary concepts of terms: **descriptive** versus **classificatory** terms and the aunt–uncle terms **bifurcate merging**, **bifurcate collateral**, **lineal**, and **generational**.

Principles of Classification

Several principles are used in classifying kin. First, **descriptive terms** refer to terms that refer to one or at most two kinds of relatives. In the United States *mother* refers to only one person; an adult female with her own children. At the opposite end of the spectrum are **classificatory terms**, those whose term cover a wide range of relatives. Thus, in the United States, the term *cousin* covers parents' siblings' offspring without further distinction. In Mexico, France, Germany and many other countries, the terms make only one distinction: by gender. In actuality, there are varying degrees between descriptive and classificatory kin.

Next are other principles that govern assignment of kinship terms. The first is **generation**, which distinguish **ascending** (parental, grandparental, and so on) and **descending** (children's, grandchildren's, and so on) kin from Ego's own generation. The second is **relative age**, in which older siblings are distinguished from younger ones. English terms make no such distinctions. The third is **gender**, in which females are distinguished from males.

The next set of principles is somewhat more complex, because many of them do not apply in our own society. The first set is **lineality** versus **collaterality**. **Lineal** kin are related in a single line, such as grandfather-father-son (patrilineal in this instance). **Collateral kin** are descended from a common ancestor with Ego, but are not Ego's direct ascendants or descendants. Brothers and sisters are collateral kin, as are cousins, aunts, and uncles. This is an important distinction in our own society.

Another set of principles concerns **consanguineality** versus **affinity**. Persons related to Ego by blood (parent-child, siblings) are known as **consanguineal kin**, whereas those related to Ego by marriage (husband–wife, parents-in-law) are known as **affinal kin**. Again, this distinction is important to our society.

Less familiar to Anglo-American societies are the terms based on **sex of linking kin**. To us, it does not matter whether your cousin is related to you through your father's brother or mother's brother; to the Yanomamö, it matters a great deal. A male must avoid his father's brother's daughter, but may—indeed has an obligation to—marry his mother's brother's daughter. We discuss this issue further in chapter 13. To most cultures of the world, this principle is essential.

Also unfamiliar to Anglo-Americans are the terms based on **bifurcation** or **merging**. **Bifurcation** refers to the practice of distinguishing relatives on the father's side from the mother's side. Apart from the distinction between father and mother, Americans recognize no such distinction. In unilineal societies, the distinction is crucial; mother's brother is often distinguished from father's brother.

Cousin Terminology

Although somewhat oversimplified, anthropologists recognize six systems of terminology. Some are consistent with bilateral descent, others with one or the other form of unilineal descent. In addition, the type of cousin marriage may influence the terminology.

The first and simplest terminology is **Hawaiian cousin terminology**, in which no distinction is made between siblings and cousins, although the terms may differ by gender. Terms applied to mother and father are applied to all aunts and uncles, reflecting **generational terminology** for all kin of the ascending generation. By the same token, sons and daughters are merged with nephews and nieces. This terminology is usually found in association with bilateral descent, and often with ambilineal descent groups.

The second terminology is **Eskimo terminology**, sometimes known as **Inuit terminology** to anthropologists aware that *Eskimo* is derived from an Athabaskan derogatory term meaning "raw meat eaters." This terminology separates the siblings from the cousins, and is associated with **lineal terminology**, which separates the parents from the aunts and uncles. Cousins are not separated except by gender, and the same applied to aunts and uncles. This terminology is associated with bilateral descent, and tends to emphasize the nuclear family.

Iroquois terminology merges brother and sister with male and female parallel cousins on either side. However, the cross-cousins are separated from both Ego's siblings and his/her parallel cousins. Mother's brother and father's sister are distinguished from father's brother and mother's sister, who are not distinguished from father or mother, a distinction known as **bifurcate merging terminology**. As an example, it is interesting that a Yanomamö male calls his cross-cousin *suaböya*, that is, "(future) wife," while she calls him *soriwa*, or "(future) husband." As we will see in chapter 13, **bilateral cross-cousin marriage** is **prescribed**. This rule of descent is associated with unilineal descent, either patrilineal or matrilineal.

Sudanese terminology is even more complex. Here, brothers and sisters are distinguished from all their cousins, and all the cousins are distinguished from each other. Thus, mothers' brothers are distinguished from fathers' sisters, and are both distinguished from parallel cousins, who are also distinguished from each other: father's brother's offspring are distinguished from mother's sister's offspring. This is also associated with **bifurcate collateral terminology**, in which father, mother, father's brother, mother's sister, mother's brother, and father's sister are all distinguished from each other. Found in many African societies (hence the name; Sudan refers to tropical Africa as a whole as well as the country), this terminology is found in predominantly patrilineal societies with some elements of matrilineality, suggesting association with double descent. It is also found among societies that tend to be **ranked** or **stratified** (see chapter 12).

Omaha terminology, along with its logical opposite, **Crow terminology**, is the most complex. Reflecting its patrilineal orientation, **Omaha terminology** (which includes its Native American namesake) is one in which a man refers to his brothers' children by the same term as his own, but his sisters' children by different terms. There is a merging of generations on his mother's side; the terms for mother's brother and mother's sister are applied not only to those relatives but also to their patrilineal offspring (maternal cousins) and *their* patrilineal offspring. Generational differences are important to Ego's own patrilineal kin (i.e., through his father), but not the mother's patrilineal kin. Aunt and uncle terminology conforms to a **bifurcating merging terminology**.

Crow terminology reflects the opposite orientation, the preference for Ego's mother's matrilineal kin over Ego's father's matrilineal kin. Ego's father's matrilineal kin are lumped together with the term for father's sister and father's brother and their matrilineal offspring, whereas there are generational distinctions for Ego's own mother's matrilineal kin. As in the Omaha system, **bifurcate merging terminology** applies to the Crow system as well.

Conclusion

As one can see, kinship regulates not only family and marriage, but also other aspects of preindustrial societies as well. For that reason, learning the types of descent affiliation, descent groups, marriage types, family types, and even types of marital alliances are essential to understanding other aspects of society. To understand cultures without understanding the principles of kinship (even societies that do not rely on complex kinship relations, such as the Inuit, and of course industrial ones) is akin to learning chemistry without the periodic tables or physics without the theories of relativity or the laws of thermodynamics.

Nor have you left the principles of kinship just yet. In economic anthropology, the logic behind exchange marriages are discussed in reviewing Mauss's three obligations of the gift; in political anthropology, the alliance patterns formed by bilateral and matrilateral cross-cousin marriage will be discussed. As stated, you cannot understand preindustrial cultures without understanding kinship. Have a nice day.

Chapter 11

ECONOMIC ANTHROPOLOGY

Introduction

We all fret about "the economy." Will the stock market plummet sometime soon? Will the unemployment rate ever go down? Will my job be shipped off to Bangladesh next year? All of these questions refer to a capitalist, market-driven economy under which we live—and all too often, we think and behave as if ours were the only economy in the world. We might recall that Russia and its allies, once upon a time known as the Soviet Union, had a "communist" economy, more accurately a **command economy**. But that is as far as we go.

In fact, there has been in the world's cultures a variety of economic systems, some of them containing markets but not dominated by one. The !Kung until about 50 years ago had no market and no money and no use for either. The Northwest Coast native people traded, but used no currency, nor was the trade primarily for economic gain. There are (or at least until roughly 50 years ago) many economies that do not (1) have stock markets, (2) have markets at all, (3) have money as we know it, (4) have businesses, and (5) have corporations. This is where our ethnocentrism and culture-bound notions dominate our conscious and even unconscious thinking.

So what, then, is an economy? Let's look at the roots of the word. *Economy* is derived from the Greek *oikonomia*, which means "household manager," which is further derived from *oikos*, house, and *nemein*, to manage. Metaphorically, then, a band, a tribe, a nation state are comparable to a house that is to be managed. One manages a household by keeping it clean and uncluttered, making best use of the food, clothing, furniture, and so on. In this light, I leave to you to evaluate how well we the people are managing our household, our nation state.

So now, in light of its derivation, **economy** might best be defined as the production and distribution of goods and services in a society. All societies have the need to produce, to exchange, and to consume, so that is about as universalistic a definition we can get. However, there is another aspect to economics that also plays a role in many societies. This is the need to **economize**, or to make the best use of the goods and services to which one has access. That, too, is the essence of good house management.

In chapter 6, we compared five basic subsistence systems, or food-getting techniques. Often, however, the literature speaks of a "herding economy" or a "hunting-and-gathering" economy. These are technological matters, not economic ones. The techniques of hunting, or clearing forests, or irrigating fields are related to technology, not economy. The focus shifts to the economic when we ask how work is organized, whether in a Yanomamö village or in a factory. When we ask who owns the hunting territory or the plots of ground being irrigated or the water used for irrigation, we are also asking questions pertaining to economics.

Thus, we begin by discussing approaches to economic anthropology, including the relationship to economics and society. We address the notion of scarcity, which forms the foundation of Western economic science, and we contrast the substantive with the formalist approaches. We then turn to the kinds of property ownership in the world's culture—where there is such a thing, that is. Organization of production is addressed next, and you may be surprised that the notion of "company time" is foreign to most cultures. We then look at exchange systems to show that market exchange is but one of many. Finally, we look at consumption, including the rights and privileges attached thereto.

Economy and Society

To begin, we need to take up the fundamental assumption of Western economics. If you are taking, or have taken, economics, you know about the **scarcity postulate**, which holds that, inasmuch as human wants (the focus of economics is on wants, not needs) are infinite and the means for satisfying them are finite, we must deal with the reality that all goods and services are **scarce**. Lionel Robbins set forth a concise definition of economics in this light: "the science which studies human behaviour as a relationship between ends and scarce means which have alternative uses" (1937). Any scarce good is therefore an **economic good**; any good that is infinite in quality (say air—let's ignore air quality for a moment) is a **free good**. Once upon a time, water was considered a free good—but have you looked at your water bill lately? Case closed!

In light of the scarcity question, about 40 years ago an acrimonious debate erupted among economic anthropologists as to the best cross-cultural treatment of a topic we call economy. On the one hand were those who held that **substantivism** is the most appropriate framework. Scarcity, the substantivists argued, was not present in all places for all goods. The !Kung have an infinite supply of building material, nor are they short of food most of the time. New Guinean tribesmen can grow all the

sweet potatoes they want without a great deal of effort. The Northwest Coast tribes had all the salmon and timber they needed. To assume otherwise was to apply ethnocentrically models of supply and demand or other economic models to societies where neither property nor scarcity was an issue.

Therefore, we must question how each society goes about providing goods and services to meet its people's needs. Moreover, economies are embedded in society. You cannot understand bridewealth without also understanding the relations among families that it bonds. The economy, wrote Karl Polanyi, himself an economic historian, is an "instituted process" (1944; 1971). Why else does the Trobriand Islander canoe with his fellow from one island to another, braving storm and sharks, just to trade a white armshell for a red necklace? Why do Northwest Coast peoples hold potlatches involving giving of valuable gifts just to validate the status of the next chief?

In rebuttal, another school advanced the notion of **formalism**. In every society, they argued, there is scarcity in some respect. The !Kung, they might argue, might have all the building material they need, perhaps plenty of food of all kinds, but what about large game? Aren't giraffes or wildebeests hard to come by? Aren't the prized mongongo nuts exhausted before the next season? As for the Northwest Coast native peoples, isn't the prestige of a chief a scarce commodity? And if the New Guinea tribesmen have enough sweet potatoes to eat, why then do they go into all the effort and expense to raise pigs to give away and consume at the next big moka (feast) every ten years or so?

Therefore, we have no choice but to recognize that every society has unlimited wants of some sort for which limited quantities of goods and services are available. Do we want prestige for a New Guinea big man? Then he must spend his waking hours mobilizing his followers to marshal the necessary pigs. Do you want your daughter to marry well? Then you must entice a well regarded family with large numbers of healthy cattle as bridewealth. Scarcity is everywhere, even in noneconomic sectors. The question, then, is how does one economize? How does one make the best use of one's resources? That is the economic question from the formalist perspective.

This debate went on for years without resolution, in part because every argument was met with a counterargument from the other side. Mainly, however, a tune by Bob Dylan sums up the issue: "You were right from your side; I was right from mine." There is something to viewing economies from a relativistic standpoint: Not all societies are market societies, and people do not behave rationally according to the rules of the marketplace. From the other side, something is scarce in every society, even if the thing that is scarce is time or prestige.

Property

One of the fundamental questions of economic anthropology is property ownership and its allocation. At first glance, we might assume that property is not a major issue to, say, foragers. As we have seen, foragers define their territory loosely, and property rights, where they exist, tend not to be exclusionary. As populations increase and assets like land and animals become more valuable, exclusionary property rights are likely to emerge.

Thus, we may develop a typology of ownership types. First is **communalism**, the property arrangements whereby everyone has access to its assets. Foragers range in more or less defined territories, though theirs may overlap with the territory of others. Among the !Kung, gatherers are free to dig their tubers, harvest their nuts, and pluck their fruits or leaves wherever they may find them. Hunters are also free to move wherever game is to be found. Private property is rarely absent, however. The food women gather is the property of her family. Such rights—the communal right of property access but the individual right of use—is known in legal terms as **usufruct**. Men who hunt down the animals "own" it, but only to give its meat away—in other words, ownership means only stewardship.

Yet even exclusive property rights may be found among foragers. Among the Owens Valley Paiute of the Nevada Basin in the western United States, piñon nut trees were particularly valued, so that families and bands claimed exclusive rights to territory containing these stands, and defended them against all intruders (Bloch 1983, cited in Scupin 2003:178). Dyson-Hudson and Smith find that the greater the predictability and concentration of resources within a territory, the more pronounced the conception of exclusive property rights (1978; Scupin 2003:178). Generally speaking, however, the main norm involves rights to all to common property for individual exploitation.

In societies with more complex technologies, communalism may remain the norm. Among the Mundurucú of Brazil's Amazonia, for example, individuals have the right to clear and plant any field not reserved to the community at large. More likely, however, control of resources tends to be **joint ownership**, or ownership by an extended family, lineage, or clan. In this case, the entity owns land, cattle, or other resource, or may exercise some regulative or protective function, while the family actually exercises ownership. Thus, the property becomes an **estate**, which we already defined in chapter 10 in discussing **corporate kin groups**.

When assets—land, cattle, or other resources—become scarce, then more restrictive forms of ownership apply. Elite clans may continue to exercise joint control, or the assets may be held in **fee simple**, that is, owned privately. Agricultural land may be claimed and owned by the chiefs, lords, or monarchs, who allocate land for their use in exchange for taxes, labor, or tribute to support the institution of their chiefdom or state. A society may be based on a **feudal** or **patrimonial** arrangement, whereby the peasant or serf provides a portion of his product and labor to his lord, who in turn provides tribute to a superior lord, and so on up a hierarchy, such as those found in sub-Saharan Africa, Japan before the Meiji restoration in 1868, or medieval Europe. Finally, there is **capitalism**, whereby production for use is displaced by production for profit. When this occurs, the products become transformed into **commodities**, goods and services offered not so much for use as for sale on the market. Ours is a commodity-based, market-driven economy, so that even labor is a commodity. It is significant, perhaps, that ultraconservatives would substitute the phrase "life, liberty, and the pursuit of happiness" with "life, liberty, and the pursuit of property."

Division of Labor

Often tied in with property arrangements (or lack thereof) is the division of labor. In most preindustrial societies not based on intensive cultivation, the division of labor is based on **gender** and **age**. As we have already seen in chapter 8, the gender division of labor varies considerably from one society to another. The only exceptions that seem to be universal are that men engage in warfare and women attend to child-care tasks. Men tend to do the heavy work, but women attend to strenuous tasks as well. No matter what generalization one makes on the gender division of labor, there are always exceptions—even on the male role in warfare if the myth of the Amazons (Newark and McBride 1991) is ever verified in archaeology.

Age also plays a role in differentiating tasks of society. The young engage in play, which in many respects prepares them for adult work. Yanomamö boys may shoot arrows at iguanas or insects, preparing them for hunting porcupines or tapir five or ten years hence. As the young reach adolescence, they take on increasingly important tasks until they reach the status of adults, as locally defined. (The rites of passage, marking adulthood in many societies, are discussed in chapter 18, on psychological anthropology.) As adults, they do all the hunting and gathering or cultivation or herding on which their band or village or nomadic tribe depends. The aged do less in the way of productive work, but they draw on their experience to advise the younger members.

Whatever the rules governing division of labor, pre-agricultural peoples engage in the primary sector of their economy full time. There may be part-time practitioners, such as shamans, or there may be individuals who are particularly proficient at making arrows or leather karosses (capes used by !Kung women to carry babies and objects), but everyone, in the end, hunts or gathers, tends to the herds, or gardens. More important, the households produce for themselves and secondarily, if at all, for exchange for products they cannot produce themselves. This is known as the **domestic mode of production**, or production for the household. When the needs are met, labor usually ceases.

With the advent of intensive cultivation, the division of labor shifts from the primary sector of cultivation to the rise of full-time artisans or craftspersons. In due course, villages transform into cities, or are absorbed by them. Guilds may arise to assure the quality of footwear, or clothing, or metal products. Some cities may specialize, as well, so that trade gradually arises. Productive resources become **capital**, resources or products that are used in further production. In due course, nonfarm workers take up a significant part of the economy. At that point, the domestic mode of production becomes displaced by any of a variety of systems whereby the peasant or craftsperson must produce for exchange, not merely for the household.

As fossil fuels displace animals as an important source of power, the division of labor again undergoes a transformation. Though high energy inputs and machinery are crucial to industrial production as we know it, equally important is the rise of **detail labor**. Up to now, the craftsperson handled all aspects of his or her craft. Industrial labor now demands that these aspects be broken down to their constituent labor processes. Whereas the shoemaker tanned the leather, cut it, sewed the parts to form a shoe, and nailed on the soles and heels, now these tasks are broken up and assigned to different workers. In his classic work *Wealth of Nations*, (1776), the Scottish philosopher Adam Smith illustrated the point using pin manufacture. Which is more efficient, he asked: five men, each cutting the wire, pointing each pin, putting a head on each, adding whiting (a preservative), and putting them on lengths of paper to be sold; or the same five men doing a single task each? The answer was clear; the second alternative is more productive. It was from this assignment of specialized tasks that the assembly line was born and society became industrialized.

Distribution and Exchange

Once a good is produced or a service is made available, the product or service must reach the consumer in some way, who in the meantime has a good or service to offer that she or he has produced. At that point, some form of **exchange** or **transaction** is about to take place. In anthropology, however, the issue is not so simple as that. We started this chapter by pointing out the embedding of economy in society. Nowhere is this as evident as in preindustrial societies.

In this section, we first discuss Mauss's three obligations of the gift, then move on to describe three principal types of exchange: **reciprocity** (which subsumes three subtypes, **generalized**, **balanced**, and **negative**), **redistribution**, and **market exchange**. Then, in this and successive chapters (especially chapter 13), we show how these exchanges become part of what Polanyi called "an institutionalized process"—in other words, how they are embedded in society (Polanyi, Arenberg, and Pearson 1957:243–244).

The Gift and Its Obligations

What, then, is the rationale of all exchange: goods, services, marriage, or otherwise? One explanation is that, in the absence of the modern state and its laws, the act of gift-giving, acceptance, and repayment is imperative, although enforced by no police or army. No one puts the matter more clearly than the French sociologist Marcel Mauss.

Mauss, nephew and student of the eminent French sociologist Emile Durkheim, attempted in 1925 a cross-cultural explanation of gift-giving and its attendant obligations, in his book titled *The Gift: Forms and Functions of Exchange in Archaic Societies* (*Essai sur le don*). His starts with the assumption that two groups (band, tribe, chiefdoms, perhaps even agricultural states) have the imperative to establish a relationship of some kind. There are three options that the two groups have when they meet for the first time: They may pass each other by and never see each other again. They may resort to arms with an uncertain outcome; one could wipe the other out or, more likely, win at great cost of men and property or fight to a draw. The third option is to (what he calls) "come to terms" with each other. In other words, they find ways to establish a more or less permanent relationship.

Groups deciding on the third option can cement relations by exchanging gifts. However, unlike our own views of making gifts, such exchanges are obligatory in societies that do not have central governments, formal law enforcement organizations, or collection agencies. The obligations, which he called "total prestations," have the force of law in the absence of law. No Dun and Bradstreet will come to collect, but the presence of conflict that could break out at any time reinforces these obligations (Mauss 1925:151).

The obligation to give is the first obligation, one that must be met if a group is to extend social ties to others. The second obligation is to receive; refusal constitutes rejection of an offer to friendship as well. Conflicts can well arise from the perceived insult of a rejected offer. The third obligation is to repay. One who fails to make a gift in return is soon perceived as being in debt, being, in essence, a beggar. Mauss (1925) offers several ethnographic cases to illustrate these obligations. Every gift confers power to the giver, expressed by the Polynesian terms *mana* (an intangible supernatural force) and *hau* (among the Maori, the spirit of the gift, which must be returned to its owner).

Reciprocity and Its Variations

Stripped to its essentials, **reciprocity** refers to the direct exchange of goods and services between indi-viduals but, more commonly, between groups of individuals (bands, families, kin groups, villages, or any other). Typically, they are economic goods and services—but their functions go well beyond the confines of an economy. There are three varieties of reciprocity: generalized, balanced, and negative.

Generalized reciprocity refers to the kind of exchange in which the receiving party (individual, family, lineage, et al.) does not repay immediately, nor is it expected to do so. Generalized reciprocity may involve the pooling of resources within a household. It may involve meeting the needs of children, with the understanding that the children will care for their parents in old age. A similar case arises among the !Kung when a hunter may fail to kill large game for several months or longer; he receives meat during that time until he finally bags an animal (Lee 1998). Dentan describes a similar arrangement among the Semai of Malaysia for pig hunting and distribution (1979:48). Overall, we find generalized reciprocity within families, or among closely related ones. Generalized reciprocity serves as a kind of social insurance; in the case of game, it ensures that the animal, which could neither be consumed by a family nor stored, will not be wasted.

Balanced reciprocity refers to the exchange of goods of nearly equal value, with the obligation to make a return within a definite period of time. This type of exchange is familiar to us all; we give and receive gifts at weddings, birthdays, and religious holidays such as Christmas or Hanukkah. We take turns buying rounds at the pub.

A classic example of balanced reciprocity is the *kula* ring in the Trobriand Islands, an archipelago located off the eastern shores of New Guinea. Two kinds of valuables are involved: white armshells called *mwali* and necklaces of red spondylus shells known as *soulava* or sometimes as *bagi*. Each trader gives the partner a white armshell, with the expectation of receiving a red necklace within a defined period; the trader giving the necklace likewise expects to receive an armshell. The white armshells move counterclockwise in the islands, and the red necklaces move clockwise.

Each of the two kinds of article varies in value, depending on their history, the well-known chiefs who possessed them once upon a time, or how many times they went the rounds of the islands, so that more recently made armshells or necklaces are of lesser value than those made a long time ago. Therefore, the trader who gives a white armshell to his partner expects to receive a red necklace of equal value. If a return gift is not forthcoming within the specified time, the debtor presents a promissory gift in recognition of his obligation. Kula exchange accompanies the trading of utilitarian objects, such as axes, knives, canoes, pottery, pigs, and others (Malinowski 1922).

Balanced reciprocity generally takes place among more distant kin or villagers who have known each other for a long time. It helps cement relationships between traders who live long distances from each other. Plattner notes that the greater the risk of economic loss, betrayal of confidence, or unfair dealing, the more important the interpersonal ties that balanced reciprocity ensures (1989).

When such confidences are betrayed, or not expected, then relations are characterized by **negative reciprocity**, or exchange conducted for the aim of gaining material advantage and the aim to get something for nothing. Tribal and agrarian societies often distinguish between the insider, whom it is morally wrong to cheat, and the outsider, from whom every advantage may be gained. Sahlins (1968) includes horse raids among Plains Indians as an extreme example of negative reciprocity; a similar example might be taken of the Masai, who view their neighbor's cattle as given to them by God—hence the raids. A joke about the second U.S.-Iraq war asks "What is our oil doing in the sands of Iraq?"

One type of exchange that falls somewhere between balanced and negative reciprocity is **silent trade**. Conducted usually between mutually hostile groups, this trade is one way for each group to provide goods the other group needs. For example, the foraging Mbuti of the Ituri Forest, Congo, exist in a state of **hostile symbiosis** with their Bantu agricultural neighbors. Yet the Mbuti need the Bantus' crafted and garden products, and the Bantu need game animals and hides that the Mbuti can provide. Thus, the Mbuti may leave, say, some hide and meat at a designated site and retire into the forest. The Bantu come, inspect the goods, and if they like what they see, they take them and leave their own product for the Mbuti, who then take it if it meets with their approval. Either party rejects the product simply by leaving it in place (Turnbull 1961, 1965). This is a common form of exchange among soldiers on opposite sides of a war.

Redistribution

The second major type of distribution and exchange is **redistribution**, or one in which goods (and services) are collected from or contributed by members of a group and then distributed to the group in forms ranging from ceremonial feast to public services. Redistribution is often found in complex societies, ranging from the Kwakiutl and other native peoples of the Northwest Coast through agricultural states to industrial societies. In the United States, April 15 of every year is a stark reminder that, through the personal income tax, we have a system of redistributive exchange, the use of whose revenue is not necessarily to everyone's liking.

The **potlatch**, a major feast held during an important occasion, such as the coronation of a new chief, is held throughout the Pacific Northwest among the Kwakiutl, Tlingit, Haida, Tsimshian, and other societies that are rich enough to support chiefs and their privileges. These are all **complex foraging** societies, based principally on a plentiful supply of salmon, which are preserved by smoking, and on other abundant food sources. For the potlatch, the members of the chiefdom donate valuable articles, such as engraved pieces of copper (probably obtained originally from shipwrecks); carved, painted wooden boxes, crests, and other such objects; blankets; food, including salmon; and others. In turn, they receive the benefits, not only of the feast itself, but also the peace between the villages that it brings and the legitimation of the chief himself (Drucker 1955). This part is described in chapter 13, describing **chiefdoms**. This is one example of an economy embedded in society.

Other more complex societies also rely on redistribution. Among the Inca of the preconquest Andes of South America, a classic example of a **command economy**, the emperor controlled much of the land in the Andes cordillera and the adjacent coastal region stretching from modern-day Peru to northern Chile. Peasants of the empire were obliged both to provide **tribute**—goods in kind—and **corvée labor**, or a labor tax; they were paid in textiles of cotton and llama wool, particularly valuable in a cold climate, in chicha (a kind of corn beer), and in other necessities in life. Markets were underdeveloped, and virtually all goods and services were distributed under the Inca administrators (Daltroy 2003). This model is also referred to as a **tributary mode of production**, in which an elite exacts services and goods from agrarian workers (Wolf 1982). The efficacy of economic planning, therefore, needs to be evaluated not only in light of the recently collapsed socialist states of the Soviet Union and Eastern Europe, but also what can be reconstructed of the Inca empire. All of these are examples of economies dominated by **redistribution**.

Market

The third major type of distribution and exchange is the *market*. The market pervades our own societies, not to mention the former socialist countries such as the Soviet Union or the modified socialist economies such as China and even Vietnam and Cuba. We buy and sell food, clothing, houses, even labor. Your success in this economy hinges on your labor skills that some employer is willing to buy— we call that hiring. If you turn out to be less than useful, the employer takes his or her business elsewhere, and you are fired.

The term **market** refers to the exchanges in which prices (usually in monetary terms) are set by supply and demand, whether or not the transaction actually occurs in a marketplace. Those familiar with eBay and other sites on the Internet know you don't necessarily have to be at a store or supermarket to be involved in market transactions. The same is true for those who buy and sell stocks and bonds online.

The "pure" market hinges on several assumptions, serving as the "invisible hand," as Adam Smith put it in *Wealth of Nations* (1776) in regulating exchange. First, unlike reciprocity, which involves two individuals or groups, market contains two "crowds": the buyers who are able and willing to make purchases (summarized by the term **demand**) and sellers who have goods and services they are willing to part with at a price (summarized by the term **supply).** Under this assumption, no one individual has control or influence over the number of buyers making their demand nor the number of sellers hawking their wares. Therefore, the greater the demand, the higher the price. The buyer can go to the next vendor for apples or oranges if the price charged by the first vendor is too high. The greater the supply, the lower the price. If there are too many oranges on the market,

sellers have no choice but to charge less. Demand and supply continue to fluctuate until these two countervailing forces cancel each other out—in other words, reach an equilibrium.

There are other assumptions. One is that the government or other third party does not intervene, such as impose a tax, fix prices, grant subsidies to sellers or buyers, or something of the sort. The second is that information about any price changes is available immediately. Still another is that buyers and sellers are free to enter and exit the market.

Probably the best ethnographic illustrations are the open air markets one finds around the world: Nigeria, Haiti, and our primary focus, Guatemala, with primary emphasis on Panajachel, as studied by Sol Tax (1952) and by Tax's student, Robert Hinshaw (1975). Tax argued that the Panajachel market showed most of the attributes of free markets as **ideal types.** There are many buyers and sellers. Entry into the market is free for buyers; sellers have to pay a small plaza tax, which is negligible. Information of price changes spreads quickly. When I was in Cantel back in 1969, my wife and I were always asked how much we paid for six oranges or a yard of broadcloth. They weren't just being nosy; they wanted to find out the going price. Except for the plaza tax, there was no government intervention (Tax 1952).

The title of the book, *Penny Capitalism,* is no accident. The market is adaptive in a location where money is scarce and exchange might often be direct, that is, made through **barter** (direct exchange of one good or service or another, rather than through cash payment). For most market participants, the aim is to exchange what one produces to obtain what one cannot produce, or can produce only with difficulty. Indeed, in highland Mesoamerica, regional markets encompass contiguous villages. They may be **rotating markets**, whereby markets move daily from location to location within a region. In the region around Quezaltenango, Cantel and San Cristóbal hold markets on Sunday, Momostenango holds markets on Tuesdays and Saturdays, Zunil holds its markets on Monday, and so on. Larger towns may hold daily **solar markets**, such as that in Quezaltenango (the second city of Guatemala), Huehuetenango toward the northwest, or Guatemala City itself.

In such markets, villages and their hinterlands tend to *specialize* in—exercise a semi-monopoly over—a particular product. Such is the case of Nahualá and Santa Catarina, which specialize in pitch pine for lighting fires; Momostenango, known for its woolen products such as chaquetes (jackets), blankets, and woven bags; Zunil and Almolonga for fresh produce; San Cristóbal for broadcloth for women's skirts, Santa Catarina Ixtahuacán for sugar cakes; and Salcajá for its alcoholic *caldo de fruta* of questionable legal status. Such semi-monopolies ensure some kind of a market for each product (Kaplan 1965; McDowell 1974). The market thereby is an extension of the **domestic mode of production**, as discussed above. Transactions can be summarized by the formula C → M → C, in which C represents "commodity" and M represents "money." The main goal is to exchange commodity for money and to use the money to obtain other commodities.

Other market participants are known as *resgatones,* or resellers, whose aim it is to sell manufactured products in regional markets for a profit; such objects include plastic containers, factory-made clothing, metal utensils—all the products no rural village can manufacture. The reseller buys his or her products at a warehouse in a city or market town at a discount and sells them at a higher price in the villages (Kaplan 1965). The reseller's aim is represented by the formula M → C → M', whereby M represents the initial outlay of money, C represents commodity, and M' (M-prime) represents increased amounts of money, that is, a profit. It is when we see this formula pervading society, particularly an industrialized society like our own, that the formula M → C → M' dominates all transactions, major and in most cases minor. Then we enter the **capitalist mode of production**, where, combined with private ownership of the **factors of production** (land, labor, and capital), the productive process is oriented toward profit. **Capital** simply comprises manufactured goods involved in further production, or the claims (stocks or bonds) for such goods. We discuss industrial society in chapter 16, which focuses on globalization and culture change.

What makes the world go around—or drives exchange further—is **money**. This refers to a durable medium of exchange, based on a standard value that is used to purchase goods and services. The dominant type of money in today's society is **general-purpose money**, which can be used for all economic transactions. There are several attributes.

First, it is portable; you can carry it around. Second, it facilitates exchange; you do not have to carry, say, a canoe to buy potatoes and figure out how many potatoes it costs, then lug the potatoes about to exchange for, say, tomatoes, and figure out their relative value. All you need to do is find out how many dollars and cents a sack of potatoes is, and make the purchase. Third, money is a store of value. It retains its value to some extent. (Once, the American dollar was king among the world's currencies. Now Americans are finding it harder to exchange dollars for the less-than-ten-year-old euro.) In this connection, it is divisible into cents or their equivalents. Finally, it is usually standardized by government fiat, making counterfeiting impossible or at least difficult.

Special-purpose money, in contrast, is used only for specific transactions. Modern bus tokens are one example; you can use it only for bus fare. In nonwestern societies, certain forms of objects can be used only for certain transactions. We have already mentioned the *mwali* (white armshells) and *soulava* or *bagi* (red necklaces), used in the exchanges between two trading partners in the Trobriand Islands. Another form of special-purpose money is located on Rossel Island, also in the Trobriand chain, which is divided into various spheres of exchange that range from facilitating the exchange of ordinary goods to the transactions involving valuable objects. Money, made of a variety of sea shells, is not divisible. Thus, ordinary products are purchased with shells in the *nko* sphere of exchange, but you cannot make the purchase and receive *nko* of lesser value in "change." As for the high-value *ndap* shells, the spheres of exchange are more mutually exclusive. You must have a specific shell for bridewealth and none other within the *ndap* category. In East Africa, cattle are another example of special-purpose money, used primarily, if not exclusively, for bridewealth. (Armstrong 1967; Dalton 1967).

Conclusion

As we have seen already in this chapter, and will see in chapters 12 and 13, the economy is embedded in society or, in Polanyi's words, an "institutionalized process." The kula exchange system is as much social as it is economic, though it may facilitate trade in utilitarian economic goods. Money cements ties between two kin groups or villages through bridewealth, though the wealth itself (cattle in traditional East Africa; money in recent years) has economic uses. The potlatch may involve blankets and other utilitarian objects, but its use is to validate a chiefly status, as we will see in chapter 13. Only in modern society does the economy become increasingly divorced from society in modern society. I buy a motor vehicle from you, pay for it, and that's the end of our relationship. Even so, we still have social distinctions between "old money," the traditional elite whose names appear every year in the *Social Register*, and the *nouveau riche*, the newly wealthy who are yet to be accepted in circles of the "right people." Even in modern society, the economy is not entirely unembedded in society.

Chapter 12

POLITICAL AND LEGAL ANTHROPOLOGY: EGALITARIAN SOCIETIES

Introduction

One of the major questions in anthropology, as in social science generally, is how societies retain social control among their constituent populations. Just as subsistence strategies concern the techniques of food-getting, and economics involves the question of the provision and distribution, of goods and services, so political anthropology is concerned with the generation and distribution of power in the social sense.

Anthropology is especially relevant here, as it was in economics, inasmuch as Western concepts that attend government—the legitimacy underlying the right to rule, the control of the sovereign state over the lives and death of its constituents—is often as inappropriate in stateless societies as Western economic concepts are in marketless societies.

We start this chapter by discussing the some of the political concepts that have some bearing on all cultures and societies, simple or complex. We then shift attention to the concept **levels of integration** and its role in understanding the relatively simple and complex systems of control through social class, use of force or threat of such use, and law—and functional equivalents of societies lacking formal institutions to implement these processes. In this chapter and the next, we discuss

in alternating fashion the types of societies with or without social class—**egalitarian societies**, **ranked societies**, and **stratified societies**—then discuss their corresponding levels of integration, namely **bands**, **tribes**, **chiefdoms**, and **states**. Throughout, we provide examples of their integrating mechanism, such as **age grades** and **age sets**, **secret societies**, **segmentary lineages**, and even **marriage alliances**. We then round out our discussion with **law**, describing the difference between informal law and **codified law**, and between **restorative justice** versus **retributive justice**.

Political Concepts

Like the invisible hand to which Adam Smith refers in analyzing the workings of a market, a dual intangible force governs the workings of politics as well: **power**, or the ability to induce the behavior of others in specified ways by means of coercion, or the use or threat of use of physical force; and **authority**, or the ability to induce the behavior of others by persuasion (Fried 1967). An extreme example of power in practice are the *gulags* (prison camps) in Stalinist Russia, the death camps under Nazi rule in Germany and Eastern Europe, and the so-called supermax prisons in the United States, such as Pelican Bay in Crescent City, California. In all these, the prisoner complies or she/he is tortured or executed. At the other extreme, in most forager societies, the group complies with the wishes of the most persuasive member—though decision is usually reached by consensus.

In actuality, the two concepts form poles of a continuum. Even Hitler had to hold the Nuremberg rallies to persuade the German population that his leadership was the way to national salvation, and the Soviet leadership felt the need to hold mass parades and rallies every May Day. At the other end of the spectrum, coercive force is not absent, as indicated by homicide among the Inuit of any character who (to them) is obnoxious in the extreme.

A related concept in both politics and law is **legitimacy**, the right of individuals to leadership in whatever form of government or law. This is particularly applicable to complex societies, those that require centralized decision making. Historically, the rights to rule have been based on varied principles. In agricultural states, such as Mesopotamia, the Aztec, or the Inca, justification has been based on rules of succession, usually of the eldest son of the ruler. Even this principle is uncertain, as was the case when the Inca emperor Atahualpa had just defeated his rival and brother Huascar when the Spaniards arrived in Peru in 1533.

Often, supernatural beliefs or their functional equivalent are invoked to justify rule by an elite. The Inca emperors derived their right to rule from the Sun God; the Aztecs monarchs had Huitzilopochtli (Hummingbird-to-the-Left) to thank for their power. European monarchs invoked the divine right to rule, reinforced by the Church of England (Britain) or the Roman Catholic Church (other countries prior to the Reformation). In India, **karma**, or the cumulative force created by good and evil deeds in past lives, serves to justify the dominance of the Brahmin elite over the other **castes**. Secular equivalents also serve to justify rule by the elite. In the Soviet Union, legitimacy rested in the promise of a worker's utopia once the state no longer proved necessary to defend the revolution. In Nazi Germany, it rested on the promise of a master Aryan race. In the United States and other democratic forms of government, legitimacy rests on the consent of the governed in periodical elections—even though the incoming president is sworn in using a Christian Bible, despite the stated separation of church from state.

At the opposite end of the political spectrum, legitimacy for an elite is absent, and even antithet-ical. To describe forager nonrecognition of political legitimacy, Christopher Boehm develops the concept of **reverse dominance**. Reverse dominance occurs when a group exercises control over anyone who tries to assert power over them. The group achieves this aim by ridicule, criticism, disobedience, strong disapproval, or even informal execution of offenders or extremely offensive males (2001). Richard Lee encountered this phenomenon when, as a going-away gift for the Dobe !Kung with whom he has worked over the past year, he presented them with a fattened ox. Rather than praise or thanks, his !Kung hosts ridiculed the beast as scrawny, ill fed, and probably sick (Lee 1969, 1979). This behavior is consistent with reverse dominance.

Even at that level, decisions have to be made. Sometimes a headman may make them, particularly among some foragers, horticulturalists, many pastoralists, and equestrian hunters. Even in that event, he is not free to make decisions without coming to a **consensus** with his fellows, that is, one in which everyone is in general agreement. So in a backhanded way, legitimacy characterizes even societies without institutionalized leadership.

Another set of concepts refers to the reinforcements for compliance with the directive and laws in a complex society. **Positive reinforcements** are the rewards for compliance: medals, financial incentives, other forms of public recognition. **Negative reinforcements** are the punishment for noncompliance with the directives or laws of a power elite: fines, imprisonment, death sentences. These reinforcements can be identified even among foragers, such as increased influence for the best hunters, or ridicule or even homicide for the nonconforming. Reverse dominance is one form of negative reinforcement.

Levels of Sociocultural Integration

If cultures at various levels are to be compared regardless of organizational simplicity or complexity, there must be some common base for comparison; in other words, all cultures must have something in common. One such basis is the concept of **levels of sociocultural integration**. This notion refers to the levels of organization in cultures, ranging from one or two among foragers—the household and the larger **band**, which we will define momentarily—to several levels in **state** societies, starting again with the household and moving through the village or nomadic tribe, through the administrative subunit equivalent to U.S. states or Canadian provinces, and finally to the empire or nation state.

Julian Steward finds that there are distinct functions at every level. At the family level of integration, which he used to analyze the Shoshone of the Nevada basin, "all features of the relatively simple culture were integrated and functioned on a family level. The family was the reproductive, economic, educational, political, and religious unit" (1955:54). Other political anthropologists, such as Service (1975), do not recognize the family as a separate unit; even the Shoshone formed larger units during certain parts of the year, when they joined in rabbit drives during the animals' rutting season.

Nevertheless, we do see many functions of the family being pre-empted by larger organizations as societies become more complex. The resources, for example, become pre-empted in the form of tribute, the educational functions are taken over by schools, and the authority structure in the family is assumed by the state. Therefore, we need to categorize the levels of sociocultural integration.

In so doing, we develop two concepts that mesh with each other. On the one hand, we conceptualize a society based on **social classes** or lack thereof. These are **egalitarian**, **ranked**, and **stratified** societies (Fried 1967). On the other hand, we mesh these concepts with four **levels of sociocultural integration**, which consist of the **band**, the **tribe**, the **chiefdom**, and the **state**. It should be emphasized that these are **ideal types**, designed to identify the essential characteristics of societies "out there," in the so-called real world.

Egalitarian Societies

In complex society, it may seem that like death and taxes, **social class** is inevitable. Clearly, one is born into wealth, poverty, or somewhere in between, and one has no say in the matter, at least at the start of life. In other words, social class is an ascribed and involuntary position in society. Is it, however, universal? This is one of the rationales of anthropology; only by a cross-cultural test can one determine if social class is everywhere found.

There are, of course, problems of definition. We humans are not equal in all things. As shown in chapter 8, the status of women is low compared to men in many societies, if not most. There is also the

matter of age. In traditional societies, the aged enjoy greater prestige than the young; in modern society, the aged are subjects of discrimination in employment and other areas. Even in Japan, traditionally known for its respect of the elders, the prestige of the aged is in decline. Finally, not all of us have the same abilities, naturally acquired or achieved through effort. Some of us are more eloquent than others; some are expert craftspersons while others are not; some are excellent at conceptual thought, whereas for the rest of us, there's always the *Dummies* series, whether in computers, computer software, or even wine and sex.

Apart from these differences, are there social classes everywhere in the world? As they say, let's look at the record we call ethnographies. We find that among foragers, there is no advantage to hoarding game; in most climates, the meat will rot before your eyes. Nor is there any particular advantage to hoarding other foods. Leadership is informal, if it exists at all.

If this is the case, then perhaps there is such a thing as a society without social classes after all. Foragers such as the !Kung, the Inuit, and the aboriginal Australians can better be described as **egalitarian** societies, or societies in which there are as many valued status positions as there are individuals capable of filling them (Fried 1967). Good and poor hunters do not belong to different strata in the way that the captains of industry do from you and me. Poor hunters still receive a share of the meat; they have a right to be heard on important decisions. As for the more complex horticulturalist, pastoralist, and equestrian hunting peoples, the egalitarian definition still applies. Headmen emerge by consensus of the entire polity: village or nomadic tribe.

Therefore, we are looking at societies that lack a government or centralized leadership. They include not only **foragers**, but also **horticulturalists**, many **pastoralists**, and **equestrian hunters**. There are two levels of integration that coexist with egalitarian society: the **band** or **band level of integration** and the **tribe** or **tribal level of integration**. First, we discuss each in turn. We show how each retains its egalitarian characteristics, the classic example of which is the New Guinean **big man.** Then we discuss some of the mechanisms whereby societies can function without a state. For bands, they are virtually nonexistent. For tribes there are integrative mechanisms based both on kin-based and on nonkin-based organizations, and we discuss them in connection with this level of integration.

Band Level of Integration

It is probably more precise to say what bands are not than what they are. Usually, they comprise **simple foragers**, who rely on hunting and gathering and are nomadic for that reason, involve low populations (rarely exceeding 100 persons), and form informal groups with a few families and shifting population. They lack formal leadership, and Lee goes so far as to say that the Dobe !Kung, at least, have no leaders. To quote one informant, "Of course we have headmen. . . . Each one of us is headman over himself" (2003:109–111). At most, leaders are *primus inter pares* or first among equals—assuming anyone is first at all. Modesty is a valued trait; arrogance and competitiveness are not. We have already described **reverse dominance**.

Nevertheless, bands are probably the original extrafamilial political unit. The type of descent is in dispute. Service (1962) argued that the patrilocal band served as the prototype on the premise that male cooperation is essential to hunting, so they had to have the men to live together, and that composite bands were anomalies when forced by environmental change or invasion of other groups to adapt their organization accordingly. M. Kay Martin (1975) points out in rebuttal that gathering, women's work, makes a higher caloric yield in most cultures and so matrilocal bands might be closer to the norm. Indeed, women and men have roughly equal status because of their important role of gathering. In societies where hunting is the primary source of food, such as the Inuit, women tend to be subordinate to men (Martin and Voorhies 1975). Generally, gender status tends to be equal, and both take a part in group decision making.

Leadership is also transient. Informal leadership often shifts with the circumstances. For example, "rabbit bosses" coordinate rabbit drives during the rutting season, but play no leadership role otherwise. Some leaders may be excellent mediators whenever two individuals dispute over some issue, while others might be better at coordinating a hunt. Still other individuals may be perceived as good shamans or seers. There are no formal offices, nor are there rules of succession.

Band-Level Law

In resolving disputes, informal means of resolution also apply. There are no formal mediators nor any organizational equivalent of courts of law. A good mediator may emerge—or one may not. Sometimes, duels are employed. Among the Inuit, for example, the disputants engage in a song duel where, drum in hand, they chant insults at each other before an audience. The audience selects the better chanter, and thereby the winner of the dispute (Hoebel 1968). Ridicule is reported among the Mbuti, in which even children berate an adult for laziness, quarreling, or selfishness. If ridicule fails, the elders try to evaluate the dispute carefully, show why things went wrong, and, in extreme cases, walk to the center of the camp and criticize individuals by name; using humor softens the criticism—the group, after all, does have to get along with each other (Turnbull 1963, 1983).

Band-Level Warfare

Nevertheless, conflict does break out into war between bands and, sometimes, within them. Usually, warfare is sporadic, and extended conflict is rare. There is not the formal leadership, let alone the manpower, to sustain conflict for long. Most of the conflict arises from interpersonal arguments. Among the Tiwi of Australia, for example, a conflict arose over the failure of one band to reciprocate another wife-giving band with one of its female relatives; the abduction of women by the aggrieved band precipitated the conflict. The resulting "war" involved some spear throwing—many didn't shoot straight and even some of the onlookers were wounded—but mostly it involved violent talk and abuses more verbal than physical. (Hart, Pilling, and Goodale 1988). For the Dobe !Kung, Lee (2003:112–118) found 22 cases of homicide by males and other periodic violence, mostly in disputes over women—not quite the gentle souls Elizabeth Marshall Thomas depicts in her *Harmless People* (1959).

Tribal Level of Integration

The next level involves not one but two or more groups, known as **segments**, and usually consisting of lineages, clans, ambilineal descent groups, or other organization. A second characteristic involves some integrative device binding them together. We illustrate the principle of tribal societies with the **big men** of New Guinea. They may involve **bilateral cross-cousin marriage** or another kin-based alliance such as a **segmentary lineage**. They may involve what Service calls **pan-tribal**

sodalities, or organizations not based on kinship ties, such as **age grades** and **age sets** in eastern Africa, **men's houses** in New Guinea, or **secret societies** such as the *poro* and *sande* in West Africa (the last is discussed in chapter 13). First, we discuss the defining characteristics of the **tribal level of integration** or **tribes**, then examine the integrative mechanisms of several segments.

Whereas bands involve small populations without structure, **tribal societies** involve at least two well defined groups linked together in some way, and often ranging in population from 100 to as many as 5,000. Despite social institutions that can become fairly complex, there is no centralized political structure nor are there offices in the strict sense of the term. There may be headmen, but there is no rule of succession, nor do sons necessarily follow in the footsteps of their father.

Leadership roles are open to any male, particularly elder males, on the basis of their personal abilities and qualities. Like bands, they do not have the means for coercing others, nor do they have formal powers associated with the position. They must persuade others to take any action they feel is needed to be taken. Among the Yanomamö, one headman says that he will never issue an order unless he knows it will be obeyed; one such circumstance occurs during war. Rather than barking out orders, Kaobawä the headman exercises his influence by example, making suggestions, and warning about consequences of taking, or not taking, action (Chagnon 1997:133–137).

Thus, we may regard tribes, as bands, to be egalitarian societies. First, property may or may not be accumulated, but not to the extent whereby others are deprived. Second, every male has a chance to become headman, and like bands, one's leadership position may be situational. One man may be a good mediator, another a great war leader; a third may be capable of leading a hunt or finding a more ideal area for cultivation or grazing herds. Thus, tribes conform to Fried's definition of an **egalitarian society** as one in which there are as many valued status positions as there are persons capable of filling them (1967).

An example illustrating this definition can be seen from the **big man** of New Guinea; the term is derived from the languages of New Guinean tribes. The big man is one who has acquired followers by doing favors which they cannot possibly repay: settle the debt of one man, provide bridewealth for another. He also may acquire as many wives as pos-

sible to create alliances with wives' families; the wives work to care for as many pigs as possible. In due course, he may sponsor a pig feast that serves to put still others in his debt and to shame his rivals. It is worth noting that the followers, incapable of repaying the big man's gifts (as Mauss predicts; see chapter 11 on obligations of the gift), stand metaphorically as beggars to him.

Nevertheless, the big man does not have the power of a monarch. First, the role of big man is not hereditary. His son has to show his own worth and acquire a following of his own; he must become a big man in his own right. Second, there are other big men in the village, his potential rivals. If another man proves himself capable of acquiring a following, then he can well displace the first big man. Third, he has no power to coerce. He has no army, no police force. He cannot prevent a follower from joining another big man, nor can he force the follower to pay up. There is no New Guinean equivalent of a U.S. marshal. Therefore, he can only have his way by diplomacy and persuasion—and this persuasion does not always work (see Oliver 1955 for an example among the Siuai, and Strathern and Stewart 1999 for an account of Ongka, the big man in a Kawelka village).

Broadly speaking, we may categorize such organizations or other integrative mechanisms by **ascription** (assignment to a social category at birth, such as gender or, as time goes on, by age) or by **achievement** (assignment to a category based on the person's own efforts, such as an occupational association or union, political party, or interest group such as the Benevolent League of Terminators). We may also divide **ascribed** categories into those that are **universally ascribed** (assignment to any category that affects everyone in all cultures, such as age or gender) or are **variably ascribed** (assignment of categories found in only some, but not all, cultures, such as ethnic or regional associations). Finally, some associations involve **voluntary recruitment** (one chooses to join an association or not) while others involve **involuntary recruitment** (one is forced to join, such as the military through the draft) (Ember and Ember 2002:184–194).

Kin-Based Systems of Integration

In addition to two or more segments, Service (1962, 1975) seeks to define tribal societies in terms of *sodalities*, or associations. For example, the Yanomamö have no association to consolidate the two intermarrying lineages, yet when villages fission, subgroups of intermarrying lineages stay together. The integrative factor is **bilateral cross-cousin marriage**. Among the Nuer, who have either no age grade and age set at all or have poorly defined ones—authorities differ—they do have a **segmentary lineage** that keeps them together without being a permanent association. So we may define a tribe minimally in terms of some device that integrates two or more segments.

Bilateral Cross-Cousin Marriage. The Yanomamö practice of **bilateral cross-cousin marriage** serves as an example of such an integrative mechanism (see Figure 12.1). As you may recall from chapter 10, this is the arrangement whereby a man marries his cross-cousin related to him through both links: his father's sister and his mother's brother.

In Figure 12.1, let X refer to all the males of Lineage X, and Y refer to all the males of Lineage Y; correspondingly, let X refer to all the females of Lineage X, and y refer to all the females of Lineage Y. Let's take a third-generation example from this diagram. X_3 has married y_3.

Now trace the relationship between X_3 and y_3 through their *matrilateral* links. Notice that the marriage link is *below* the two figures, because on the diagram this couple is at the opposite extremes of this chart for this generation. Try linking *them* with an equal sign! Note that X_3's mother is x_2. Her

brother is Y2, whose daughter is y3. Therefore, y3 is X3's mother's brother's daughter. *Review this paragraph several times and refer it to the diagram.*

Now trace the **patrilateral** links of this couple. X3's father is X2, X2's sister is x2; she has married Y2, which makes her daughter y3—therefore, his father's sister's daughter. Again, review this description several times and compare it against the diagram.

Now do the same thing with Y3. Trace his **matrilateral ties** with his wife x3. Notice that his mother is x2, her brother is X2 and so his mother's brother daughter is x3. Now trace Y3's **patrilateral** ties with his wife x3. His father is Y2, his sister is y2 who has married X2, making his daughter x3. Again, concentrate on these two descriptions and compare them with the diagram.

As you can see, the **ideal type** of **bilateral cross-cousin marriage** is that a man marry a woman who is **both** his mother's brother's daughter and his father's sister's daughter. In other words, the man's matrilateral cross-cousin and patrilateral cross-cousin is one and the same woman! Retrace both links until you grasp the workings of this arrangement.

Viewed from Mauss's model of gift-giving, the lineages have discharged their obligation in the same generation. Lineage X provides a daughter to Lineage Y, and Lineage Y reciprocates with its own daughter. Each of the lineages therefore retains its potential to reproduce into the next generation. The obligation incurred by Lineage Y from taking X's daughter in marriage has been repaid by giving a daughter in marriage to Lineage X.

This type of marriage is what Robin Fox, following Claude Levi-Strauss, calls **restricted exchange** (1967:182–187). Notice that two, and only two, lineages can engage in this exchange. Society remains relatively simple because it can only expand by splitting off—and as we will see later—when daughter villages split off, the two lineages move together.

Finally, it is plain that not all marriages can conform to this idea. Often, the patrilateral cross-cousin is in real life not one and the same person; there may be two or more persons. Furthermore, a man may marry either a matrilateral or patrilateral cross-cousin, but not both. Chagnon (1997) provides numerous examples. The function of ideal types is to explain the logical outcome of cross-cousin marriage. Villages tend to remain in two sets, even though bilateral cross-cousin marriage is more the ideal than the real.

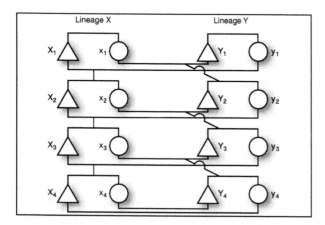

FIGURE 12.1
Bilateral cross-cousin marriage.
Trace the relationship between X_3 and y_3 and Y_3 and x_3. You can see that in both cases the bride is the groom's mother's brother's daughter *and* his father's sister's daughter. Therefore, sister exchange marriage is possible.

Segmentary Lineages.   Another type of kin-based integrative mechanism is a **segmentary lineage**. Because all lineages do **segment**, or divide into two or more daughter lineages, this may seem a redundancy. Conventional use, however, assigns a distinct meaning to this term.

A **segmentary lineage** is a hierarchy of lineages that exists for a limited purpose. At the base are several **minimal lineages** whose members trace their descent from their founder back to two or three generations. At the apex is the founder of all the lineages, of which there may be two or more **maximal lineages** derived from the lineage of the founder. There are several **intermediate lineages** at various levels between the maximal and minimal lineages. For purposes of simplicity, we will include in this discussion only the maximal and minimal lineages.

One characteristic of segmentary lineages is **complementary opposition**. To illustrate, consider the following chart, which has been simplified to make the point; in reality, there may be ten or more generations of lineages, each lineage embedded into an ever larger lineage. Here, Lineage I and Lineage II have segmented from the one established by the Lineage Founder. After a period of time, Lineages A and Lineage B have segmented from Lineage I and Lineages C and D have segmented from Lineage II. Still, the members of Lineages A and B retain their affiliation to Lineage I, and Lineages C and D retain their affiliation to Lineage II, they all retain their affiliation with the founder's lineage, which includes all its daughter lineages. Now Lineages A1 and A2 segment from Lineage A, Lineages B1 and B2 segment from Lineage B, and so on with Lineages C and D. The following diagram shows the relationships between the maximal lineage of the founder, the minimal lineages A1 and A2 through D1 and D2, and the two sets of intermediate lineages (Lineages I and II and their daughter lineages A through D).

Suppose that A1 starts a feud with A2, say, for cattle theft. Being of the same intermediate lineage A, it is likely that the feud will be contained within it. B1 and B2 ignore the conflict; it is no concern of theirs. Now suppose A2 attacks B1 for cattle theft. Now A1 unites with A2 to feud with B1, whom B2 joins in defense. The feud, in other words, involves everyone in intermediate lineage A against everyone in intermediate lineage B. Finally, suppose B2 attacks C1. Now, everyone belonging to Lineage I (including Lineages A and B) will be at war with everyone belonging to Lineage II (including Lineages C and D). The greater the scope of the war, the wider the involvement of the lineages. Nor is that all. Suppose an outside tribe attacks any one of the minimal lineages, say A1 or perhaps D2 or any of the others. The entire body of lineages affiliated with the Founder's Lineage will rise up to attack the outside tribe (Sahlins 1961:322–344; 1968).

Segmentary lineages occur but rarely in the world's cultures, usually among pastoralists. Classic examples include the Nuer, as described by Edward Evans-Pritchard (1940), the Tiv by Paul Bohannan (1989), and the Bedouin (Murphy and Kasdan 1959). They often develop in an environment of other tribes, whose hostility induces its members to retain their ties, mobilizing their kin as external conflicts arise, such as the Nuer among the Dinka. When the conflict is over, the segmentary lineage dissolves back to its constituent units. This also maintains another attribute of segmentary lineages, **local-genealogical segmentation**, in which closer lineages also dwell more closely with each other, serving as a physical reminder of their genealogy (Sahlins 1961:322–344). A Bedouin proverb summarizing the philosophy behind segmentary lineages runs as follows:

I against my brother

I and my brother against my cousin

I, my brother, and my cousin against the world

Lineage Founder							
I				II			
A		B		C		D	
A1	A2	B1	B2	C1	C2	D1	D2

Although segmentary lineages function to regulate warfare, it also serves to regulate inheritance and property rights. Often the population of tribes with segmentary lineages may approach 100,000 persons, as Sahlins indicates for the Nuer (1961).

Nonkin Systems of Integration

Sometimes known as **sodalities**, these systems function to cut across kinship ties to maintain larger groups. In a way, they represent a transition from localistic kin to wider societies. Among age grades, for example, men's loyalty to their own clans is tempered by their loyalty to their fellows of the same age, regardless of kin affiliation. In this section, we discuss several cross-cutting sodalities (age-based organizations, single-sex associations, and secret societies) and their role in maintaining societies that are not centralized as yet.

Age Grades and Age Sets.   In one sense, all societies are divided into age categories. In the U.S. educational system, the age of every child is matched with the grade in which he or she is placed—or should be placed according to education planners. If a child is six years of age, she or he should be in grade 1; if 13 years, grade 8.

However, the herders of most East African cultures support a more or less dual age-based structure: permanent **age grades**, to which all males are assigned, and **age sets**, movable categories to which men of a certain age range are assigned. The age grades often have duties and age-related assignments to them, and as age sets advance, the men in each set assume these roles.

One tribal society whose age grades and sets conform closely to the ideal type is the Tiriki of Kenya, as described by Walter Sangree (1965). From birth to about 15 years, boys become members of an age set then open for membership. When the last boy is recruited, the age set closes and a new one is open. There are seven named age sets that move along seven age grades.

The youths and men of the Juma age set in 1939 had become warriors by 1954. The Mayima who were warriors became elder warriors during that period. In precolonial times, the men of the warrior age grade defended the herds of the Tiriki and conducted raids. In fact, by 1954, they were most likely wage or salaried workers, if they worked at all. The age set of warriors moved on to be elder warriors, now acquiring cattle and houses and taking on wives; one recurring report is that the husbands are much older than their wives, who marry early, often as young as ages 15 or 16. Solid citizens of the Tiriki, the elder warriors also handled the decision-making functions of the tribe as a whole; their legislation affected the entire village, while also representing their own kin group.

Other age sets also moved up in the 15-year period (Table 12.1). The elder warriors in 1939 (Nyonje) moved on to become the judicial elders of the Tiriki by 1954. Their function is to resolve disputes that arise between individuals, families, or kin groups—of which some of the elders are a part. The Jiminigayi who were judicial elders in 1939 became ritual elders in 1954. The ritual elders handled the supernatural functions that involved the entire Tiriki community. In the meantime, the Kabalach in 1939, now devoid of members, moved down to load up on the boys in 1954. Thus, there were four functional age grades and three more reflecting either enculturation or retirement; the age sets moved in continuous cycles, each one completed over 105 years.

Now, if the diagram conforms to this description, here is what it should look like:

TABLE 12.1   Idealized Age Grades and Age Sets among the Tiriki

Traditional Duties of Age Grade	Age Sets 1939	Age Sets 1954	Age Sets 1979	Age Sets 1994
Retired or Deceased: 91-105	Kabalach	Golongolo	Jiminigayi	Nyonje
Ritual Elders: 76-90	Golongolo	Jiminigayi	Nyonje	Mayima
Judicial Elders: 61-750	Jiminigayi	Nyonje	Mayina	Juma
Elder Warriors : 46-60	Nyonje	Mayima	Juma	Sawe
Warriors: 31-45	Mayina	Juma	Sawe	Kabalach
Initiated and Uninitiated Youths: 16-30	Juma	Sawe	Kabalach	Golongolo
Small Boys: 0-15	Sawe	Kabalach	Golongolo	Jiminigayi

TABLE 12.2   Actual Tiriki Age Grades and Sets Based on Original Table (Sangree 1965:71)

Traditional Duties of Age Grade	Age Sets 1939	Age Sets 1954	Age Sets 1979	Age Sets 1994
Retired or Deceased: 91-105	Kabalach	Golongolo	Jiminigayi	Nyonje
Ritual Elders: 71-90	Golongolo	Jiminigayi	Nyonje	Mayina
Judicial Elders: 56-70	Jiminigayi	Nyonje	Mayina	Juma
Elder Warriors : 41-55	Nyonje	Mayina	Juma	Sawe
Warriors: 26-40	Mayina	Juma	Sawe	Kabalach
Initiated and Uninitiated Youths: 11-25	Juma	Sawe	Kabalach	Golongolo
Small Boys: 0-10	Sawe	Kabalach	Golongolo	Jiminigayi

However, this (Table 12.2) is the diagram based on the original actual diagram offered by Sangree (1965:71).

The reader will notice the discrepancies between Sangree's description of age grades and sets—15 year for each, totaling a cycle of 105 years—and his chart (1965:71) from which the one above is extrapolated to 1994. First, the age grade "small boys," is 10 years, not 15. Second, the age grade "ritual elders" is 20 years, not 15. Why this discrepancy exists, Sangree does not answer. This discrepancy demonstrates the questions raised when **ideal types** do not match all the ethnographic information. For example, if the Jiminigayi ranged 15 years in 1939, why did they suddenly expand to a range of 20 years in 1954? By the same token, why did the Sawe age set cover 10 years in 1939 and expand to 15 years in 1954? It is discrepancies such as these that raise questions and drive further research.

Another potential issue is the question of transition. We see that all the initiated and uninitiated boys and youths of the Juma age set in 1939 became warriors by 1954. What has happened in the intervening years? Did some Juma become warriors in the meantime, or did the oldest youths have to wait until the youngest reached age 26 for them all to make the transition? On this matter also, Sangree does not say (1965:65–72). A partial answer might be provided by the Karimojong of northeastern Uganda, also a pastoralist society. There, four major age sets comprise 20 to 25 years of males, but it is subdivided into five subsets each. Even so, the entire generation of the five age-set has to wait as a unit until being promoted into the next generation set. No doubt the seniormost age set have exhausted their patience by the time they assume the duties of the senior generation set (Dyson-Hudson 1966). It is likely that, among the Tiriki, there is no transition; the entire age set had to wait until the most junior members of the Juma age set reached the age of 16 before becoming warriors. The extreme disparity between the ages of husband and wife also points to this likelihood.

Bachelor Associations and Men's Houses. Among most tribes of New Guinea, if not all, men's houses serve to cut across the clans that comprise each village. Typically, horticulture combined with pig raising. New Guineans are decentralized, but the households are not autonomous. Perhaps one of the most fastidious cases of male association in New Guinea is the bachelor association of the Mae-Enga. A boy becomes conscious of the distance between males and females even before he leaves his home at age five to live in the men's house. Women are regarded as potentially unclean, so strict codes minimizing male-female relations are enforced. The *sanggai* festivals reinforce this division; every youth of age 15 or 16 goes into seclusion in the forest with additional restrictions, such as avoiding pigs (cared for by women) or avoiding his gaze on the ground, lest he see female footprints or pig feces (Meggitt 1964:202–224). One can see, therefore, that every boy commits his loyalty to the men's house early in life, though he remains a clan member.

Men's houses represent the center of male-centered activity. It is in the men's houses that warfare is planned and strategies are drawn. It is the seat of ritual activity, where magic is performed and ancestral spirits are honored. It is also the place where the periodic pig feasts are planned and rituals rehearsed.

Tribal Law

Tribal societies generally lack **codified law**, a system of law whereby damages or crimes are specified and the remedies or punishments are spelled out. Only the state can determine, usually by writing, which behavior is permissible and which is not, and this we discuss in the next chapter. Nor is there a system of **law enforcement**, whereby some agency—police, sheriff, army—can enforce a law enacted by some appropriate authority. As already shown, no headman nor big man can force his will on others.

In tribal society, as in any society, conflicts arise between individuals. Sometimes, the issues are equivalent to **crimes**, or the taking of property or commitment of violence that is not considered legitimate within a given society. Other issues are disagreements over questions of ownership or damage of some property, or accidental death. In tribal society, the aim is not so much to determine guilt or innocence or criminal or civil responsibility as it is to resolve a conflict.

There are several ways in tribal society to resolve a conflict. Two individuals or parties may choose to avoid each other. Indeed, bands, tribes, or kin groups often move away from each other, and it is much easier for them to do so than for people living in a complex society.

Guilt or Innocence: Oaths and Ordeals

One issue in tribal societies, as in all societies, is guilt or innocence. Often, the offense was committed in the absence or unreliability of witnesses. In the absence of forensic technology—fingerprint, blood-type, or DNA matches—tribal societies may rely on supernatural means. An **oath** is the act of calling on a deity to bear witness to the truth of what one says; we see the oath in court as a holdover from this practice. An **ordeal** is a means used to determine guilt or innocence by submitting the accused to dangerous, painful, or risky tests believed to be under supernatural control. One example is the poison oracle used among the Azande of the Sudan, who assume that most misfortunes are induced by witchcraft (which in this case does not involve ritual but rather ill-feeling of one person toward another). A poison oracle is used—a chicken is force-fed a concoction containing strychnine known as *benge* just as the name of

the suspect is called out. If the chicken dies, the suspect is deemed guilty and a means of punishment or reconciliation is initiated (Evans-Pritchard 1976).

Negotiation and Mediation

A more commonly exercised option is to find ways to resolve the dispute. In small groups, any unresolved question quickly escalates to violence and to disruption of the group. The first step is often **negotiation**, whereby the parties attempt to resolve the conflict by direct discussion in the hope of arriving at an agreement. Sometimes the offender, particularly if he or she is sensitive to community opinion, will make a **ritual apology**. In Fiji, for example, the offender will make a ceremonial apology called *i soro*, one of the meanings of which is "I surrender." An intermediary speaks, offers a token gift to the offended party, and asks for forgiveness. The request is rarely rejected (Koch et al. 1977:169–170).

If negotiation or ritual apology fails, often the next step is to recruit a third party and engage in **mediation**, whereby the third party tries to bring about a settlement in the absence of an official who has the power to enforce a settlement. One classical example in the anthropological literature is the **leopard skin chief** among the Nuer, who is identified by wearing a leopard skin wrapped about his shoulders. The man is not a chief but a mediator. The position is hereditary, has religious overtones, and has the responsibility for the social well-being of the tribal segment. Often he is called if there is a serious matter, such as a murder. The culprit immediately goes to the residence of the chief, who then cuts the culprit's arm until the blood flows. If the culprit is afraid of vengeance by the dead man's family, he will remain at the leopard skin chief's residence, which is considered sanctuary. He then acts as a go-between for the perpetrator's family and the dead man's family.

Throughout the process, the leopard skin chief cannot force a settlement, nor enforce the settlement if it is reached. The source of his influence is the desire for the parties to avoid a feud, which could well escalate to an ever-widening conflict involving kin descended from different ancestors. He urges the aggrieved family to accept compensation, usually in the form of cattle. When an agreement is reached, the chief collects the cattle—40 to 50 head—and takes them to the dead man's home, where he performs various sacrifices of cleansing and atonement (Evans-Pritchard 1940:291); Haviland cites in this study (2002:212).

This discussion largely reflects the preference of other societies to mediate, given the alternative of a long-term feud. Even in state societies, mediation is often preferred. In the agrarian town of Talea, Mexico, even serious crimes are mediated in the interest of preserving some degree of local harmony. Often the national authorities will tolerate local settlement if it maintains the peace (Nader 1991).

Tribal Warfare

What happens, then, if mediation doesn't work and the leopard skin chief cannot convince the aggrieved clan to accept 40 or 50 cattle in place of their loved one? You go to war. In tribal society, war varies in causes, competence, and duration, but in the absence of large populations and technology, they tend to be less deadly than those run by the state, as we shall see.

Compared to bands, tribal societies engage in warfare more often, both within (internal) and between (external) tribes. Causes vary. Among pastoralists, theft of cattle or attempts thereof may spark conflict, and it is the pastoralists who have the reputation to be most warlike among prestate societies. Horticulturalists, however, also engage in warfare, as the film *Dead Birds*, about warfare among the highland Dani of west New Guinea (Irian Jaya), attests. There is also a "protein debate" about the causes of warfare. Among the Yanomamö, Marvin Harris (1989) claims that a protein deficiency, reflected in scarcity of game, is the cause of warfare, and Kenneth Good (1997) supports this thesis in part by finding that the game a Yanomamö village brought in barely supported the village there. (He could not link this variable to warfare, however.) Nevertheless, note Chagnon's rebuttal that abduction of women, not fights over hunting territory, is the efficient cause (1997:91–97), and findings from other cultures tend to agree.

Tribal wars vary in duration. A frequent type of war is the **raid**, involving a short-term use of physical force that is planned and organized to achieve a limited objective, such as the acquisition of cattle (pastoralists), other forms of wealth, and often the abduction of women, usually from neighboring communities (White 1988). Longer in duration is the **feud**, a state of recurring hostilities between families, lineages, or other kin groups. The responsibility to avenge is the responsibility of the entire group, and the murder of any kin member is considered appropriate, because the kin group as a whole is considered responsible. Among the Dani, for example, vengeance is an obligation; spirits are said to dog the victim's clan until its members murder someone in the perpetrator's clan (Heider 1970).

Conclusion

Societies without states, then, are generally small-scale. Leadership, where it exists at all, is situational, and involves a *primus entre pares*, a first among equals. Though egalitarian, tribal societies are more structured and organized than bands, whose membership shifts almost daily. They comprise at least two segments—lineages, clans, perhaps ambilineal descent groups—that are integrated with other kin ties, or non-kin associations. Law focuses primarily on the resolution of disputes, even where it might involve homicide. Reconciliation is not inevitable, however, and among New Guinean groups such as the Dani, whose supernatural beings demand revenge, reconciliation is impossible or extremely unlikely.

Chapter 13

POLITICAL AND LEGAL ANTHROPOLOGY: RANKED AND STRATIFIED SOCIETIES

Introduction

We have seen, therefore, how societies not only can exist without social class and state, but have done so for millennia. Indeed, the first state society does not make its appearance until 8000 B.C.E. in the Near East, 2,000 years after the first confirmed instance of plant and animal domestication called the Neolithic in 10,000 B.C.E. Early states tended toward a high degree of centralization, frequent expansionary warfare, extensive exploitation of its subject populations, and harsh punishment for those breaking or resisting the law established by these states. Time has not seen significant change. Despite the spread of democratic governmental structures—elected parliaments or national assemblies, elected executives, and appointment of judiciaries by executives or sometimes by popular vote—ways have always been found to circumvent the democratic aspects of these institutions.

When did states form and persist? Evidence suggests that they may have undergone a transition through **ranked societies** and **chiefdoms**. Gradually, minorities gained control of basic or strategic resources—resources that sustain life, such as land, water in arid regions, and manufactured products intended for further production (namely,

capital)—in other words, became **stratified**. **States** emerged along with the stratification process. We discuss the characteristics of **ranked** societies and its association with **chiefdoms**. We discuss their association with sodalities that are shared with **tribes**, such as the *poro* and *sande* societies across west African chiefdoms. We then turn to **stratified societies** and the **state**. Next, we discuss **war** as an integrative mechanism and conclude with the role of **law** as found in association with centralized political structure.

Ranked Societies and Chiefdoms

Ranked Societies

Unlike **egalitarian societies**, **ranked societies** (sometimes called "rank societies," as if they had a stench) involve greater differentiation between individuals and the kin groups of which they are a part. These differences may be inherited, and often are. Nevertheless, there are no significant restrictions on access to basic resources, and all individual can meet their basic needs through membership in kinship groups. Rather, the differences are based on **sumptuary rules**, or norms that permit persons of higher rank to wear distinctive clothing, jewelry, and decorations denied those of lower rank. One may therefore define a ranked society as one in which there are fewer valued status positions than persons capable of filling them.

Chiefdoms

This definition leads us directly to the characteristics of **chiefdoms**. The position of **chief** is, unlike the position of **headman**, an **office**, that is, a permanent political status that demands a successor when a given chief dies. Put another way, there are two concepts of **chief**: the man himself (women rarely occupy these posts), and the office. Thus, the expression "The king is dead; long live the king" reflects the dual meaning of both *king* and *chief*. If one contrasts this with the New Guinean **big man**, we see at once that the death of the big man is also the end of his status; other big men will arise to take his place, and there is no rule that stipulates his eldest son—or any son—must succeed him. For the post of chief, however, there *must* be a successor and there must be a rule of succession.

Usually, the exchange system known as **redistribution** accompanies political centralization, which begins with chiefdoms. As noted from chapter 11, redistribution entails the flow of goods and services from the population at large to the central authority, represented by the chief. It then becomes the task of the central authority to return the flow of goods in another form.

These principles are exemplified by the **potlatch** of the several chiefdoms concentrated along the Northwest Coast of North America, which stretches from the extreme northwest tip of California through the coasts of Oregon, Washington, British Columbia, and southern Alaska. As stated in chapter 11, the potlatch observed major events, such as births, deaths, or marriages of important persons, or the installment of a new chief. Families prepared for this event by collecting food and other valuables such as fish, berries, blankets, animal skins, carved boxes, and copper. At the potlatch, several ceremonies were held, dances performed by their "owners," and speeches delivered. The new chief was watched very carefully, the eloquence of his speech noted, the grace of his presence observed—including any mistakes, however egregious or trivial.

The distribution of gifts came next. Again the chief was observed in that process: Was he generous with his gifts? Were the value of his gifts appropriate to the rank of the recipient, or was he giving valuable presents to those of lower rank? Did his wealth allow him to offer valuable objects?

The next phase was critical to the chief's validation to his position. Visitor after visitor arose to give long speeches evaluating the worthiness of this successor to the chieftainship of his father. If he had performed to expectation, if his gifts were appropriate, the guests' speeches would praise him accordingly. They would be less than adulatory if the chief did not perform to expectation, and indeed the eligibility of the successor was not sufficient. He had to perform. If he did so, then the guests' praise not only legitimated the new chief in his role, but also it ensured some measure of peace between villages. Not only was the event festive, but it also involved legitimation and diplomacy (Drucker 1955).

Much has been made of the **rivalry potlatches**, competitive gift-giving by rival pretenders to the chieftainship. Philip Drucker argues that the competitive potlatch was a product of sudden demographic changes among the Northwest Coast native peoples. As smallpox and other diseases decimated thousands, the hereditary successor or his brothers as likely as not died out, leaving several potential successors who might be eligible for the chieftainship. Thus, competition became extreme, with blankets being repaid with ever larger piles, coppers being met with ever larger quantities, and valuables being destroyed in an effort to demonstrate one's wealth. So raucous did the events become that the Canadian government outlawed these displays in the early part of the 20th century. Prior to this period, it was sufficient to present appropriate gifts by a successor who had been chosen beforehand (1955:134–143).

Kin-Based Integrative Mechanisms: Conical Clans

With the centralization of society, kinship is most likely to continue playing a role, albeit a new one. Among Northwest Coast native peoples, for example, the ranking model has every lineage ranked, one above the other, siblings ranked in order of birth, and even villages in a ranking scale. Drucker (1955) points out that the further north one goes, the more rigid the ranking scheme is. The most northerly of these coastal peoples trace their descent matrilineally; indeed, the Haida consist of four clans. Those further south tend to be patrilineal, and some show characteristics of an ambilineal descent group. It is still unclear, for example, whether the Kwakiutl *numaym* are patrilineal clans or ambilineal descent groups.

Kin-Based Mechanisms: Matrilateral Cross-Cousin Marriage

Another mechanism that tends to reinforce ranking—and perhaps stratification—is matrilateral cross-cousin marriage (Figure 13.1). On the chart you constructed, you may note that in this arrangement, male Ego marries No. 36, his mother's brother's daughter. Her brother could not marry Ego's sister; she would be his patrilateral cross-cousin (father's sister's daughter), which a prescriptive matrilateral cross-cousin marriage precludes.

This diagram (Figure 13.1) shows four patrilineages (A, B, C, and D), in which male B2 has married female a1. As you an see, they are linked together by a1, ego's mother, and her brother, A1, making a2 his mother's brother's daughter or matrilateral cross cousin. Their daughter, b3, will have to marry C3, because she is C3's mother's brother's daughter. Trace their links through b2 and B2. Try the same with other matrilateral pairs.

Viewed from the top in the form of a flow diagram (Figure 13.1), the four lineages are marrying in a circle and, indeed, you need at least three lineages for this arrangement to work. The Purum of India, who practiced matrilateral cross-cousin marriage, had seven lineages. Notice that B cannot return A's daughter with one of its own; if A2 married b2, he would be marrying his patrilateral cross-cousin, linked to him through A1, his sister a1, and her daughter b2. So b2 has to marry C2—trace their links to find out why.

This means that lineage B can never repay lineage A for the loss of their daughters. Because they cannot meet the third of Mauss's obligation (chapter 11) to repay, B is a beggar relative to A. By the same token, C is a beggar to B. Paradoxically, however, A, who gives its daughters to B, is a beggar to D, because Lineage D is where Lineage A obtains its brides. We seem to have an equality of inequality in this scheme.

This system operates in a complex society in highland Burma known as the Kachin. In this system, the wife-giving lineage is known as *mayu* to the wife-receiving lineage known as *dama* to the lineage that just gave it one of its wives. Now, in addition to other mechanisms of dominance, the higher-ranked lineages maintain their superiority by giving a daughter to the lower-ranked lineages.

Thus, the relations among social classes, already differentiated by other means, are reinforced through the *mayu-dama* relationship. (Leach 1961); Fox cites this information (1967:215–216).

Other Marriage Forms

The Kachin are not alone in interclass marriage as reinforced dominance. The Natchez peoples of the Mississippi region of North America, a matrilineal society, were divided into four classes: the Great Sun chiefs, the noble lineages, the honored lineages, and the inferior "stinkards." Unlike the Kachin, however, marriage was a way to upward mobility. The child of a woman marrying a man of lower status assumed his/her mother's status. Thus, if a Great Sun woman married a stinkard, the child would become a Great Sun; likewise, if a noble woman married a stinkard, their children would become nobles. If, however, a stinkard woman were to marry a noble (Great Sun) man, the child would

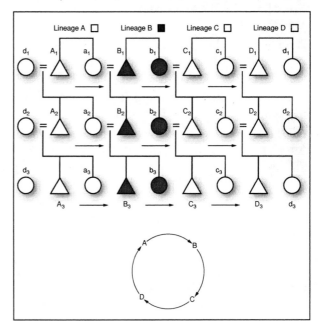

FIGURE 13.1
Matrilateral cross-cousin marriage.
Trace the relationship between B1 and a1. You will notice that the bride is the groom's mother brother's daughter. Lineage B cannot reciprocate Lineage A with B1's sister b1, because she would have to marry A1 as his patrilateral cross-cousin, which is forbidden. Therefore, she has to marry into Lineage C. Why? Look at the relationship between C1 and b1. There must be at least three lineages for matrilateral cross-cousin marriage to work. Why?

drop down to the third class, an honored lineage. Only two stinkard partners would maintain that stratum, which was continuously replenished with people in warfare (Le Page du Pratz 1958; Scupin 2003:239).

Other societies maintain their status in other ways. We have already mentioned brother–sister marriage in the royal lineages of three societies: the Inca, the Ancient Egyptians, and the Hawaiians, all royal lineages, all seeking to keep their lineages "pure." Another, more common type of marriage was the **patrilateral parallel cousin marriage**, already described in chapter 10. Often found among Middle Eastern nomadic societies, such as the Rwala Bedouin, a chiefdom, it serves to consolidate the herds of a man's son and his brother's daughter, an important consideration between lineages wishing to maintain their wealth (Lancaster1997; Service 1978).

Non-Kin Integrative Mechanisms: Associations

Chiefdoms, lacking the means to enforce their power by resource control or by monopoly over the use of force, rely on the integrative mechanisms similar to non-kin associations that cut across kinship groups. We provide some examples here.

Poro and Sande Secret Societies. Secret societies are one such example. The *poro* and *sande* secret societies, for men and women respectively, are found in the Mande-speaking peoples of West Africa, particularly Liberia, Sierra Leone, the Ivory Coast, and Guinea. Though illegal under national law in Guinea, they are not only legal elsewhere, but membership is universally mandatory under local law. They play roles both in the political and religious sectors of society. One may legitimately ask as to how they can possibly be secret if all men and women have to join? For the Kpelle of Liberia, according to Beryl Bellman, himself a member of a *poro* association, the standard is an *ability* to keep secrets; only when members learn to do so can they be entrusted with the political and religious responsibilities associated with that society (1984).

There are two political structures in both societies: the "secular" and the "sacred." The secular structure consists of the town chief, the neighborhood and kin group headmen, and elders. The sacred structure (the *zo*) comprises a hierarchy of "priests" of both *poro* and *sande* in the neighborhood. Among the Kpelle, the *poro* and *sande zo* take turns in dealing with in-town fighting, rape, homicide, incest, and land disputes. Not unlike the leopard skin chief, the *zo* play important roles in mediation.

The *zo* of both the *poro* and *sande* are held in great respect, even fear. Some authors suggest that both secret societies strengthen the hands of secular political authority because chiefs and landowners occupy the most powerful positions in the associations (Little 1965:349–365; Bledsoe 1980); Ember and Ember cite these studies (2002). This suggests the formative elements of a stratified society and a state, as we shall see in the next section.

Stratified Societies

Opposite from the **egalitarian society** in the social class spectrum is the **stratified society**, which may be defined as one in which a minority controls the strategic resources that sustain life. The Kpelle of Liberia, described above, are the closest of ranked societies that fall short of being stratified, and one might argue that it is a transitional society. By **strategic resources**, we refer to such resources as water in states that are dependent on irrigation agriculture, land in the **feudal mode of production** or patrimonial society, and oil in industrial society. **Capital**, or products and resources used for further production, is a **mode of production** that, in industrial society, is reliant on oil and other fossil fuels, such as natural gas.

Caste Systems

Operationally, **stratification** is, as the term implies, the structure of society that involves two or more largely mutually exclusive layers of population. An extreme example is the **caste** system of traditional East Indian society that draws for its legitimation **Hinduism**, of which more will be said in chapter 15. A **caste** is a form of social class in which membership is determined by birth and remains fixed for life. **Social mobility**, or movement from one social class, either upward or downward, within a lifetime is not an option. Nor can a person of one caste marry another person of a different caste; they are **endogamous**; marriage is allowed only within a caste. Although efforts have been made to abolish castes since India achieved its independence in 1947, they still predominate in rural areas.

The caste system consists of four **varna**, or pure, castes, plus one that is collectively known as **Dalit**, sometimes also known as *Harijan* and known in English as "untouchables," reflecting the notion that to touch, or even see, a Dalit is to pollute oneself. The topmost *varna* caste is the **Brahmin**, or priestly caste. They comprise the priests, as the name denotes, but also governmental officials and bureaucrats at all strata, and other professionals. The next highest is the **Kshatriya**, or warrior castes, which include soldiers and other military personnel, coupled with police and its equivalent. Next come the **Vaishya**, or craftsmen and merchants, followed by the **Sudra** [pronounced "shu-dra,"], which include peasants and menial workers. Metaphorically, they represent the parts of Manu, who is said to have given rise to the human race through dismemberment: the head corresponding to the *Brahmin*, the arms to the *Kshatriya*, the thighs to the *Vaishya*, and the feet to the *Sudra*.

Several variations occur; the most important source is the occupational subcaste, known as **jatis**, of which there are hundreds if not thousands. Wheelwrights, ironworkers, landed peasants, landless farmworkers, tailors of various types, barbers—all of them belong to different *jatis*. Like the broader castes, *jatis* are endogamous and one is born into a specific subcaste. They form the basis of the **jajmani** relationship, involving the provider of a particular service, the **jajman**, and the recipient of the service, the **kamin**. Although training is involved, one does not choose his vocation; it is **ascribed** or predetermined by birth. Furthermore, the relationship between *jajman* and *kamin* is determined by previous generations. If I provide you, my *kamin*, with haircutting services, it is because my father cut your father's hair. In other words, you are stuck with me, however poor a barber I am. This is perhaps another example of the economy as instituted process, the economy embedded in society.

The system extends to those excluded from the *varna* castes, the "untouchables," or **Dalit**, that we shall use henceforth. Under the worst restrictions, *Dalits* were thought to be polluting of the other castes, so much so that if the shadow of an untouchable fell on a Brahmin, the latter immediately went home to bathe. Thus in various times and locations, the untouchables were also unseeable, being able to come out only at night. (Long 1987; Maloney 1987a, 1987b). *Dalits* were born into the jobs that were considered polluting to other castes, particu-

larly work involving dead animals. Such work included butchering (Hinduism precludes consumption of meat, so the clients would be Muslims, Christians, and other religions), skinning, tanning, shoemaking using leather, and so on. It should be pointed out that contact of an upper caste person with another person of any lower caste, even if "pure," is also considered polluting, and any bodily contact between, say, a *Brahmin* and a *Sudra* is strictly forbidden.

The theological basis of caste relations involves *karma*, or the belief that one's caste in this life is the cumulative product of the person's acts in past lives. The concept extends to all beings, from minerals to animals to even gods. Therefore, if soul class mobility is nonexistent within a lifetime, it is possible between lifetimes. Brahmins justify their station by claiming they must have done good in their past lives; however, there are indications that the untouchable Dalits, not to mention other lower castes, are not so convinced of this legitimation (Khare 1984). We discuss the theology of *karma* and the related concept of *dharma* ("path of duty" assigned to each caste) in chapter 15.

Although the most extreme, India is not the only society with a caste system. In Japan, a caste known as *Burakumin* is similar in status to the *Dalits*. Although no different in physical appearance from other Japanese, this population has been forced to live in ghettos for centuries. They are descendants of peoples who worked in the leather-tanning industry, a low-status occupation, and still work in leather industries, such as shoemaking. Marriage between *Burakumin* and other Japanese is restricted at most, and their children are excluded from public schools (Scupin 2003; Befu 1971).

Social mobility of a greater or lesser extent characterizes all societies, but even the so-called **open-class societies** are not quite so mobile as one might think. In the United States, despite the Horatio Alger and rags-to-riches myths, actual movement up the social ladder is rare. Stories of individuals "making it" through hard work ignore the majority of persons whose hard work does not pay off or who actually experience downward mobility. On the other hand, in India, a **closed-class society**, there are exceptions to the caste system in the ideal sense. In Rajastan, for example, those who own and control most land are not of the warrior caste, as one might expect, but of the lowest caste; their tenants and laborers are, by contrast, Brahmins (Haviland 2002:314).

State Level of Integration

The **state** is the most formal of the four levels of integration under study here. In the state, political power is centralized in a government that exercises a monopoly over the legitimate use of force (Fried 1967). It is important to understand that such exercise constitutes a last resort; indeed, one hallmark of a weak state is the frequent use of physical force to maintain order. States exist in societies with large populations—hundreds of thousands or more—and a complex economy, either a command economy or a market driven one; social stratification; often an ethnically diverse population; and an intensive agricultural or industrial base.

Several characteristics accompany the monopoly over the use of legitimate force in a state. First, like tribes and chiefdoms, states occupy a more or less clearly defined **territory**, or land enclosed by boundaries that mark it off from other political entities that may or not be a state. Egypt was a state bounded to the west by desert and possibly foraging or tribal nomadic peoples. Mesopotamia was a series of city-states competing for territory with other city-states.

Second, there are heads of states, who may be individuals known as kings, emperors, or monarchs, with other names. Others may be democratically elected, in fact or in name—even military dictators may be known as presidents. Usually, there is some board of councilors (the cabinet in the United States, the politburo in the former Soviet Union). Often the council may be supplemented by a legislative assembly, and sometimes two. Rome, an empire, had a senate (which originated as a body of councilors) and up to four assemblies that combined patrician (elite) and plebian (general population) influences. Today, almost all countries have some sort of an assembly, however often they may rubber-stamp the decision of the executive.

Third, there is an administrative apparatus, a bureaucracy that handles the public functions provided for by executive order or legislation or both. Formally, the offices are typically arranged in a hierarchy, with the top offices delegating specific functions to lower ones. The arrangement of personnel within any branch mirrors the hierarchy of offices in general. Generally speaking, the relations tend to rely on interpersonal relations in agricultural

states, and principles of rational hierarchical organization in industrial ones (e.g., Weber 1997).

Fourth, there is the power to tax, adding power to the system of **redistribution**, whereby everyone from proletarian or plebe to peasant has no choice but to participate. This power comes in various guises, from the *mitá* or labor tax of the Inca to the tributary systems of Mesopotamia to the monetary tax known to us and to many other subjects throughout the history of the state. Control over others' resources is another mechanism undergirding the power of the state.

Fifth is the presence of ideology, designed to reinforce the right of the powerholders' right to rule. Ideology may manifest itself in philosophical forms—the Divine Right of Kings in preindustrial Europe, karma and the caste system in India, the consent of the governed in the United States, the metaphorical family in Imperial China. More often, ideology is more indirect, less perceptible as propaganda. We may watch the Super Bowl or follow the latest Martha Stewart interior designs, oblivious that both are diversions from the reality of power in this society. Recruits may be lulled into the Iraq war, as their parents were into the Vietnam War, in the belief that military life is a way out of unemployment (or underemployment at Wal-Mart). In thousands of ways and across different cultures, Plato's parable of the shadows in the cave—that watchers misperceived the shadows as reality—have served to reinforce political ideologies.

Finally, there is the delegation of the coercive power itself. The necessity to use power betrays an important weakness—that a wide portion of the subjects or citizens do not recognize the powerholders' right to rule. Even where the legitimacy of power is not questioned, force serves to maintain the state, and the functions are delegated. The police force serves to maintain the internal order of the country, whereas the army and its military cohorts are defending the country against enemies, perceived or real, or often expanding the country's borders.

State and Nation

The frequent interchangeability of **state** and **nation** often obscures the distinction between a coercive institution and an ethnic population. A *nation* refers to a usually geographically contiguous population sharing a single ethnicity and language; whereas a *state*, as defined above, is a society with a head or heads whose power is derived from the monopoly of the exercise of legitimate force. Nations without territories are *diasporas*. Statistically, there are about 200 states in the world, many of which did not exist before World War II. In contrast, there are possibly 5,000 nations, each with a language, territorial base, history, and political organization. (Clay 1996); Haviland cites Clay (2002:336). Few states are coterminous with a nation. Even in Japan, whose millions of people are of one ethnicity, there is a significant indigenous minority known as the **Ainu**, at one time a distinct biological breeding population as well as an ethnic group. Only recently has Japanese society included migrant minorities such as the Koreans and Taiwanese. Otherwise, most states, including the United States, comprise multiethnic societies.

Nor do all ethnicities have their own states. The Kurds are a nation without their own country, located as they are in adjacent areas of Turkey, Syria, Iraq, and Iran. In the colonial era, the Mande-speaking peoples range across at least four west African countries, and the borders were drawn without respect to the tribal identity of its population. In addition, there are **diasporas**—peoples of one ethnicity scattered across the globe. Ashkenazi and Sephardic Jews are classic examples, but others include Armenians, various African nations uprooted by slavery, overseas Chinese, and, in recent years, many others, as refugees are forced to flee their homelands.

Formation of States

States fall into two categories according to how they are formed. The **pristine states** are those that develop where none has existed before, so that causal factors do not include modeling after, or adapting to the presence of, existing states. Historically, there are no recorded or well documented examples of states forming where none existed before. **Secondary states** are those that develop amid other states, which do serve as models and may exert pressure for a society to develop a government of its own, partly to prevent being conquered

How do states form? One precondition is the presence of a **stratified society**, one with an elite minority controlling life-sustaining strategic resources. Another is the increased productivity of agriculture which, in turn, is capable of supporting a larger population. Nevertheless, neither is a suffi-

cient cause. One group, dissatisfied with conditions in the home region, has the motivation to move someplace else—unless there is no place to move to.

This is where **circumscription** enters the picture. The region may be hemmed in by mountains or desert, and any migrant community would have to change its subsistence strategies from agriculture back to foraging, herding, or horticulture. Indeed, the Inca empire never colonized on a massive scale beyond northern Chile to the south or into the Amazon, because the indigenous people there simply picked up and moved elsewhere. Even so, the majority of the Inca population did not have this option. Circumscription also results when an adjacent desirable region is already taken by other states or chiefdoms (Carneiro 1970, 1981).

The State and Peasantry

Who, then, are the subjects of the state? One short answer is **peasants**. Derived from the French *paysan*, which means "countryman," one thinks of a landed yeomanry who have long constituted the foundation of an agricultural state. Yet peasantry has entered relatively late in the anthropological literature. In his 800-page tome titled *Anthropology*, Alfred L. Kroeber defines peasantry as "part societies with part cultures" (1948). Robert Redfield defines peasantry as a "Little Tradition" set against a "Great Tradition." Louis Fallers argues against calling African cultivators "peasants" because they have not lived within the context of a state-based civilization long enough (1961:108–110).

This sample indicates that peasantry is defined in reference to some larger society, usually an empire or a state or a civilization. In light of this development, Wolf (1966) seeks to place the definition on a structural footing. Using a funding metaphor, he compares peasants with what he calls "primitive cultivators." First, both primitive cultivators and peasants have to provide for a caloric fund: grow food and, by extension, provide for clothing, shelter, and all other necessities of life. Second, both must provide for a replacement fund, that is, not only reserve seed for next year's crop, but also make repairs on the house, replace a broken pot, rebuild a fence, and all the rest. Third, both primitive cultivator and peasant must provide for a ceremonial fund, whether a rite of passage for the *poro* rites or the fiesta for a Mesoamerican village.

Where peasant and primitive cultivator part ways is that the one lives within a state and the other does not. The state exercises a domain over the peasant's resources for which he or she must provide a fund of rent. The fund of rent comes in many guises—tribute in kind, taxation in money, or *corvée labor* to some empire or lord. The primitive cultivator, in Wolf's conception, is free of these obligations. In chapter 16, we will see how this process operates in the process of *peasantization*, from which even the primitive cultivator cannot escape.

The State and the Landless

Not all subjects, however, are landed. Indeed, as we will see in chapter 16, landless populations have a long history. To begin with, **slavery** has long coexisted with the state. Forced labor without compensation is a long tradition that reaches back to chiefdoms—the Kwakiutl had slaves. Long before Portuguese, Spanish, and English seafarers added slaves to their trading along the west coast of Africa, Arab slavers took Africans both west and east of the continent (Stavrianos 1974).

Among peasantry, loss of land has been a continuous process. As we shall see in chapter 16, **proletarianization** has been a continuous process, as were the **enclosures**, whereby the last of the landed gentry found sheepherding more profitable than the tributes of peasants (Perelman 2000:38–59). We will also see how this process works for Guatemalan peasants.

Law and Order

At the level of the chiefdom, and particularly the state, law becomes increasingly a formal process. Procedures become more and more regularly defined, and categories of breaches in civil law and of crime emerge, together with their remedies. Agricultural states came to formalize legal decision and punishments through legal codes, formal courts of law, police, and legal specialists such as lawyers and judges. Mediation may still be practiced, but often they are supplanted by **adjudication**, where the judge's decision is binding on all parties. The decision may be appealed to a higher judge, but any final decision must be accepted by all concerned.

The first known system of codified law was enacted under the warrior king Hammurabi in Babylon, located in the present state of Iraq. This law was based on standardized procedures for deal-ing with civil and criminal offenses, and subsequent decisions were based on precedent, or previous decisions. Crimes became offenses not only against other parties but also against the state. Other states developed similar codes of law in China, Southeast Asia, and even in the state-level societies of the Aztec and Inca.

Two interpretations, not necessarily mutually exclusive, have arisen about codified law. Fried (1978) argues from his analysis of the Hammurabi codes that these laws reinforced a system of inequality by protecting the rights of an elite class while keeping the peasants in a subordinate status. This is consistent with a stratified society, as already defined. Another interpretation has it that the maintenance of social and political order is crucial for agricultural states. Any disruption within the state would lead to neglect of agricultural production, which would prove deleterious to all members, regardless of social status. Civil law ensures, at least in theory, that all disputing parties will get a hearing—assuming that high legal expenses and bureaucratic logjams do not cancel out this process—and criminal law ensures protection of all citizens from offenses ranging from theft to homicide.

However valid the ideal of formal procedural law, there are circumstances in which such law fails to realize its aims. For example, the United States has one of the highest crime rates in the industrial world. More homicides occurred in New York in 1990 than deaths from colon and breast cancer or all accidents combined. (Roberts 1993); cited in Harris and Johnson (2003:186). Although the violent crime rate declined during the mid-1990s, this was possible only with the construction of more prisons per capita (in California) than of schools. Nationwide, there are more than one million prisoners in state and federal correctional institutions, making this country one of the highest imprisoned populations in the industrial world (Butterfield 1996); cited in Harris and Johnson (2003:186).

Warfare

Warfare occurs in all societies, even among foragers, but at no level of integration does it involve as widespread a population as at the state level of integration. Indeed, warfare was integral to the formation of the agricultural state. As governing elites accumulated more resources, warfare came to be one of the major means of increasing their surpluses (Childe 1950; cited in Scupin 2003:263). Often, as the wealth of states themselves became the target of nomadic pastoralists, the primary motivation for warfare shifted from control over resources to control over neighboring populations (Otterbein 1994; cited in Scupin 2003:263).

A further shift comes with the advent of industrial society; industrial technologies, driven by fossil fuels, enabled countries to invade distant countries. One of the primary motivations for these wars has been to establish economic and political hegemony over foreign populations. Wars of the past century, particularly World War I, World War II, and the lesser wars that have taken place since then, have generated ever higher levels of war-related technology, such as wireless communication devices, tanks, stealth aircraft, and nuclear weapons. Competition among nations has led to the emergence of the United States as militarily the most powerful nation in the world.

This has not come without costs. All nation-states have involved civilians in military adventures, and almost everyone has been involved in some way in their countries' wars—if not as military, then as member of the civilian workforce in the military industries. World War II created an unprecedented armaments industry in the United States, Britain, Germany, and Japan, among others, and the aerospace industry underwent expansion in the so-called Cold War that followed. In chapter 16, we look at the process of globalization, and explain how the United States, now a unicentered empire, has influenced the peoples of other countries in the world.

Stability and Duration of States

It should be noted that states show a clear tendency toward instability, despite trappings designed to induce awe in the wide population. Few states have lasted as long as 1,000 years. The American state is 230 years old, yet the increase in extremes of wealth and poverty, escalating budgetary and trade deficit, a war initiated under false pretenses, and escalating social problems are indications that it could collapse before long. Jared Diamond's recently released book *Collapse* (2004) draws parallels between complex societies such as Easter Island, Chaco Canyon, and the Maya with contemporary societies such as

our own, and finds that overtaxing the environment has been an efficient cause in all these societies. Chalmers Johnson argues similarly that the states of perpetual war, loss of democracy, systematic deception, and financial overextension contributed to the decline of the Roman Empire and are also likely to contribute to the demise of the United States "with the speed of FedEx" (2004:285).

Why states decline in due course is not hard to fathom. The extreme disparities in wealth, the use of force to keep the population in line, the stripping of people from their resources (such as the enclosures in England), the harshness of most laws, all should create a general animosity toward the elite.

Yet no one is out in the streets calling for the president or Congress to resign. Here is the paradox: Though widespread, this animosity does not automatically lead to the dissolution of the state nor the overthrow of the power elite. Thomas Frank addresses this issue in *What's the Matter with Kansas?*, which shows that, despite the fact that jobs have been shipped abroad, that once-vibrant cities like Wichita are virtual ghost towns, and that both Congress and the state legislature have voted against social programs time and again, Kansans continue to voting into office the very Republicans who are responsible for these conditions in the first place (2004). Nor is this confined to Kansas or the United States. That slaves themselves—blacks, and many before them—tolerated slavery for hundred of years (despite periodical revolts), that workers tolerated extreme conditions in the factories and the mines long before unionization, that there was no peasant revolt strong enough to reverse the enclosures—all of these demand an explanation. Frank himself discusses reinforcing variables—the propaganda of televagelists and Rush Limbaugh, for example—but offers little explanation besides them (Frank 2004).

Conclusion

Over the last two chapters, we have examined the levels of sociocultural integration, the types of social class (from none to stratified), and the kinds of social control exercised from interpersonal relations of the foragers to the state exercised within agricultural and industrial societies. Reasons have been suggested, and the bibliography offers many more. There are many more questions than answers. Explanations have been advanced and debated why socioeconomic inequality arises in the first place, and how states serve to reinforce (or perhaps are generated by) them. Societies without states have lasted far longer—about 100,000 to 150,000 years—than states with them (roughly 8,000 to 10,000 years). All the greater mystery, then, as to why they persist to this day, despite the demonstrable disadvantages they present for the majority.

Chapter 14

PSYCHOLOGY AND CULTURE

Introduction

Of the various fields in anthropology, psychological anthropology (sometimes referred to by one of its subfields, personality and culture) tends to emphasize the individual rather than the group. It involves the nature of the personality (some psychological anthropologists would dismiss culture-and-personal studies altogether, an example of the professional warfare that goes on in any discipline), how children are enculturated (acquire their personality, skills, knowledge, and beliefs), and the sources of people's personality—genetic, environmental, or some combination of both. Mental and personality disorders and how cultures handle them are also part of the questions considered in the discipline. Some anthropologists would go so far as to say that psychological issues are epiphenomenal to the socioeconomic structure of societies, and that their practitioners are little more than space cases.

All these are considered in turn, but first we start with the elements of personality. Just what are the elements of personality? We then consider an area that is fundamental to enculturation, namely language acquisition, relying heavily on Chomsky's model. Following these, we look at Piaget's structural model of child development and the two types of personality formulated by the Whitings and

Child Six-Cultures study. We then compare the environmentalist versus biological models of personality, followed by cross-cultural approaches to mental and personality disorders.

Elements of Personality

One matter that is poorly covered in many introductory anthropology textbooks is the elements of personality. For example, Haviland hints at them when he defines **personality** as the way a person thinks, feels, and behaves (2002:490), but that is as far as he goes. Interestingly, he points out that the term comes from the Latin word for *mask* (the dictionary reads *persona*, which means "actor's mask), and it is this *persona* that we need to analyze.

The first element of personality is **perception**, namely what an individual obtains through his or her five senses. Except for some disability, we all have the senses of vision, hearing, touch, taste, and smell. Nevertheless, none of these is acute. As we indicated in chapter 2, primates do have better vision than other mammals, but the acuity of our vision can never compare with that of hawks, eagles, or other predatory birds, which can spot their prey a mile away. As for hearing, we cannot compare with animals with sonar, such as bats, and dogs can hear sounds we cannot. Dogs and other mammals also have better senses of smell than we do, and drug-sniffing dogs are well known in the popular culture. Several reports have it that animals sensed the coming of the tsumani of 2004, and ran away into safer territory long before humans were warned—if they were warned at all.

Therefore, our perception is not perfect, and we often have to fill in the blanks. This function is taken up by **cognition**, namely our thought processes, how we conceive of things we perceive. As humans, we have conceptual processes denied to or limited in other animals. Our capacity for **displacement** enables us to conceive of objects that are not present, or even of relationships that contain no objects at all—can we think of pi square or the Pythagorean Theorem as objects? How about the Second Law of Thermodynamics or the General Theory of Relativity? Again, most of us may not have the discipline of a mathematician or physicist in our thinking, and so cognition is not perfect. They may include a person's aptitudes, abilities, intellectual capacities, or skills.

The third source of personality involves what we feel, that is, our **emotions**, or one's affective response to, or feelings about, perception or cognition to a given situation. They run the gamut from happiness to sadness to anger. They provide a motivation to act in some way. Indeed, emotion can often distort one's perception or cognition within a given circumstance. Rightly or wrongly, emotions may fill in the gaps. Does discovering that a spouse is having lunch with another man or woman imply adultery? Emotions often lead to the conclusion that it does. Emotions over the picture of a gruesome murder scene often lead a jury to an emotional leap that the defendant committed the crime, whatever the facts of the case.

The fourth source of personality is **behavior**, which can represent the outward manifestation of the first three elements of personality. We cannot get inside the head of another person—we do not know what he or she perceives, thinks, or feels. Only the behavior gives us some idea, and even then not a perfect one at that.

The four elements combine to form the personality of each individual, a *persona*, so to speak. We might add to the definition *stability* and *patterning*, inasmuch as, unlike a mask, one cannot slip a personality in front of one's face. Some individuals are more analytical than others, or handier with tools; other individuals may be given to anger, or depression, or cheerfulness. Still others may be more outgoing, or reticent, than others.

Enculturation

The question that governs the next several sections of this chapter concerns the way personalities develop, whether child rearing has much or little to do with the personality one acquires, and whether biology or environment plays the greater role. Of course, all this is mediated by language.

Language Acquisition

As we emphasized in chapters 4 and 5, the layer that mediates between the culture that the individuals belonging to the species *Homo sapiens* acquire and their biological capacity for culture is language. We have seen that the brain is structured to enable speech, understanding, and association with various senses. We have also seen that the articulatory mechanisms of the mouth, combined with the lingual muscles and hypoglossal nerve, all contribute to our capacity to use language. If there is any validity to Chomsky's notion of a universal or generative grammar, this is the biological basis for it.

It is axiomatic that children learn the rules of grammar early in life, although they do not know what a noun or verb is, nor can they diagram a sentence. In the babbling stage, the infant utters a wide range of possible sounds. Then as he or she hears the mother talking, and adults engage in conversation, she or he puts strings of sounds together, eventually uttering the first word. In due course, the child strings the words together to form sentences and gradually acquires the language that his or her parents speak. However, this does not mean that language is merely a trial-and-error process, nor is the child's mind a tabula rasa, a blank slate waiting for whatever content comes along.

Chomsky argues that the child has an inborn capacity known as **universal grammar**, which serves as a template, or model, with which a child matches and sorts out the patterns of **phonemes** and **morphemes** that she or he will use over life. The child also learns the subtle distinctions needed to communicate in any language. The universal structure of the human mind enables the child to acquire language and produce sentences never heard before; thus, as defined in chapter 5, language has **productivity**.

Nevertheless, the child must acquire language in what Chomsky calls a critical period, between birth and the onset of puberty. If children are not exposed to language in that period of time, they may never learn it, or they may learn it only in a very rudimentary fashion. In his view, the human brain contains genetically programmed modules for learning a language, and they form a child's growth (Chomsky 1980; cited in Scupin 2003:104–105).

Cognitive Development

Beyond language is the question as to how children develop their cognitive abilities. The Swiss psychologist Jean Piaget investigated the ways children acquire their cognitive capacity to learn, and how they perceive the world. In his view, the first phase of a child's cognitive development is the **sensorimotor phase**, in which the infant explores the world through touching, sucking, listening, and other sensory modes; the phase lasts from birth to approximately two years of age. The second, the **preoperational phase**, involves the period in which symbols, including language, are first used. They learn to attach meanings and names to their specific environment, but they have not yet conceptualized the world in general terms. This phase lasts from age two to seven years.

The ability to use logic defines the **concrete-operational phase** at ages seven through eleven. They begin to connect events in terms of cause and effect, and they begin to manipulate symbols in a more nuanced way. At this phase, children are also capable of taking the perspective of another person, allowing them to engage in complex activities that involve several participants. At the **formal-operational phase**, which begins at age twelve, children develop the capacity to think for themselves, and to think of themselves and the world in highly abstract terms (Piaget 2000).

Several anthropologists have evaluated Piaget's model using cross-cultural data. For example, Bloch finds that all humans have intuitive capacities to perceive time and space in the same way. Unlike Westerners, who perceive time in a linear fashion from past to present to future, East Indians perceive time cyclically, seeing the creation and destruction of the universe over millions of years. Yet both the Western and Hindu cultures perceive time both cyclically and lineally in relation to the cycle of seasonal changes or the life cycle of an individual through biological aging (Bloch 1985). Cole and Scribner find that the thinking processes are similar across cultures, using similar patterns of logic and developing an understanding of cause-and-effect relationships (1974; cited in Scupin 2003:80–81).

Dependence and Independence Training

Other studies have focused on children's independence versus dependence on one's group or family. Conducting a six-culture study, John and Beatrice Whiting, in collaboration with Irving L. Child, found that two different patterns of child rearing recur consistently across the cases: **dependence training** and **independence training**. In **dependence training**, children promote compliance in the performance of assigned tasks and favors keeping individuals within the group. The pattern is found in association with extended family households, one comprising a minimum of three generations of married kin, and with an economy based on subsistence farming. In contrast, **independence training** promotes independence, self-reliance, and personal achievement on the part of the child. It is typically found in association with nuclear families, comprising of husband, wife, and children, and is particularly characteristic of industrial societies, such as the United States. In actuality, both types of training are found in most societies, and exist in a continuum rather than as mutually exclusive options. (Whiting and Child 1953).

Personality and Culture: Genetic and Environmental Models

Once the child is an adult, other questions arise as to the relative contribution of the cultural environment versus the genetic composition toward one's personality. Benedict and Mead (1950) saw a relationship between child rearing and the child's personality, but differed in the direction of causality between personality and culture: Is a culture "personality writ large," as Benedict puts it, or does culture condition child rearing, as Mead argues? What role does biology play? Is the Freudian analysis valid at all in specifying id, ego, and superego as the child develops? What about the alleged role of race or nationality in intelligence, however defined? Do we need a dominant personality type for cultures to function, or are cultures capable of accommodating all personality types? We consider these questions in turn.

Cultural Determinants

Ruth Benedict and Margaret Mead were among the first anthropologists to link child rearing and personality with the culture in which the child is born. In her book *Patterns of Culture*, Benedict made her famous definition of culture as "personality writ large" (1934). In other words, culture represents the sum total personality of its constituents.

To argue this point, Benedict developed four personality types—Apollonian (after the sun god in Roman mythology), Dionysian (after the god of wine), megalomaniac, and paranoiac—and applied them to four cultures. The Zuñi exemplify the formalistic Apollonian, a personality given to formalistic relations, distrustful of the orgiastic behavior of the Plains Indians, whom she categorized as Dionysian. As for the Kwakiutl, whose rivalry potlatch was by then well known, she categorized them as megalomaniac, one whose chiefs exhibited self-aggrandizing behavior in their massive gifts of blankets and other valuable objects. Finally, she regarded the Dobu islanders, located in the Trobriand Islands, as paranoic, distrustful of their neighbors and highly defensive of their property. Hers was the prototype of the **modal personality** that Kardiner was later to develop (Benedict 1934).

Margaret Mead found that cultures were the determinants of personality, starting first with adolescent girls of American Samoa, whom she thought sexually promiscuous but free of the *Sturm und Drang*, the period of turmoil found among U.S. adolescents (Mead 1961 [1927]). Derek Freeman was later to write a refutation of this thesis, as described in chapter 2 (1980). Later, she found that in New Guinea and other islands of Melanesia, personalities varied considerably among cultures. Among the Tchambuli, for example, the gender roles were the reverse of those expected between the genders in North America; Tchambuli men exhibited behavioral traits expected of women in North America, and Tchambuli women did the same in reverse (1950). Later, in collaboration with Geoffrey Görer, she argued for national character of personalities in Japan and Russia.

Biological and Genetic Explanations

What induced Franz Boas, one of the founders of American anthropology, to send Margaret Mead to the South Pacific in the first place was his reaction against the ideology of eugenics, popularized by the English biologist Francis Galton in the 19th century. According to this ideology, personality traits are the products of innate characteristics (genetics had not been developed as a science at the time). According to this belief, the intelligent should be allowed, even encouraged, to breed offspring, whereas the feebleminded should be discouraged from breeding, and even sterilized. The eugenics movement had as one offshoot the Nazi policy of propagating Aryans while eliminating "inferior" peoples, such as Jews, homosexuals, and the feebleminded.

One of the first attempts to ground human behavior in biology was Freud's structure of personality. According to his model, there are three components in personality: the id, which is pure psychic energy based on the sex drive; the ego, the part that mediates the personality with the real world; and the superego, the moral component. (It is worth noting that *ego* is Latin for the first person singular "I," so that *superego* suggests a group value beyond the ego, or "I"). All psychic energy originates in the id, and the other two components modify this energy according to pragmatic adaptation or moral constraint. Using the same model, Freud argued for child development in three phases: oral, anal, and oedipal; the last is the stage whereby the five-year-old male would murder his father and mate with his mother, following the mythical Oedipus the King, who is said to have committed these acts (1943).

Freud's model has been questioned and often dismissed. He explained the incest tabu by a undocumented incident, whereby a horde of men, jealous of their father's monopoly over its women, murdered the father. Then, overwhelmed with guilt, the sons vowed to take their wives from other hordes. The book that set forth this thesis, *Totem and Taboo*, was criticized at the moment of its publication (1913). Nevertheless, the Freudian models have influenced much of psychological anthropology.

Other genetically based theories have arisen since. One of the more egregious attempts is *The Bell Curve* (Murray and Herrnstein 1994), which claims a correlation between breeding populations and intelligence, in which East Asians score the highest in intelligence tests, Euro-Americans the next highest, and blacks the lowest. Several critiques have attacked the methodology of sampling and the use of culture-bound tests.

Another test of genetic determinism of behavior comes in the form of studies of twins, both **monozyotic** (twins conceived in the same ovum or egg; also known as identical twins) and **dyzygotic** (twins conceived in separate ova or eggs). According to the logic of the studies, twins who are separated at birth should display similar behaviors though reared in separated environments. In one study, monozygotic and dizygotic twins were compared with unrelated (adopted) siblings reared in the same household. Results revealed that, in the author's words, "the very modest IQ similarity between [unrelated siblings], despite their common rearing, suggest that the shared environment has a very small effect on intellectual development and supports the position that individuals respond to environments in ways consistent with their genetic predispositions." They also indicated that monozygotic twins displayed more similar intelligence test results than the dizygotic twins and unrelated siblings (Segal 1997:381–390). Other results tend to be more mixed.

Comparative Cognition and Culture

Other studies have involved cross-cultural analyses of cognitive patterns, some of which may involve genetic variables. One of the longest-standing analyses is color categorization, as conducted by Berlin and Kay (1969). The researchers studied the color-naming practices of informants from 98 globally distributed language groups, and found that societies differ considerably in the number of basic color terms they possess, ranging from two (black and white) in New Guinea to eleven in the United States. They show a consistent pattern. For example, a language that identifies only two colors divides the spectrum between black and white; those with three identify the spectrum as black, white, and red; those with four will identify black, red, white, and either green, yellow, or blue. This pattern, Berlin and Kay suggest, indicates an evolutionary sequence: Those with only two color terms have a simple technology; those with eleven basic color terms have a complex technology (1969; cited in Scupin 2003:81–82).

Still other studies reveal that folk taxonomies of natural life may not vary much from taxonomic schemes in biology. Boster found that people from different societies classify birds in similar ways. For example, the Jívaro native population of South America classified species of native birds in a way corresponding to the way scientists classify those bird; running a test among University of Kentucky students with no scientific training or familiarity with South American birds, Boster found that they classified the birds in the same way as the Jívaro and the scientists (1987; cited in Scupin 2003:82). These and other findings suggest that, despite differences in cultures, the human mind appears to organize the world in nonarbitrary ways (Scupin 2003:82).

Another strain in cognitive analysis in psychological anthropology involves **evolutionary psychology**. Based on ethnographic research, psychological experiments, and evolutionary theory, researchers in the field seek to demonstrate how the brain developed and how it influences cognitive processes and behavior. According to *The Adapted Mind*, a volume edited by Jerome Barkow and colleagues (1992), modules in the brain enable humans to understand intuitively how nature operates, including motion, force, and the functioning of plants and animals. **Modules** are independent units in the brain that enabled ancestral sapient forms to adapt to Paleolithic conditions; these modules predispose humans to perceive, think, and behave in ways that allow for adaptation. One example is the language module, which governs language acquisition and use, as reviewed in this chapter and chapter 3. Other specialized modules regulate abilities to understand basic emotions, relations between the sexes, and cooperation among individuals (Barkow et al. 1992; cited in Scupin 2003:83–84).

Culture and Personality

Another strain in psychological theory addresses the relationship between individual behavior and culture as shared by a group with common language, practices, and values. As stated earlier, Benedict attempted to link behavior with culture, but was criticized for simplistically reducing cultures to behavior. Drawing on this model and adding elements from Freudian analysis, Kardiner developed the concept of **modal personality**, in which, statistically speaking, personalities of certain types dominate a culture; this allows for personality variation within cultures. Personality structure, he argued, comprises a constellation (not unlike a constellation of stars) of emotional, cognitive, and behavior traits that form patterns. Primary institutions are those in a culture associated with social development of the child: initially nurturing and later training in skills, attitudes, and values—although he does not offer a comprehensive list.

Secondary institutions reinforce the primary ones. This combination of individual propensities and cultural forces yield the personality type that statistically dominate any culture (Kardiner and Linton 1939).

Francis Hsu offers a different model that similarly combines social forces with those underlying individual behavior, which meet in each person's *jen*, which roughly is translated as "personage" (1971). The internal forces of each individual comprise the unconscious, the subconscious, and the conscious; these interact with the influences from one's intimate society and culture (family and kin), the instrumental society and culture (village or band), wider world (region) and the outer world (nation state, international system of states and economy) ions, to create a personality—or personage—that reflects both major sets of influences. The personage itself ranges between the subconscious, conscious, and intimate society and culture (Hsu 1971:23–44).

Others would find that one need not assume a dominant personality at all. For example, Anthony F. C. Wallace argues that culture is not so much a collection or structure of personalities as a mediator between personality types, one that serves as an "organization of diversity" (1956). In his view, culture serves as a traffic cop, ensuring that everyone within a culture obeys the rules of the road, but otherwise displays a diversity of personalities. Viewed in this way, he contends, one avoids the risk of simplistically reducing cultures down to personality types or modal personalities (1970).

Mental Disorders

Across the world's cultures, as in our own, there are mental disorders that are both identified as such by the *Diagnostic Statistical Manual of Mental Disorders* Vol. 4 (DSM-IV), issued by the American Psychiatric Association (1994), and identified as such within individual cultures. Societies vary by the nature of the disorders, their interpretation, and ways that they are treated or otherwise handled. Benedict early argued, in her *Patterns of Culture*, that what we identify as mental disorders, such as "sadism or delusions of grandeur or of persecution, there are well described cultures in which these abnormal function with ease and with honor and apparently without danger of difficulty to the society" (1934; cited in Scupin 2003:86). Benedict herself cites cases in which an individual heard loud voices and was plagued by dreams of falling off cliffs and being devoured by yellow jackets, a species of wasp. The individual went into a state of trance, lay rigidly on the ground, shortly recovered, and danced three nights in a row. In Western society, this behavior would be classified as a mental disorder; among the Native American peoples of which the person was a part, this particular individual (gender is not identified) was respected as a medicine practitioner (Benedict 1934; cited in Scupin 2003).

Other disorders familiar to us are interpreted as a supernatural phenomenon. Northerners are familiar with cabin fever, in which long periods of activity confined in a cabin or other structure leads one to extreme irritability and restlessness. An extreme form called *pibloktoq*, or arctic hysteria, is found among indigenous individuals throughout the circumpolar (Arctic circle) region. Among the Inuit, both men and women, but particularly women, become extremely irritable or withdrawn, then behave with violent emotion. Subjects may scream as if terrified, run out into the snow, tear the clothes off, jump into a fire, and "speak in tongues." Subjects may have convulsive seizures and in due course fall asleep. Upon wakening, a subject may have no memory of what happened (Wallace 1992; cited in Scupin 2003:87). A similar behavior described among the Reinder Tungus is taken as a sign that the person (usually a woman) has had contact with the spirit world and was selected to become a shaman, one capable of diagnosing (and sometimes treating) illness (Eliade 1964; Czaplicka 1914; Service 1978).

Other disorders are culturally defined disorders. For example, *amok* refers to a culture-specific behavior describe in Malaysia, Indonesia, and parts of the Philippines among middle-aged males. Following a period of withdrawal and brooding, sometimes followed by a perceived insult, the man undergoes a wild outburst marked by rage; he grabs the nearest weapon such as a machete and attacks any person or animal in his path. These attacks are followed by prolonged exhaustion and amnesia; like the victim of *pibloktoq*, the *amok* subject does not recall what happened (Bourguignon 1979; cited in Scupin 2003). Another disorder, one specific to males among the Chippewa, Cree, and the Montagnais-Naskapi Indians of northeastern Canada, is **windigo psychosis**, in which an individual feels he has become possessed by the spirit of a windigo, a giant cannibal giant with a heart or entrails of ice. In due course, he feels he becomes a windigo himself and attempts to kill and eat other individuals. Cases of homicide and cannibalism have indeed been documented among these populations (Barnouw 1985; Marano 1982; cited in Scupin 2004:86–87).

Medical factors may account for some of these behaviors. For example, *windigo psychosis* may be related to the experience of starvation and famine that often occurs during the winter in northeastern Canada—but if so, there is the added question as to why this disorder does not occur elsewhere in the northern woods, such as the Athabaskan peoples of western Canada and Alaska. Wallace suggests that the occurrence of *pibloktoq* may reflect a calcium deficiency or the drastic annual variation in daylight, which becomes limited or nonexistent in winter (1972; cited in Scupin 2003:87).

Also an open question is whether these disorders represent cultural interpretations of mental illness as classified in the DSM-IV. According to critics, culture-specific disorders may be panic disorders, persecution complexes, hysteria, or other psychoses that occur in all societies in one degree or another. Some may be the products of biochemical disorders often inherited genetically (McMahon and McMahon 1983; cited in Scupin 2003:87).

However, most psychological anthropologists contend that the content of these behaviors are local interpretations of disorders that may or may not appear across the world.

Conclusion

A defining characteristic of culture is that it is shared among groups defined by language, distinct lifeways, and value orientations. There has been a temptation among anthropologists to argue that personalities are shared traits as well. As we have seen, anthropologists such as Anthony F. C. Wallace find these notions simplistic and unmindful that individuals and their personalities, after all, do vary within cultures.

Nevertheless, several commonalities cannot be ignored. Everyone has a language, and how children acquire a language is an important issue. There also remains the question whether children acquire their values genetically, through training by their parents, or some combination of both. Students of cognitive psychology have also argued for many intercultural commonalities in such cognitive issues as natural taxonomies, color categories, and adaptive behavior. The relationship between the individual and his/her culture thus remains a question for which much research is to be done.

Chapter 15

ANTHROPOLOGY OF THE SUPERNATURAL

Introduction

Belief in the **supernatural**, or beings, objects, and forces that occur beyond nature, or the range of the five senses and their extensions, exists in all cultures. We cannot see an entity called God, or *mana* believed to exist among the Polynesians, or the being *di* among the Trobriand Islands, but people somewhere in the world believe that they are there. Americans, or at least some of them, separate the supernatural from the natural as handily as the U.S. Constitution separates church from state; but there are many peoples around the world who treat the supernatural as real as the tree in front of their house or the pigs they tend or the sun in the sky. In point of fact, there is much we do not know. We have no idea where we "came from" (other than a woman's womb and a man's sperm), nor do we know where we go after death (if we go anywhere, that is) or what happens to us (if anything other than becoming a feast for the worms).

Hence it is hardly surprising that, despite the many answers science has given us, religions and belief in other areas of the supernatural remain with us. In this chapter, we start with some fundamental definitions (including the differences between magic and religion, which overlap), then review some of the commonalities and differences in belief

systems. We summarize some case studies and have a look at some shared components of supernatural ritual. We then ask what functions supernatural beliefs and belief systems fulfill, concluding this chapter with a look at revitalization movements.

Defining the Supernatural

One of the fundamental distinctions in the supernatural involves that between magic and religions, a distinction that James Frazer made in his classic work *The Golden Bough* but, because of conceptual and practical difficulties of the distinction, has fallen into disuse. The fact remains, however, that some belief systems involve maintaining the relations between humankind and its gods and the divine world, and that others involve manipulating unseen beings and forces.

World View and the Supernatural

Thus, we may define **magic** as a religious ritual involving manipulative means to induce spirits or forces to produce the effect desired by the practitioner. One may define **religion** as a social process that orders the relationship between humankind and the supernatural world, whether dominated by a single God, multiple gods, spirits, forces, ghosts, demons, or some combination thereof.

Often, though, in order to separate the manipulative from the supplicative, there are overlaps in all religious beliefs. Thus, we may see the Balinese Eka Desa Rudra, held every hundred years to ensure that the destructive demons transform themselves into the creative forces, as a religious act; it involves priests, and unites every Balinese on the island. Yet it is also manipulative by the very rituals that are supposed to effect the transformation. How many devout Catholics ask St. Jude, the Saint of Lost Causes, for favors, and thank him in newspaper advertisements for favors rendered? **Magic** has its subtypes—and perhaps we are violating the very norms brought up the last sentence—but to cite an intended pun, what the Hell? Often, magic has its evil side. Thus, **sorcery** refers to the manipulation of supernatural beings and forces to bring harm to others (although some definitions do not include harmful intent). **Witchcraft** refers to the ability to harm others by harboring malevolent thoughts about them, but without using ritual for that end (some definitions would conflate witchcraft with sorcery in the malevolent sense). To make the distinction between good and evil, some definitions would invoke **white magic**, or the rituals intended to benefit another person through supernatural means. (**Black magic** is usually synonymous with **sorcery**.) Finally, **shamans** are individuals who are perceived as intermediaries between the material and spirit world, but who themselves are not recognized officials of any organized religion.

Religion, too, has its subtypes. Among prestate societies, the most common forms of religions are **cosmic religions**; the concepts, beliefs, and rituals of these religions are integrated with the natural environment, seasonal cycles, and all living life-forms (Scupin 2003:220). One of the earliest recognized forms of cosmic religion is **animism**, first identified by E. B. Tylor. The term refers to the belief that there is a spirit world populated by spirits, demons, ghosts, and other beings. According to Tylor (1976), dreams represent an entry point into this world; one leaves the body while sleeping and wanders in an space whereby every natural object—trees, rocks, sun, sky, water—has a conscious being. A second interpretation was offered by a researcher identified only as R. Marratt (1914), who contends that forces rather than beings are behind the natural objects and events. This is close to the Polynesian concept of **mana**, or supernatural powers that render certain objects **tabu**, or forbidden to most people as too dangerous to handle.

One example of animism is the Australian Aborigine notion of **dreamtime** (Stanner 1979; cited in Scupin 2003:188). Dreamtime exists in the "other world," one associated with the time of creation, where a person goes in dreams and visions, and after death. Consistent with Tylor's model, the belief has it that, at the time of creation, the ancestors dropped souls of all living things near watering holes, eventually embedding beings in all matter, from rocks and water to trees and humans. We describe dreamtime among the case studies below. In another variation of the animistic theme, the Inuit (so-called Eskimo) do not believe in a separate, omnipotent supreme being, but do believe that every living creature possesses a soul that is reincarnated after death. The spirits of animals allow themselves to be hunted and are reincarnated into other animal forms (Balikci 1970; cited in Scupin 2003:189).

Ranked societies retain many aspect of animism, but often formalize their beliefs in the form of **theocracies**, societies ruled by chiefs (or kings) who derive their legitimacy by their place in the society's moral and sacred order. In Polynesia, for example, the power of a chief is reinforced by a system of **mana**, a supernatural force (somewhat equivalent to electricity in the material world) deemed to be powerful and sometimes dangerous. Accompanying **mana** is an elaborate **tabu** system that reinforces social inequalities through a set of rules of elaborate deference and extreme expressions of humility on the part of commoners. Paramount, or supreme, chiefs are said to have a great amount of **mana**, subsidiary chiefs lesser amounts, and commoners almost none at all. To violate a *tabu*—for example, touching a member of the chief's family—is to result in death, from the power of *mana* itself. The term *mana* is often used generically in reference to any nonpersonified supernatural force (Scupin 2003:241–242).

At the other end of the social spectrum stand highly structured, formal, and organized religions, which become increasingly intertwined with stratification and the state. The religious traditions that develop in agricultural states are known as **ecclesiastical religions**, whereby no distinctions are drawn between religion and state. Modern examples include the Jewish state of Israel, the Anglican-sanctioned state of Great Britain, and until recently the Catholic Church and Spain. Early civilizations included formal religion as part of the state apparatus: Mesopotamia, Egypt with its divine pharaohs, the Aztecs and Inca with their respective sun gods,

China dominated by Confucian ideology, and the Greeks and Romans with their divine pantheons led by Zeus or Jupiter (Jove). Religions become standardized, often as hierarchical in the supernatural realm as societies are in the culturally defined material world (Scupin 2003).

Also developing in agricultural states are **universalistic religions**, those purporting to represent all of humankind rather than a specific nation-state or empire. Two major branches emerged: One emerged in the Middle East and spawned the historically related religions of Judaism, Christianity, and Islam; the other arose in southern Asia and spawned Hinduism and Buddhism. Despite their claims to universality, many assumed the guise of ecclesiastical religion, the Roman Catholic church becoming the state religion of France, Ireland, Italy, and Spain, among others. Indeed, the doctrine stipulating the separation between church and state that underlies the First Amendment of the U.S. Constitution is unusual in the world's nations. In industrial states, many churches have become **secular**, religions that admit the validity of science in their cosmos, and during the Soviet phase, Russia and Eastern European republics endorsed atheism as state ideology.

Denizens of the Supernatual

Cutting across the societies are gods, spirits, and ghosts, who themselves are often dichotomized as benevolent or malevolent. **Gods** refer to beings that are divine in origin, that is, not of the earth, who display human attributes. In **polytheistic religions**, they may specialize in different realms of human existence, such as the chief executive (Zeus or Jove in Greek and Roman mythology, or Siva in Hinduism), wealth (Mammon in Greek and Roman mythology or Ganesh in Hindu society), war (Ares or Mars), erotic love (Aphrodite or Venus), and metalworking (Hephaestus or Vulcan). In **monotheistic** religion, there is one God, often of a jealous sort ("Thou shalt have no gods before Me.") or vengeful (the Bible contains divinely ordained atrocities by which the Holocaust, the Rwanda genocide, or the Abu Graib incident pale in comparison), but often is said to be loving ("Praise Allah, the merciful, the compassionate"). Whatever the variations, the shared perception is that this god is omnipresent (everywhere), omniscient (all-knowing) and omnipotent (all-powerful).

The gods (or god) of morality or creation have their antithetical beings, of which Satan is a well-known example in all three universalistic religions of the West. Demons are typically antithetical to multiple gods, or perhaps the support staff of a monotheistic god, the angels. Among the Balinese, as in other religions originating in southern Asia, the demons are perceived not so much the purveyors of evil as of dissolution. To the Balinese, the task is not so much to secure the triumph of good over evil as to maintain the balance between the forces of creation versus the forces of decay. Even the demons have their place (Lansing 1983).

Other supernatural beings have their origins on earth, as deceased humans. The term **ghost** applies generically to all spirits of human origin, although many glosses refer to them as **spirits** as well. They are the objects of veneration in many societies. The Day of the Dead, held throughout Latin America at or toward the beginning of November every year, welcome their (not so) departed relatives with their favorite food, drink, and ornaments. Similarly, the Lugbara of Uganda, Africa, retain their deceased kin within their lineages, often communing with their elders no longer living (Middleton 1960; cited in Scupin 2003:222).

Often ghosts turn malevolent. Sometimes, their malevolence is the product of neglect. Among Mexican Nahuatl-speakers, departed spirits may bring misfortune on kin who do not erect shrines or make offerings on the Day of the Dead (Berdan 1982). Among the Lugbara, a son who does not offer food to his departed father later suffers sickness, as may his wife and children. "The sickness is that of the ghosts, to grow thin and to ache throughout the body; these are the sicknesses of the dead" (Middleton 1960:46, cited in Scupin 2003:222). Ill will also may arise over some issue in life that has remained unresolved.

Coexistence or No Existence: Gods and the Spirits

Even the monotheistic gods coexist with other supernatural beings in most societies, if not all. Spirits, or more local beings, also usually of nonhuman origin, are found everywhere. Even in postconquest Latin America, one finds local spirits hiding behind the names and images of saints. The Virgin of Guadalupe, the national patron saint of Mexico, has shades of a fertility goddess, Tonantzin or Coatlicue. This process of combining supernatural beliefs from two or more different belief systems is known as **syncretism**. Syncretism is becoming less and less tolerated. In Cantel, as in other parts of Guatemala and Latin America at large, *catequistas* (catechists) have espoused the standard interpretations of Christian Roman Catholicism; at the same time, the evangelical Protestants have undergone a phenomenal expansion (McDowell 1974).

Practitioners of the Supernatural

Where there are supernatural beliefs, there are practitioners. We have already mentioned **shamans**, whose role it is to make direct contact with the spirit world. Often hallucinogens may be used, such as *ebene* among the Yanomamö to contact the *hekura*, the unseen spirits of their world (Chagnon 1997). Similarly, the Jivaro use a tea known as *natema* containing alkaloids somewhat similar to the LSD (lysergic acid diethylamide) to gain access to spirit helpers, or *darts*. Some shamans sent their helpers to inflict illness on their enemies; others sent them to cure illnesses (Harner 1972; cited in Scupin 2003:220).

We have already mentioned the practitioners of **sorcery**, whose aim is to bring harm to others through ritual. Among the Navajo, for example, **sorcerers** (referred to in the source as **witches**) were thought to bring harm to others by transforming themselves into animals, eating human flesh, and grinding human flesh (especially of children) to make poison. The poison was then thrown into the houses or the persons of their enemies, which would then act to bring diseases to the victims. Antidotes were the galls of certain animals, such as bears or eagles, which were carried about to forestall these attacks. Wealthy individuals were often thought to use witchcraft for their ill-gotten gains, such as grave robbing and stealing jewelry from the dead; the wealthy could exonerate themselves only by sharing their surplus. In Clyde Kluckhohn's view, witchcraft accusation was one route to wealth redistribution or leveling (1967: cited in Scupin 2003:221).

However, one might endure witchcraft accusations without working at it. Such was the view of the Azande, whose poison oracle has already been discussed in chapter 12 in law by ordeal. Witches were thought to become witches because of an inherited bodily organ or blackish substance called *mangu*. It was said to be sex-linked; a man could inherit *mangu* from another male, a woman from another woman. Once the *benge* was administered to the chicken, the chicken dead from the concoc-

tion, and the suspect identified thereby (see chapter 12), attempts were made to correct the balance. On death, the Azande performed autopsies to determine whether witchcraft was carried in a family line (Evans-Pritchard 1940; cited in Scupin 2003:220–221)

The practitioners of organized religion, for whom the generic term **priest** applies, has a role primarily to interpret written texts: the Bible in Christianity, the Qu'ran in Islam, the Torah and the extended Talmud in Judaism. In Bali, a novice became a priest only after years of studying the sacred texts of Hinduism and the local writing of the Lantar, named after a tree of the same name, the palm leaves on which the texts were written (Lansing 1983). Often the priests became the official custodians of the religious cosmology and had official roles in the political hierarchy. They presided over state-organized rituals called **rites of legitimation**, which reinforced the divine authority of the ruler (Parrinder 1983: cited in Scupin 2003:265).

The Supernatural: Some Case Studies

We have seen some attributes of the supernatural at various levels of complexity. We have not, however, examined theologies or cosmologies of the beliefs themselves. It might be worth one's while to see just what they are. In this section, we look at some of these cosmologies: Dreamtime of the Australian Aborigines, the Azande conception of their cosmology, the so-called Three Worlds of Bali, and the beliefs of Islam.

Dreamtime

As mentioned before, the Aborigines of Australia believe in an animistic world they call **dreamtime** in their indigenous languages. The world of dreamtime existed before they were created, and it continues today. At the time of creation, the ancestors deposited souls of all living forms near waterholes—most Aborigines lived in the hot and dry interior known as the Outback—and all objects eventually acquired souls. If anything, the birth of the universe resembles a fall from the dreamtime, roughly analogous to the Fall of Man from grace in the Western religions (Stanner 1979).

The dreamtime exists today, and the ancestors continue to live in this world of spirit. They act as intermediaries between the dreamtime and the profane, everyday world of human affairs. These ancestral beings intervene in life, controlling plant, animal, and human life and death. Dreamtime is a complex system of spirits that embraces the period of creation in the past and has particular significance for the present and future. It is as if the kingdom of the dreamtime were within you—but without the kingdom.

The dreamtime, then, is a complex animistic cosmology among Aboriginal peoples. All objects, from rocks to water to animals to humans, are infused with souls that, at the creation, were "dropped" from dreamtime to the profane world. Behavior is cognizant of the moral standards of dreamtime, as if one learned from evil to live the ideal life.

Hinduism and the Balinese

Balinese religion relies heavily on the Hindu tradition that once dominated the Indonesian archipelago until the spread of Islam; the island of Bali was the last refuge for Hindus. Although it shares the broad outlines of Hinduism, the Balinese have added their own interpretation of the belief, which also contains strains of Buddhist belief.

As mentioned in the section on the caste system of India, the ideology of *karma* serves to reinforce the absolute separation of castes and the domination of the higher castes over the lower. The forces of karma operates in the belief that all existence on earth and in the cosmos is an illusion, or *samsara*. *Samsara* is the realm of life, death, and rebirth in cycles that will continue until the individual perceives that this seemingly endless process is based on an illusion and breaks through it. This discovery, this enlightenment, is known as *nirvana* or other names. It is not so much the belief in heaven as the liberation from this prisonlike samsara. Until the liberation, all beings must perform their duties in whatever plane of existence they find themselves, that is, perform their *dharma*.

Although the Balinese accept the basic tenets of Hinduism—karma, samsara, dharma, and nirvana—they offer several new twists of this basic ideology. First, they perceive the cosmos as comprising three worlds: the world of creation represented by the gods dominated by Siva, the world of decay personified by an infinite number of demons dominated by Rudra, and the world of the human plane. The cosmic task of the human race is to keep the forces of creation and destruction in a state of balance. Their numerous festivals function toward that end, and their art and literature, such as the puppet shows known as *wayang,* serve to interpret the cosmos for the people, in the understanding that no human can perceive the gods, the demons, and the forces they represent directly. Art, the dances, theater—all of these are integral to the cosmological balance between creation and destruction (Lansing 1983).

Their belief suffuses the entire society. For example, their agricultural techniques reflect the balance between creation and destruction. Irrigation of rice fields is timed according to the temple festivals. As the festival at one temple begins, the surrounding fields are flooded and remain so until the festival ends; water is then shut off and reallocated to lands whose temple is now sponsoring the next festival. During the flooding, algae is formed, contributing nitrogen to the field; later, ducks eat the algae and their droppings add to the fertility of the topsoil.

Nevertheless, the Balinese perceive that the cosmos must be renewed periodically, specifically every hundred years. Eka Desa Rudra serves to make this renewal. The entire Balinese population takes part by providing offerings, ranging from finely crafted sculptures, made from such ordinary materials as pig fat, to animal sacrifices. The rudras—demons ruled by the supreme demon Rudra—descend on the earth, and it is up to the people to transform these beings of decay into gods, the beings who represent the forces of creation. Things are reduced to their elements and recombined to make a more perfect universe. If the people, led by the priests, fail in this task, the world will come to an end (Lansing 1983).

Islam

Although stereotypically thought to be an Eastern religion—and indeed the nation containing the largest Muslim population in the world is Indonesia—Islam is as much a part of the Western tradition as Judaism and Christianity. Like the Jews and the Christians, the Muslims accept Adam, Abraham, and Moses as true prophets of God. They are monotheists—there is no God save Allah, and Muhammad is his prophet. Unlike the Balinese conception, and that of Hinduism and Buddhism generally, good and evil cannot coexist. Good ultimately must triumph over evil, and the personification of evil—Satan—will be cast into Hell, along with all other evildoers.

"Islam" comes from the Arabic and means "submission," namely to the will of God. Every true Muslim has five obligations called the Pillars of Islam. The first Pillar is to declare daily one's acceptance of God. The second is to pray five times daily, washing one's hands while going into the place of worship and bowing in the direction of Mecca, the place where Mohammad received the Suras from the Angel of Gabriel that eventually made up the Qu'ran (often spelled as the Koran), Islam's most holy book. The third Pillar is to observe the month of Ramadan, which includes abstention from food and drink from sunrise to sunset. Because the Muslim calendar consists of lunar months, Ramadan moves regularly to different times from year to year; the month may occur in summer one year and in winter seven years later. The fourth Pillar is to provide alms for the poor, especially if one is earning an income adequate for living expenses and for keeping out of debt. The fifth and final Pillar is, if financially possible, to make a pilgrimage, or *Hajj*, to the sacred city of Mecca at least once in a lifetime.

There are other well publicized rules of Islam. Consumption of drugs and alcohol is strictly forbidden. Representational art is strictly prohibited, so that most Islamic art and architecture emphasize geometrical forms rather than images, which to them is idolatry. No man may marry more than four wives. (In pre-Islamic Arab society, men typically married far more than four women.) Less well known is the history of tolerance with other religions; under Ottoman law, for example, Jewish and Christian communities were allowed to exist, although they were taxed more heavily than Islamic communities. Islamic universities made many contributions in medical science, astronomy, chemistry, and mathematics, among other scientific disciplines; Arabic numbers came from their namesakes and included the concept of zero, displacing the ponderous Roman numeral system. Indeed, one may say without exaggeration that Islamic universities preserved much of the Western culture that was jeopardized when Greece, then Rome, collapsed. In short, there is much about Islam that goes against today's stereotype of violent Muslims on a *jihad*—holy war—against Western "infidels."

Explaining the Supernatural

Studying questions of religions often inspires skepticism from a scientific standpoint. We are dealing, after all, with attributes of things and events whose very existence cannot be tested. Did the volcanic Mount Agung erupt in 1963 because the Balinese priesthood, under pressure from the then-Indonesian president Achmed Sukarno, attempted to conduct the Eka Desa Rudra ceremony before the proper time had arrived—or would Mount Agung have erupted anyway? Did the explorers who opened King Tutankhamen's tomb die because of King Tut's curse, or did they meet their demise from some locally contracted disease? What about the black sands of Hawaii, whose curse is said to bring ill fortune to those who take away a handful? These are untestable hypotheses; we cannot go back in time and see whether Mount Agung would not have erupted if the priests had shown more backbone, or the fate of Richard Carter had he not opened Tut's tomb.

Nevertheless, we can ask why religions exist or, less charitably, why people believe in all that stuff. Several explanations have been brought forth. First, we might ask what functions they serve. Are religions indeed the opiate of the people, as Karl Marx would have it? Do they serve to promote social solidarity, as the sociologist Emile Durkheim would argue? Several such explanations have surfaced in recent years. Second, one might ask an epistemological question: Do religions fill in the conceptual gaps left behind by science, however defined and however unsophisticated or sophisticated? Do they explain the universe in areas that science cannot, whether the scientist is a thoughtful Azande tribesman or a philosopher of science at Harvard or Oxford? Third, and as a theme and variation of Marx's opiate theory, do supernatural cosmologies offer comfort to those uncertain as to what death is like and what the afterlife holds for them, if any?

First, religion fills in the gaps of knowledge. It serves to connect what is known and knowable to that which is unknown and unknowable. The Azande interpretation of witchcraft connects the known "how questions"—how cattle die off from the rindepest, how a beer hut burns down—with the unknown "why questions"—why a specific family lost its cattle, why *that* particular man's hut burned down—which the less empirical witchcraft explanation fills. Origin myths fill the void that conception explanations can never fill; the subjective events after death are filled with explanations of karma or visions of heaven and hell or visions of a future dreamtime.

Second, because of the uncertainty of knowledge beyond the five senses and their extension, some individuals or social groups manipulate others into the acceptance of behavior that the individual or social group desires. A case in point is the behavior of Quasalid, a Kwakiutl shaman who as an apprentice observed trickery among his mentors. For example, when treating a patient, they put a piece of down in their mouths before performing the ritual to exorcise the disease-causing object, then toward the end, bled in the mouth by biting the tongue. They extracted the bloody down at a crucial moment to "prove" they had extracted the harmful object. This ensured that the "patients" would come back and spread the shaman's efficacy by word of mouth.

A theme and variation of this manipulation is commonplace in complex societies. There, the power elite use religion to justify their position of power, as we have seen in chapter 13 dealing with **legitimation**: the divine right to rule among European monarchs, the notions of *karma* in India, the semidivine justification of a master race in Nazi Germany. This is what Marx alluded to when he called religion "the opiate of the masses"; promises of a better afterlife contribute to the quiescence of the masses of the injustices in the here and now.

Third, religion, partly because of the unknowability of the supernatural, serves to reinforce the notions of right versus wrong. We have already seen for the Australian Aborigines that the dreamtime models acceptable behavior. Among the Yanomamö, there are supernatural punishments for stinginess, and, among the Maori, individuals risk harm from the *hau* that accompany a gift until it is repaid (Mauss 1925). All the major religions prescribe moral behavior, and are remarkably parallel. Theft, murder, adultery, and bearing false witness are all proscribed. Indeed, even in a polity—the United States—that does not recognize an established religion, witnesses and public officials routinely swear on a Christian Bible.

Fourth, religion serves to maintain social solidarity. Emile Durkheim, in his *Elementary Forms of the Religious Life*, divides society into the sacred and the profane (his term for the ordinary or mundane). It is the sacred that reinforces the commitment of members to society (1995). The sacred may be outside the religious; the American flag is one sacred object and is not to be desecrated in U.S. society. Another sacred object was the Golden Stool, the seat of government (literally and symbolically) of the monarch of the Ashanti of West Africa. It was (and remains) so sacred that no one has ever sat on it and it has never touched the ground. When, after conquering the Ashanti in 1873, the British commander sat on the Golden Stool, the outraged Ashanti launched an unusually brutal revolt, killing every British soldier on sight and decapitating many. It took three years to suppress the revolt (Schildkraut and Gelber 1987).

Fifth, the supernatural is found where there is fear and insecurity. One adage puts it that "there are no atheists in a foxhole"; where there is war, there are appeals to the deity. Malinowski finds that, for the Trobriand Islands, all magic is focused on the construction and launching of seagoing canoes rather than the small craft that ply the shallow lagoons in the atolls and adjacent islands. The reason is not hard to fathom. The open seas are fraught with dangers; storms could capsize the canoe, there are real sharks and imagined monsters that devour the seafarer, and there is no guarantee that, upon arrival, the trading partners will be as friendly as originally thought. Magic applies to all these situations (Malinowski 1922). Closer to the present, Drury argues that the Project for a New American Century includes fear appeals and propagation of religion (which the designers do not believe in themselves) in its strategies of control (Drury 1999).

Revitalization Movements

Over the past five centuries, Western countries and their powers elite—Western Europe, the United States, and for a time imperial Japan—have expanded their economic and political influence over the rest of the world. Changes have generated widespread insecurity among non-Western peoples over widespread regions, generating among other things **revitalization movements**. Such movements occur during times of extreme change, in which religious leaders emerge to bring forth change, positive or negative. One may consider the definition offered by Anthony F. C. Wallace, who defined the term as "deliberate and organized attempts by some members of a society to construct a more satisfying culture through rapid acceptance of a pattern of multiple innovations" (1970: cited in Harris and Johnson 2003:255)

According to Wallace, most revitalization movements follow a more or less regular pattern of five phases.

1. A society is in a state equilibrium.
2. A society is pushed out of equilibrium by various forces, such as a climatic or biotic (biological environmental) change, epidemic disease, war and conquest, economic restructuring, and other factors.
3. The society undergoes disorganization and its members disillusionment that accepted norms no longer function.
4. Social deterioration sets the stage for a revitalization movement to bring about a society more satisfying to its constituents.
5. An individual or group constructs a new, idealistic model of culture that forms the basis of social action. If the movement is successful, the society reaches a new steady state (Wallace 1970).

Examples abound during the late 1880s and 1890s, the Paiute Indians of the Nevada Basin began a movement, the **Ghost Dance**, sparked by a charismatic leader known as Wovoka, which spread into the plains. Wovoka and his followers envisioned a day in which all the ancestors would return to life and bring about a life of plenty. The Lakota (Sioux) reinterpreted this vision and initiated a version of the Ghost Dance that included the return of the bison and the extermination of whites under a massive landslide. Although the followers believed these events would emerge on their own, they confined their activities to leading pure lives and refraining from violence. Nevertheless, settlers, fearing an uprising, called for preemptive action. The U.S. Army captured and assassinated Sitting Bull, one of the Lakota leaders and legendary warrior-chief, then massacred 200 members of the Lakota, mostly women and children, at Wounded Knee, South Dakota, on December 29, 1890 (Mooney 1965; cited in Harris and Johnson 2003). Although the Ghost Dance itself was effectively ended, the revitalization movement became more introspective and passive. Other movements developed. The Native American Church is one, emphasizing visions through peyote use, singing, and ecstatic contemplation, followed by a communal breakfast. They do not envision the return of the buffalo or extermination of whites (Stewart 1987; cited in Harris and Johnson 2003:279). More recently, a Red Power movement has emerged, with a second confrontation at Wounded Knee and using activists, lawyers, novelists, and tactics to

maintain and regain their stolen lands (Deloria 1969). In various guises, the revitalization movement sparked by the Ghost Dance has persisted to the present.

Another set of revitalization movements are a variety of **cargo cults** throughout Melanesia and parts of New Guinea. Initially generated by the presence of U.S. troops during World War II, with their reputed generosity and hiring of Melanesians in important jobs, Melanesians typically hope for the return of their ancestors aboard ships or aircraft bearing similar gifts and amenities. Some of the movements stressed the return of the Americans. In one cargo cult, the John Frum movement on the Island of Tana in the New Hebrides (now Vanuatu), the followers worshipped an old GI jacket as the relic of a John Frum, whose identity is otherwise unknown. They built landing strips, bamboo control towers, and grass thatch cargo sheds; in some instances, they kept beacons ablaze at night, and "radio operators" waited with tin-can microphones in hand to guide the planes to safe landing. Explanations by British and Australian colonists failed to convince the Melanesians that such wealth could come only with hard work—the colonists were wealthy and they weren't working. As Harris and Johnson put it, "In one sense, the natives were entitled to the products of the industrialized nations, even though they couldn't pay for it. The cargo cult was their way of saying this." The John Frum movement persists to this day (Worsley 1968; Burridge 1995; Trompf 1991).

Nor are Westerners free of their own revitalization movements. Jim Jones and his followers developed and maintained an intentional community called Jonestown in Guyana; in 1978, under pressure of congressional investigation, the 800 followers committed mass suicide by drinking grape Kool-Aid laced with cyanide. A similar millenarian community, Heaven's Gate, ended in suicide in San Diego, California, more than two decades later. The Branch Dravidians, under a leader self-named David Koresh, formed a community in Waco, Texas, that, in 1994, was destroyed by fire after a two-month siege from the FBI and other federal agencies; the circumstances of that incident are still unclear. Some revitalization movements have arrived at Wallace's "new steady state"; thus the Church of the Latter Day Saints, initially expelled from several towns in its history, finally settled at the present site of Salt Lake City, Utah, and has since become one of the major established churches in the United States. Its rejection of an earlier practice of polygyny no doubt has helped.

Conclusion

In this chapter, we have examined a dimension that many cultures do not recognize as separate from the everyday reality we see around us. Supernatural phenomena (sometimes known as **noumena**, or things and events said to occur beyond the five senses and their extensions) are as routine in daily living among some cultures as eating or sleeping is anywhere. In a sense, this may reflect a culture-bound bias of our own. We cannot empirically test for ghosts, mana, gods (one or many), spirits, sor-

cery, or witchcraft; these are outside the ken of science. Yet because we cannot test for these things and events, how do we know they are not there? We cannot test for emotions (love, hate, anger) except through behavior; these qualities are intangible. At one time, it was thought that the sun went around the earth or the earth was flat, showing in both instances that our ordinary perceptions of these phenomena are wrong.

As these considerations show, there is much about this world to be learned. That all cultures recognize the supernatural demonstrates how much there is to know—perhaps much more than we do know. Even what we know is uncertain. Who would guess from unaided observation that a gold ring is made up of atoms?

Chapter 16

GLOBALIZATION, SOCIOCULTURAL CHANGE, AND APPLIED ANTHROPOLOGY

Introduction

Received wisdom has it that anthropologists have a public responsibility toward the people they study, and that one way to fulfill that responsibility is through applied anthropology. To do so, scholars in the field must know something about culture change. Traditionally, the anthropological focus has been on change at the personal, perhaps family, and usually at the local levels. And change is nothing new. As the English novelist and satirist Jonathan Swift put it, "There is nothing in this world constant but inconstancy." Put in the modern vernacular, the only constant is change.

Nevertheless, the anthropological focus has all too often excluded the extralocal sources of change. Medical science, for example, has facilitated the reduction of disease. The reduction of disease, however, has led to population increases beyond the capacity of land to support this increase. There has also been a distribution problem, and the larger economies have led to an extremely unequal distribution of wealth, whether in land or capital. Corporate globalization has exacerbated this maldistribution. Unequal terms of trade, whereby less developed countries (LDCs) are unable to import their manufactured wares to more developed countries (MDC), add to the equation of inequality, not only locally or nationally, but at a worldwide scale.

These commonplaces reveal the fallacies underlying many studies of culture change and applied anthropology. In an effort to "help" a "target" or "client" culture, policymakers and implementers of technical and social programs, however well intended, all too often make things worse. Technology bears a price. To be sure, tractors and fertilizer increase crops astronomically, but their costs are equally astronomical. Cash crops that initially yielded large monetary returns fail to do so when the market collapses.

Perhaps the time has come that anthropologists take some of their own advice and apply the holistic principle to integrative levels beyond the band, tribe, or village to ever wider sociopolitical entities. What forces Yanomamö villagers off their plots or Guatemalan peasants off their lands originates well beyond their communities—in the boardrooms of New York and London and the powers residing in Washington, London, and Paris—not to mention Tokyo.

In light of these developments, this chapter first surveys the landscape of changes occurring worldwide. They include the spread of corporate domination throughout the world, the militaristic means for reinforcing this domination, and the hazards of resource depletion and environmental pollution that have accompanied this spread. These developments have occurred for centuries, so the chapter goes on to outline their effects: extermination of many of the world's peoples, the enslavement of others, and, more recently, the peasantization and proletarianization of the remainder. Theories of sociocultural change are advanced and given critical review, and principles of applied anthropology are evaluated in light of global domination and ecological decline.

Globalization and Its Discontents

Once considered a paranoiac construct among Leftist scholars and ideologues, globalization is now acknowledged across the political spectrum and among the power elite and non-elite alike. Few events can be understood without taking the entire global entity into account. Therefore, the structure and function of a **global level of integration** must be understood, no less than the earlier levels of integration of the band, tribe, chiefdom, and state. Their positive and negative influences need to be considered: productivity and distribution capacities induced by unprecedented levels of manufacturing, transportation, and communication technology, coupled with the prodigious consumption of energy, mostly petroleum-derived, that threaten the globe both with resource depletion and environmental collapse.

Global Level of Integration

The motor of the global level of integration is the **global system of production**. In chapter 11, we noted that one of the markers of the **capitalist mode of production** is the breakdown in the division of labor to **detail labor**, whereby the tasks of production are analyzed to their constituent parts, then assigned to individual workers (Braverman 1974). With the transformation of transportation (thanks to container vessels capable of shipping large cargos never before dreamt possible) and communication (whereby you can, with your computer, access any website anywhere in seconds), labor tasks can be shipped worldwide.

Perhaps you experience this fact in your daily life. The labels indicate your pants are made in Pakistan, and your shirt or blouse in Hong Kong; your car is assembled in Mexico. You lost your job ten years ago when the company sent it down to Mexico along with 6,000 other jobs; then you found out in today's newspapers that the same jobs were re-sent to China, probably at some prison labor camp. You think about improving your skills, only to find that another company will send its high-tech jobs to India, for people who took exactly the same training you were contemplating. Enjoy your hamburger-flipping job at McDonald's—if you have one. There is always the National Guard, and you might get to enjoy the warmer climes of Iraq. (Ever wonder why Jessica Lynch joined the army? She couldn't be hired at Wal-Mart.)

Transnational Corporations.   The driving engine of the global mode of production is a longstanding institution known as the **corporation**. Under commercial law, the corporation is defined as a legal person, with limited liability. This means that the corporation may be sued for its assets held in its name, but not for the personal assets of the members—corporate executives, its staff, and its shareholders. This stipulation limits its accountability to the public. Thus, if the U.S. and Indian courts ever do hold Dow Chemical responsible for its now-subsidiary Union Carbide's failure to prevent the Bhopal, India, disaster in 1984, whose gas leak killed 4,000 people and maimed thousands more, the liability will only extend to the company's assets, not the personal assets of the executives and the stockholders.

Freed from public accountability of the executives and stockholders, corporations have progressed from competitive to monopolistic enterprises. The number of U.S. automobile manufacturers decreased from 35 in the early 1900s to three by the 1950s, and the same pattern persists in other industries (Scupin 2003:280). At the same time, corporations have become international in scope. Although **multinational corporations** (corporations with operations in two or more nation states) have existed at least since the 1600s—the British East India Company, for example—they have increased in scope and efficiency during the past century. **Transnational corporations**, or multinational corporations with highly integrated operations across the nations, have become the norm.

At the base of all industrial power is the need for high-energy sources, of which fossil fuels, namely coal, natural gas, and principally oil, are the only reliable and relatively safe (that is, compared to nuclear power) sources. As Savinar (2004) points out, "almost every current human endeavor—from transportation to manufacturing to electricity to plastics and especially food and water production—is inextricably intertwined with natural and natural gas supplies (2004:5). The culture of consumption demands ever-increasing inputs of fossil fuels, forcing the United States to become ever more dependent on foreign sources (Bodley 2001:85; National Research Council 1975). Somehow, these sources need to be protected.

Military Reinforcement: A System of Bases
These operations do not lack institutional support. It is no surprise that many transnational corporations base their headquarters in the United States, and that the U.S. government backs the corporations with military force. In his book *The Sorrows of Empire*, Chalmers Johnson shows that U.S. bases span the globe from Latin America to East Asia to the former Soviet republics such as Uzbekistan; ignoring the secret figures for espionage operations, the number of U.S. military personnel abroad totals 474,312 (2004:155,161). Among the aims of this worldwide system of bases is the protection of oil sources (2004:152).

Economic and Legal Mechanisms.   Nevertheless, as the continuing hit-and-run attacks in Afghanistan and Iraq demonstrate, an overwhelming military force is no guarantee that the occupied country will behave itself. As pointed out in chapters 12 and 13, there must be some patina of legitimacy to any relations of power. The most effective means of legitimacy rests in economics and law. The economic argument concerns the "trickle-down effect," whereby everyone benefits from economic expansion around the globe. The legal arguments concern the need for order in an otherwise chaotic world.

There are two phases of this control. The first is **mercantilism**, dominant in the 16th to 18th centuries. This is the direct administrative control over the economy of another state. When administrative costs rose and countries sought independence, the second means of control, **imperialism**, or the domination of one country over another by economic means, took its place. A combination of foreign investment and unfavorable terms of trade—low tariff barriers for raw materials, high tariff barriers for finished products—took its place (Stavrianos 1974). Attempts by LDCs to regain control over their own resources led to coups d'etats, usually supported from the MDC. The his-

tory of Iran's attempt to control its oil under Mossadegh, only to be aborted in a CIA coup, illustrates the point (Kinzer 2003). Guatemala affords a similar illustration (Immerman 1986).

Since then, the reins of domination have become tighter. First, transnational corporations have outsourced their operations in their home countries to **maquiladoras** (sometimes called **maquilas**), which are branch plants that form a transnational production system, from processing raw materials to manufacturing finished products. The fear of job loss tightens the power of transnational corporations over LDCs. As Naomi Klein observes for a settlement of 200 maquiladoras in Cavite, home of an export-processing zone 90 miles south of Manila, the Philippines, "fear pervades the zones. The governments are afraid of losing their foreign factories, the factories are afraid of losing their brand-name buyers, and the workers are afraid of losing their unstable jobs" (2000). Like swallows, as maquiladora jobs are called in Guatemala, jobs can fly away at any time (2000:206). As this example illustrates, the LDCs do not benefit from outsourcing.

Second, countries in debt have been forced to surrender the right to manage their own affairs. Through institutions such as the World Bank (formally known as the International Bank for Reconstruction and Development), the International Monetary Fund, and the World Trade Organization, LDCs are compelled to accept loans on the condition that they privatize public services, limit or eliminate social programs, and accept services and manufactures only from developed countries. Nor is that all: the Trade-Related Intellectual Property Rights Agreement (TRIPS), which was designed to prevent underdeveloped countries from copying or stealing proprietary technology, also claims proprietary rights over the LDC's natural resources. Even rainwater may not be collected in areas where water is sold, as was the case in Cochabamba, Bolivia, before a revolt in 2000 forced a consortium controlled by Bechtel, the beneficiary of water privatization there, out of the city (Olivera and Lewis 2004).

Environmental Consequences of Globalism

In the meantime, there are severe environmental consequences of the globalization process, particularly through the global economy's heavy dependence on oil. Alternative energy sources have been attempted, but they are either too dangerous (nuclear energy, particularly with the long half-live of the primary elements uranium and plutonium), or too unworkable or unreliable (wind and solar energy). Consequently, we rely on oil, both a dangerous pollutant primarily responsible for global warming and a nonrenewable source whose depletion is likely to come sooner or later (see Heinberg 2003).

Environmental Pollution.   Oil, together with its products, is one of the principal pollutants of the world's atmosphere. For one thing, automobile and factory emissions, along with the burning of tropical rainforests and methane gas emissions, are creating an overload of carbon dioxide. According to this model, after the solar rays enter the atmosphere, the carbon dioxide traps the heat and prevents it from going back into the atmosphere. The average temperature in the globe increases, and the secular (long-term) trend is toward the melting of long-standing glaciers and ice caps. Evidence of such warming has accumulated over anecdotal accounts of migratory birds remaining in the north longer than usual, longer growing seasons in Alaska and northern Canada, the loss of glaciers in Greenland, and the inability of arctic ice to support Inuit hunters and their dog sleds. The thinning of the ozone layer exacerbates the warming trend (Bodley 2001).

Furthermore the world population has grown exponentially over the past century. From about 10 million people toward the end of the Paleolithic period, the world's population grew to 300 million in the Neolithic period. By 1850, a hundred years after the start of the industrial revolution, the world population was one billion. Since then, the world population has increased to 6 billion as of the year 2000, and is expected to reach 10.5 billion by 2050 (Hassan 1981; Scupin 2003:426–427). China's one-child policy has slowed the rate of population growth but has not reversed it, and has created new demographic problems, such as the unbalanced sex ratio in favor of males (World Population Sheet 1991; Evans 2001; Scupin 2003:428–429).

Peak Oil.   Finally, a new problem may provide a partial solution to environmental air pollution, but has the potential of inducing die-offs in a world overdependent on oil; this resource is likely to be depleted before long. **Peak oil** refers to the point in the cycle of oil production and use where oil ceases to be cheap and plentiful and begins to be more expensive and scarce. Peak Oil is now expected to occur, depending on scenario, between 2000 and 2010. (Heinberg 2003; Savinar 2004).

China and India: The End of Unipolarity?

Recent developments suggest that other countries, especially China and India, may challenge U.S. global hegemony. In recent years, China and India have emerged as developing countries in the true sense of the term. Both are developing diversified economies, with factories proliferating in Beijing, Shanghai, and Guangdong in China, and Mumbai (formerly Bombay) and Mysore in India. Outsourcing of high-technology operations has benefited at least these two countries.

One result has been the increased demand for oil in both countries. China consumes 6.5 million barrels of oil per day, a figure expected to double by 2020, and it is now the world's largest oil importer after the United States. India consumes 2.2 million barrels per day, with expectations for the figure to rise to 5.3 million barrels daily by 2025 (Pocha 2005:20). To meet the demands, China and India have had to emulate the United States in acquiring foreign oil, and they are both competing with the United States to secure oil exploration rights in Africa, Southeast Asia, Central Asia, and Latin America (Pocha 2005:20–21).

The rising power of Asian countries, including China and India, was recognized as early as 1995. According to Andre Gunder Frank in his book *ReOrient*, Asia outstripped the European power in economic and military strength until the so-called Age of Discovery, and may come to enjoy hegemonic status again. As of 1995, for example, the U.S. balance of trade was $395 billion, whereas China's balance of trade was $17.5 billion and Japan's stood at $128 billion (Frank 1998). This unfavorable balance of trade has increased, and today the United States is indebted to both China and Japan. Despite its military power, the U.S. status as an economic powerhouse is being compromised.

Nevertheless, U.S.-based corporations are attempting to get in on the action. Both countries have invited foreign investors to their oil industries. ExxonMobil, for example, already owns 19 percent of the Sinopec company, one of the largest operations in China, and is helping the company to construct 500 gas stations across the country and build two refineries in the southern region (Pocha 2005:21). This question remains ambiguous, and may require new models specifying the independence of transnational corporations from the United States.

Globalization: Local and Regional Effects

These are examples of global trends that neither anthropologists nor other microlevel social scientists can ignore. The remainder of this chapter examines theories of social change, their limits, and implications for the underdevelopment of "developing" countries and the formerly preindustrial societies that compose them.

Economic and political globalization goes back to many centuries, perhaps millennia (Frank and Gills 1993). Since the creation of state-level societies, nation-states or empires have always vied for dominance within a region and always with the aim of extracting resources and precious minerals—gold, silver, gemstones—from the vanquished. Only with the commodification of land, resources, and labor has globalization assumed its modern guise. The impact has varied with history, but the non-elite population—the subjects of most anthropological studies—have felt the impact of globalization in four basic ways.

The first is **extermination**. Entire tribes were extinguished as the North American settlers moved westward from the Atlantic seaboard. Even before western expansion, the Beothuk of Newfoundland were wiped out entirely. The Tasmanians of Australia suffered a similar fate from the hands of the migrants from Britain (many of them resettled convicts). Others were nearly exterminated, but survived. Today, the United States, Canada, Australia, and New Zealand are occupied by settlers who had the illusion that they were occupying "empty space," space that had sustained large populations before they were killed off either by settlers or disease (Scupin 2003:306, 332–333, 406).

The second major change is **slavery**, principally of the peoples from the African continent. Some were captured directly, first by Arabs, then the Portuguese and Spaniards, then by the British and to a lesser extent by the French. Most were the products of warfare between the states of West

Africa, the conquering nations enslaving those of the vanquished and selling them off to the traders who plied the African coast. Although most slaves came from West Africa, no small number of East Africans were also taken by Arab traders (Scupin 2003:333–334). Davidson points out the difference: Arab traders allowed their slaves rights, including maintaining their extended families; European traders treated slaves as property, with no more rights than cattle (1988).

The third major change is **peasantization** (sometimes called *de-agrarianization*), or the forced integration of formerly independent cultivators, herders, or foragers into a state policy (Bryceson 1996). The classic example of this process was the monetization of the Tiv in Nigeria, an experience duplicated in other cultures and other continents (Bohannan 1971:132).

The Yanomamö, long accustomed to using machetes, now find themselves having to work for the nearby Salesian mission to obtain them (Chagnon 1997). In so doing, they became more dependent on missions; they were trained in new agricultural techniques (which involve fertilizer and equipment obtainable only from outside), and so became ever more tightly integrated into the national and world economy (Chagnon 1997: 243–250; Hurtado et al. 2000).

The fourth trend is **proletarianizaton**, in which cultivators (or herdsmen or foragers) lose their land entirely. An early example are the Enclosures, which Moselle describes for southern England in the early 19th century (1995). Most contemporary peasants (see chapter 13 for a definition) throughout the world, however, are finding themselves deeper in debt, dependent on ever-shrinking plots of land, facing ever-increasing population density and, in the end, losing land or other strategic assets through foreclosure. Lacking land and employment opportunities, most former peasants are forced to migrate to places offering greater opportunity, which are mainly in cities and larger towns. Hence the widespread phenomenon of **rural-to-urban migration**. Breen presents a modern-day example of the process brought about by the Internet (2005).

From Peasant to Proletarian: The Case of Guatemalan Mayan

Guatemala represents a case study of the underdevelopment process. Colonized in the 16th century,

Guatemala began as a backwater country. Unable to find gold in Central America, the Spaniards soon lost interest. For 400 years, the country consisted of regions dominated by haciendas with a labor reserve of Indians. Then in 1871, the Liberals came to power, discovered coffee and bananas, and soon became a test case for economic imperialism. Everything MDCs could do to LDCs, they did do to Guatemala. This section traces the sequence of cultures arising from this history.

Colonization and Colonialism

Before Pedro de Alvarado and his troops of Spaniards and Tlaxcalans defeated the Quiché emperor Tecun Uman on the Plains of Xelajú (now Quezaltenango), the highlands were dominated by warring city states with no fewer than 22 languages. Organized into patrilineal clans, they lived in more or less scattered hamlets. Conquest was not unknown to them; in C.E. 927, Toltecs had invaded the Mayan region, constructed Chichén Itzá's Toltec monuments, and exacted tribute until the Mayan collapse around C.E. 1200. The Spaniards were not the first conquistadores.

Their impact, however, was thoroughgoing. Hamlets were consolidated into towns laid out in the Spanish grid with a central plaza, and Indians, by force or persuasion, were herded into them. Lacking administrative manpower, the Spaniards set up a town hall to be run by the Mayan elite, known in the Spanish/Nahuatl gloss as *caciques* (chiefs), while the friars set up a religious apparatus also comprising Indians and a church to match. Towns were exacted quotas of tribute and labor, and it was up to the Indian elite to mobilize both. *Alguacils*, police combined with messenger boys, gathered up both men and goods to meet their quota. The Spaniards also appropriated the land, but deeded a square league of terrain to each new town (Jones 1940; Carmack 1995).

By the 1600s, the Spaniards realized that Central America was no El Dorado, and took most of their administrators and churchmen to the more lucrative gold and silver mining regions in Mexico and Peru. Perennially understaffed, the captaincy of Guatemala made fewer visits to the rural districts, and the Native population appropriated the town hall and church for their own uses (Carmack 1995).

One outcome was the emergence of community structures consistent with Wolf's description of **closed corporate peasant communities**. As corporate entities, the communities' estate was in the form of land, held by the community, but let out to their constituent townspeople at a low rate. Land could neither be bought nor sold. Among the obligations was to serve in a **cargo**, which in Spanish means both office and burden, for a year without pay, and often attended by expenditures from the holder's own pocket. There were fiestas to sponsor, new clothes to purchase for the saints, food and drink to provide, and bands to rent. By the end of the year, the office holder would be poor in resources but, at least, rich in prestige (Cancian 1965; McDowell 1977; Wolf 1957, 1959).

The community was closed as well; rules of village endogamy were strict, clothing styles marked one community off from another, and even linguistic nuances betrayed the speaker as being from Almolonga or Cantel or Zunil or any of hundreds of other communities across the country. Regional markets, as described in chapter 11, dotted the countryside. A conservative elite emerged, and except for trade in cacao, then red and blue dyes, the country remained relatively isolated from the outside world. The communities formed an army of reserve labor for the haciendas (Jones 1940; Woodward 1999; McDowell 1994).

Liberal Reforms

All this changed in the years beginning in 1871. Consistent with the pattern elsewhere in Latin America (Burns 1980), the Liberals under Justo Rufino Barrios ousted the Conservatives under the half-Indian Rafael Carrera, and embarked on land and labor policies that destroyed some Indian communities and compromised others. First, he introduced coffee as a cash crop; of all others he tried, this was the only one that proved lucrative (Woodward 1999). Because coffee requires extensive amounts of land, Barrios abolished communal ownership of land and deeded it to anyone who filed a claim for the now-declared "vacant" tracts. Communities in lands ideal for coffee were invaded and transformed into plantations. Even lands unsuitable for coffee were taken over by speculators. Forced labor was also instituted, restoring the quota system the Spaniards had instituted shortly after the Conquest. Although the quota system was abolished by the turn of the century, other systems of forced labor took their place: the growing system of debt peonage followed by the vagrancy laws of 1931, which required all able-bodied men to work. Bananas joined coffee as the country's leading cash crops, and infrastructure—roads, railroads, telecommunication systems (Jones 1940; McDowell 1994).

Although a ten-year reformist hiatus interrupted this trend toward a commerce-driven country, Conservative forces aided by the U.S. Central Intelligence Agency overthrew the reformist Arbenz government in 1954 and established a series of largely military-led or controlled regimes. Disparities of land ownership grew apace, death squads suppressed every movement from labor to peasant to cooperatives, and even social program directors might receive such messages as "Don't worry about your funeral; it's all paid for, down to the flowers" (Jonas 1974; Carmack 1976). A civil war ensued, with leftist guerrillas assassinating plantation owners and the National Police and army repaying with massacres in village after village (Carmack 1988; Manz 1987). Although a truce in 1996 stopped or lessened this carnage, Guatemalans still refuse to talk about those years of violence (Wilkinson 2002).

To the Neoliberal Present

Today, maquiladoras dominate the country. Several South Korean textile factories have set up shop in Guatemala City, and farms specializing in cauliflower and snow peas are growing around the province of Chimaltenango. Rural-to-urban migration remains the norm. It may seem paradoxical, but Guatemala came into the neoliberal project late; the reluctance of investors to enter is linked to the violence in the country (Petersen 1992; Chase-Dunn et al. 2001).

Theories of Socioeconomic Development

One occupational hazard of anthropology is its **localocentrism**, the tendency in anthropology and other social science disciplines to explain cultural change primarily with local rather than external variables. We focus on three general theories of change—a stage theory of development, psychological factors, and culture contact through diffusion—to illustrate.

Stage Theory of Economic Growth

One theory posits a fivefold stage theory of economic development from the traditional to the age of high mass consumption. In his *The Stages of Growth: A Non-Communist Manifesto*, Walt Whitman Rostow argues that economic development can occur in cultures if certain preconditions are met. At the *traditional stage*, the economy of a society cannot grow because persistent traditional attitudes prevent it; traditionalism places great emphasis on family and community relationships, inhibiting individual initiative and enterprise. At the stage labeled *preconditions for take-off*, the society has undergone culture and value changes that permit individuals to take initiative, and entrepreneurs emerge to take on the necessary risks for economic progress. At the *take-off stage*, the rates of investment and savings increase and provide the context for the development of industrial-capitalist society. At the *drive to (economic) maturity stage*, the members of the society intensify economic progress, mass education is implemented to promote advanced skills and modern attitudes, and the "march of compound interest" begins. Finally, at the *age of high mass consumption*, society attains a high standard of living, characterized by mass production and consumption (1991).

This model pays scant attention to the varieties of "traditional" societies and argues a dichotomy (separated by a continuum) between traditional and modern economies. It also fails to examine the structural barriers that LDCs face, namely the tariff barriers in MDCs that shut off any market for products any industry might develop.

Need for Achievement

In the psychological realm, David McClelland in *The Achieving Society* (1961) develops a concept called *need for achievement* (abbreviated *n-ach*) to explain development; the term refers not so much to the desire for more material goods as to an intrinsic need for satisfaction in achieving success in some enterprise. In his view, populations with high *n-ach* are more likely to benefit from development programs than those with low *n-ach*.

The problem, then, is to develop indicators that measure this quality. Some of the more interesting indicators are folk tales that exhibit this need. One example come from Turkey, and may be familiar to mathematics and computer science students: A boy walks into a grocery store and offers to work for the storeowner for one cent the first day, two cents the second day, four cents the third day, and so on, doubling the previous figure every day. Clearly mathematically challenged, the storekeeper accepts his offer. By the end of the month, the boy owns the store and the grocer works for *him*. In this scenario, the boy clearly shows a willingness to take risks—start by working for low wages—with the aim of realizing large gains for his initiative. Communities with high *n*-ach members are likely to succeed in any development project that is implemented there (McClelland 1961)

McClelland's model betrays a reductionist fallacy. Will a nation advance because the sum total of its villages comprises mostly high *n*-ach individuals? Will they be able to surmount barriers preventing their products from entering MDCs because of high tariffs? Can one realistically expect that the high-achieving citizens of the LDC can surmount the debt burden and redirect the country's surplus to reinvestment—if there is any surplus, that is? The localocentric orientation of the psychologists, like those of sociologists and economists, fail to appreciate the global structural barriers to LDC development, as described above. Furthermore, few would accuse indigenous peasants of Guatemala or Peru of lacking a need to achieve, yet in the absence of economic opportunities, material improvements have not been forthcoming.

Diffusion of Innovation

One of the explanations of change for which anthropologists are most noted is **diffusion**, or the spread of culture traits from one society to another. Often the advantages of the new trait are evident: fertilizer that yields greater crops, powered hand plows that turn the soil faster than do hoes or foot plows, medication that cures dysentery or diarrhea—the list goes on. The **demonstration effect** refers to the desire by the client or target group to accept an innovation whose advantages are obvious, or at least apparent—apparent because the costs of obtaining the fertilizer, powered plow, or medication are not evident until later. Your foot plow or hoe may take longer to turn the soil, but at least you do not have to pay for the gas.

Even without these hidden costs, the evident advantage of an innovation is no guarantee of acceptance. For example, in the village of Tzintzuntzan, the team of anthropologists and government agents who tried to found a potters' cooperative ran into considerable resistance. Few were willing to take the risk of producing their wares for marketing in Guadalajara and Mexico City. George Foster, the lead anthropologist in this project, examined the barriers to change behind this resist-

ance. The first barrier he conceptualized as the **image of limited good**. This refers to the peasants' perception that all desirable things or qualities exist in fixed quantities. Commitment of one's resources in one undertaking reduces their amount for another undertaking. This zero-sum perception pervades other aspects of Tzintzuntzeño life, Foster found. If a woman grows her hair too long, he reports, little energy is left to maintain the rest of her body and she becomes sickly. Therefore, it would be a hard sell to convince potters that they would earn more if they marketed their wares in cities (1987).

Another barrier to change, Foster (1967) argues, is the **dyadic contract**. Almost all agreements among Tzintzuntzeños involve two persons, and only two persons. If a man makes a deal with another, it does not imply that his wife is involved. If he defaults, his wife is not liable for her husband's failure to keep his end of the bargain. It is because of just such contingencies that Tzintzuntzeños are not prepared to join multistranded arrangements such as a cooperative. Distrust is pervasive; why join an organization whose treasurer might abscond with the funds?

Dependency and World-Systems Theory

Growing numbers of social scientists are perceiving the limits of localocentric change models and are drawing upon more macrolovel models. One such school of thought is **dependency theory**, originated by the economist Andre Gunder Frank. According to Frank, underdevelopment is an active process; countries (the LDCs) are poor because richer countries (the MDCs) exploit their cheap labor and raw materials. So long as an LDC cannot use its own resources to develop, its underdevelopment will deepen. Debt exacerbates the process because (as shown above) much of the country has to pay at least the interest, leaving less to pursue development projects or other public ends (Frank 1965, 1972). Here, Foster's "image" of limited good becomes the *reality* of limited good.

Critics of this thesis point out that some former LDCs have made rapid gains in recent years; the so-called Asian Tigers come to mind—Thailand, Hong Kong, Taiwan, and South Korea. Known as **newly industrialized countries**, they all have developed a sophisticated industrial and financial industrial infrastructure, even while trading with the United States and other MDCs. South Korea even has its own automobile industry. Other critics argue that internal problems have kept LDC underdeveloped, such as political unrest, overpopulation, and excessive centralized economic control (Scupin 2003:304–305).

A related model is world-systems analysis. First presented in *The Modern World-System* by Immanuel Wallerstein in 1974, the model presents a threefold typology of nations: **core countries**, with industrial, highly diversified economies that exercise economic and political domination over other countries; **peripheral countries**, whose resources are dominated by core countries and that lack little control over their own economies; and **semiperipheral countries**, which are industrialized to some degree and sometimes act as intermediaries between MDCs and LDCs. Wallerstein contends that under specific historical circumstances, LDCs can develop economically: the Asian Tigers are examples (1974, 1980). The main criticisms of this approach center around its overreliance on economic factors as opposed to political, religious, and other cultural factors in explaining both development and underdevelopment (Shannon 1980; Scupin 2003:305–306).

Applied Anthropology

One of the major disciplines in anthropology is **applied anthropology**. This refers to the use of anthropological findings to solve practical problems affecting the health, education, security, and prosperity of human populations in diverse cultural settings (Harris and Johnson 2003:2). Because this discipline draws findings from the other four fields, however, I shall retain the four-discipline definition provided in chapter 1.

Applied anthropology has sprouted in different subdisciplines. From physical anthropology and archaeology comes **forensics**, or the science of crime scene reconstruction using skeletal and dental analysis, together with the cause of death—gunshot wounds, blunt instruments, or other means. From a combination of physical and cultural anthropology comes **medical anthropology**, which applies findings about folk medical beliefs to actual treatment, including such areas as biomedicine, ethnomedicine, and alternative systems of medical care. Other applied areas involve business, demographic issues, and advocacy for low-income populations, including the homeless (Harris and Johnson 2003:302–313).

However, the science of anthropology too often becomes compromised as an applied discipline, as Kathleen Gough suggested when she wrote, "anthropology is a child of imperialism" (1968:403–407). Both at home and abroad, the overarching role of applied anthropology has been to induce diverse peoples to adjust to the demands of a capitalist economy. The barriers to change cited for Tzintzuntzan highlights the mistrust villagers have toward outsiders, including anthropologists. The applied literature is rife with "target populations," "clients," "directed change," "change agents," and other terms that betray a message: "You must adjust to the realities of a modern economy and society." Even when such programs are well intended and prove themselves effective, they are seldom implemented if they support autonomy in the process. This point can best be illustrated by a program that actually seems to have served the "client" population, yet was not extended.

The program, officially named the Cornell Peru Project (CPP) and best known as the Vicos Project, was carried out in Vicos, Peru, a hacienda with a surrounding community comprising 1,703 peasants whose economic condition was characterized as serf-like. Directed by the anthropologists Allen Holmberg and Mario C. Vasquez, with the help of the biomedical researcher Carlos Monge Medrano, the Vicos Project sought to transform the hacienda into a functioning plantation run by the Vicosinos themselves. It was an exercise of planned change. Over this period, nearly 100 American and Peruvian specialists (anthropologists, agronomists, nutritionists, educators, photographers, psychologists, and many students) trained the Vicosinos in every aspect of running a commercial farm, from seed selection and fertilizer use to financial administration and marketing. By the time the project ended in 1966, the Vicosinos were running the operation themselves (Doughty 2004).

However, the very success of the project betrayed its limitations. On the heels of the CPP, hundreds of thousands of peasants demanded similar programs. A combination of bureaucratic foot-dragging, police repression, and promises that went unfulfilled effectively stopped that movement. A land invasion also was suppressed and the land returned to their former owners (Country Studies, Peru n.d.: *www.country-studies.com/peru/ landlords-and-peasant-revolts-in-the-highlands.html*). (Gorin 1985: *www-lib.usc.edu/~retter/guillen1.html*).

These incidents show that even successful programs, which the Vicos project seemed to be, are limited by the realities of the world economy. This raises the question: What good are demonstration projects if they are cut off by the very agencies that initiate them?

Resistance Movements

Several attempts to reverse the spread of global corporatism have been made over the past century, and they persist today. Socialist revolutions took place in Russia in 1917, China in 1949. Cuba in 1959, and other countries in later years; all of them have either failed (Russia in 1991), become isolated (North Korea), or have been severely compromised (China, Vietnam, even Cuba, all of whom have signed deals with foreign investors). Venezuela is on a drive to achieve autonomy, and despite three attempts to overthrow it, the Chavez administration appears as strong as ever. After the collapse of the economy in 2001, Argentinians appear to be attempting to control their autonomy. Worker takeovers of more than 200 factories as of 2003 (Lewis and Klein 2004; see also Magnani 2003) are one indication. In Bolivia, Indians have resisted the privatization of the water works in Cochabamba (Olivera and Lewis 2004), threw out one president, Gonzalo de Lozada, over his attempt to privatize the country's liquid national gas, and pressured his successor, Carlos Mesa, not to privatize LNG or any other resource. Meantime, the Islamic revolt appears to be spreading with the Shi'a victory in Iraq in January 2005, and other resistance movements may well be spreading.

One fertile field for applied anthropology, then, seems to be analyses of these movements. Land invasions have occurred in Brazil, Guatemala, Mexico, and elsewhere. The Ejécito Zapatista Liberación Nacional (EZLN) has brought about land reform and community development in several Mayan communities in Chiapas after its symbolic takeover of several cities on January 1, 1994, including the state capital Tuxtla Guitierrez and San Cristóbal de las Casas (Ross 2000; Hayden 2001). Clearly, the rapid developments throughout the world make it clear that students of cultural change and applied anthropology will need to initiate rapid changes in these disciplines as well.

Conclusion

The future of applied anthropology, and culture change overall, is an open question. It seems that as a cross-cultural discipline, anthropology is in a unique position to compare past societies that serve most or all its people, and then come up with several scenarios for a society workable not for a power elite but for all. Will it? With practicing anthropologists working for the corporations, other areas of the for-profit private sector, and every agency from military intelligence to law enforcement, the prospects do not appear promising. We shall see.

EPILOGUE:
A CRITIQUE AND PROSPECTUS

Anthropology has the potential to become a science of humankind. The declared commitment to cultural relativism renders the discipline a science, in the true sense of the word, if only there is the will to turn that declaration to reality. So far, however, the discipline has become fragmented into hundreds of thousands of little hobby horses called research projects. The discipline and its findings lack coherence and unity.

This is not to say that the discipline has failed to make contributions. Some have yielded insights into how human cultures operate; others have proven useful in forensics or community development or health improvements. How many have yielded positive benefits in either area is anyone's guess.

The overall results, however, have proved disappointing. The policymakers in Washington have learned nothing from what anthropologists could have, or should have, offered. We are in the midst of a disastrous war in Iraq; the Pentagon seems to know nothing about guerrilla warfare despite 60 years of study. Poverty is widespread and increases every year. Where are the anthropologists with their insights about cross-cultural economics? Third World states remain basket cases—where are the political anthropologists with their knowledge ready to be applied to reform failed states? AIDS

threatens to wipe out an entire continent. Where are the cross-cultural medical practitioners to mitigate this disaster?

Stanislav Andreski had much to say about this shortfall in the social sciences generally. Despite more than a century's existence, the social sciences' yield in the way of results has been paltry (1972). So-called postmodernists have gone so far as to give up any prospects of a science of the social. We are condemned to a discipline of partial truths, many of them Eurocentric, and if we deny it, we are just being ethnocentric (Nanda and Warms 2004:55–56).

However, there are limits to an extreme cultural relativism. In ethics, such a perspective too often leads to **ethical relativism,** a view that, taken to absurd lengths in its logic, means that public policymakers should tolerate headhunting, cannibalism, mass murder, and human rights violations from China to the Sudan to Afghanistan (Bagish 1981; Hatch 1983; Edgerton 1992). Perhaps the United Nations' Universal Declaration of Human Rights is ethnocentric; if so, why do its signatories represent all regions of the world? Why is it the most translated document in the world, from Abkhaz to Zulu?

By the same token, should we not be striving for a set of regularities predicting the social? We all, after all, have a capacity for language. We all have a capacity for technology. Every one of us has a capacity for culture in all its other aspects. The maxim that we be sensitive to the perceptions of other cultures and their people does not preclude a search for cultural principles that apply to all.

Where the social sciences have gone wrong is the attempt to use physical science, in many instances biological sciences, and even linguistics as metaphors to guide social science, and then to forget that these are only metaphors. It is time to develop a methodology for the social sciences in its own right. We cannot control human behavior or the social systems that govern them in laboratories. We are not dealing with atoms or molecules, or parts of organisms. We are dealing with human individuals and the populations that comprise them. This is one area where holism becomes relevant. Why aren't the researchers and practitioners in anthropology taking this principle seriously?

Here is where anthropology is in a unique position. The concept of cultural relativism in its scientific sense is a special instance of scientific detachment. We do not apply our own cultural norms in researching other cultures any more than we apply our religious values to evolutionary biology or notions of alchemy to physical science. All scientists compare phenomena to verify or reject hypotheses. Why shouldn't social scientists do the same?

On that note, we now have a rich body of ethnographic data against which to evaluate all hypotheses regarding the social sciences. Anthropology is in a unique position because it has the power to compare. The time has come to use the principles of holism and cross-cultural comparison as methodological guides, and to synthesize the findings from the field.

BIBLIOGRAPY

Abd Allah, Mahmud M. 1917. "Siwan Customs." Harvard African Studies 1:1–28.

American Psychiatric Association. (1994. Diagnostic Statistical Manual of Mental Disorders Vol. 4. Washington, DC: American Psychiatric Association.

Andreski, Stanislav. 1972. Social Science as Sorcery. Harmondsworth, UK: Penguin.

Armstrong, W. E. 1967. "Rossel Island Money: A Unique Monetary System." In Tribal and Peasant Economies. George Dalton, ed. Pp. 246–253. New York: Natural History Press.

Bagish, Henry. 1981. Confessions of a Former Cultural Relativist. Santa Barbara, CA: Santa Barbara City College Publications.

Balikci, Ansen. 1970. The Netsilik Eskimo. New York: Natural History Press.

Barkow, Jerome, Leda Cosmides, and John Tooby eds. The Adapted Mind. Oxford, UK: Oxford University Press. 1992.

Barnouw, Victor. 1985. Culture and Personality. Homewood, IL: Dorsey Press.

Bellman, Beryl. 1084. The Language of Secrecy: Symbols and Metaphors in Poro Ritual. New Brunswick, NJ: Rutgers University Press.

Benedict, Ruth. 1934. Patterns of Culture. Boston: Houghton Mifflin.

Berdan, Frances. 1982. The Aztecs of Central Mexico: An Imperial Society. Belmont, CA: Wadsworth.

Berdan, Frances, Edward A. Stark, and Carey Van Loon. 2004. EthnoQuest: An Interactive Multimedia Simulation for Cultural Anthropology Fieldwork, Version 3.0. Upper Saddle River, NJ. Prentice Hall.

Befu, Harumi. 1971. Japan: An Anthropological Introduction. San Francisco: Chandler.

Berlin, Brent, and Paul Kay. 1969. Basic Color Terms, Their Universality and Evolution. Berkeley: University of California Press.

Binford, Lewis. 1983. In Pursuit of the Past. New York: Thames and Hudson.

Bledsoe, Caroline H. 1980. Women and Marriage in Kpelle Society. Stanford, CA: Stanford University Press.

Bloch, Maurice. 1983. Marxism and Anthropology. Oxford, UK: Oxford University Press.

Bloch, Maurice. 1985. "From Cognition to Ideology." In Power and Knowledge: Anthropological and Sociological Approaches. Richard Fardon, ed. Pp. 21–48. Edinburgh: University of Edinburgh Press.

Bodley, John. 2001. Anthropology and Contemporary Human Problems. Mountain View, CA: Mayfield.

Boehm, Christopher. 2001. Hierarchy in the Forest: The Evolution of Egalitarian Behavior. Cambridge, MA: Harvard University Press.

Bohannan, Paul. 1971. "The Impact of Money on an African Subsistence Economy." In Tribal and Peasant Economies. George Dalton, ed. Pp. 123–135. Garden City, NY: Natural History Press.

Bohannan, Paul. 1989. Justice and Judgment Among the Tiv. Prospect Heights, IL: Waveland Press.

Bordes, François. 1961. "Mousterian Cultures in France." Science 134:803–810.

Boster, James. 1987. "Agreement Between Biological Classification Systems Is Not Dependent on Cultural Transmission." American Anthropologist 89(4):914–919.

Bourguignon, Erika. 1979. Psychological Anthropology: An Introduction to Human Nature and Cultural Differences. New York: Holt, Rinehart and Winston.

Braidwood, Robert. 1960. The Agricultural Revolution. Scientific American 203(3):130–148.

Braverman, Harry. 1974. Labor and Monopoly Capital: The Degradation of Labor in the Twentieth Century. New York: Monthly Review Press.

Breen, Marcus. 2005. Proletarianization: The Web's Contribution to "Immaturity." Paper presented at the International Conference on Technology, Knowledge, and Society. Berkeley, California, February 20.

Broad, William, and Nicolas Wade. 1983. Betrayers of the Truth: Fraud and Deceit in the Halls of Science. New York: Simon and Schuster.

Brown, Donald E. 1991. Human Universals. New York: McGraw-Hill.

Bryceson, Deborah Fahy. 1996. "Deagrarianization and Rural Employment in Sub-Saharan Africa: A Sectoral Perspective." World Development 24(1):97–111.

Burns, E. Bradford. 1980. The Poverty of Progress: Latin American in the Nineteenth Century. Berkeley: University of California Press.

Burridge, Kenelm. 1995. Mambu. Princeton: Princeton University Press.

Butterfield, Fox. 1996. "Study Finds Disparity of Justice for Blacks." New York Times, February 13: 8A.

Cancian, Frank. 1965. Economics and Prestige in a Maya Community: The Cargo System of Zinacantan. Stanford, CA: Stanford University Press.

Carmack, Robert. 1988. Harvest of Violence; Guatemala's Indians in the Counterinsurgency War. Norman: University of Oklahoma Press.

Carmack, Robert. 1995. Rebels of Highland Guatemala: The Quiche-Mayas of Momostenango. Norman: University of Oklahoma Press.

Carneiro, Robert. 1967. On the Relationship Between Size of Population and Complexity of Social Organization. Southwest Journal of Anthropology 23:234–243.

Carneiro, Robert. 1970. "A Theory of the Origin of the State." Science 169:733–738.

Carneiro, Robert. 1981. Chiefdom: Precursor to the State. In The Transition to Statehood in the New World. Grant Jones and Robert Kautz, eds. Pp. 37–75. New York: Cambridge University Press.

Centre for Atmospheric Science. The Ozone Hole Tour. n.d. Cambridge University. www.atm.ch.cam.ac.uk/tour/

Chagnon, Napoleon. 1997. Yanomamö. 5th ed. New York: Holt, Rinehart and Winston.

Chase-Dunn, Christopher, Susanne Jonas, and Nelson Amaro. 2001. Globalization on the Ground: Postbellum Guatemalan Democracy and Development. Lanham, MD: Rowman and Littlefield.

Childe, V. Gordon. 1950. "The Urban Revolution." Town Planning Review 21:3–17.

Childe, V. Gordon. 1951. Man Makes Himself. New York: New American Library.

Chomsky, Noam. 1965. Syntactic Structures. London: Mouton.

Chomsky, Noam. 1975. The Logical Structure of Linguistic Theory. New York: Plenum Press.

Chomsky, Noam. 1980. Rules and Representations. New York: Columbia University Press.

Chomsky, Noam. 1995. The Minimalist Program. Cambridge, MA: MIT press.

Clay, Jason W. 1996. "What's a Nation?" In Talking About People. William Haviland and R. J. Gordon, eds. P. 188 2nd Edition. Mountain View, CA: Mayfield.

Cohen, Mark N. 1977. The Food Crisis in Prehistory: Overpopulation and the Origins of Agriculture. New Haven, CT: Yale University Press.

Cole, Michael, and Sylvia Scribner. 1974. Culture and Thought: A Psychological Introduction. New York: Wiley.

Czaplicka, Marie Antoinette. 1914. Shamanism in Siberia. Oxford, UK: Clarendon Press.

Dalton, George, ed. 1967. Tribal and Peasant Economies. New York: Natural History Press.

Daltroy, Terrence N. 2003. The Incas. Oxford, UK: Blackwell.

Darwin, Charles. 1975 [1859]. On the Origins of Species. Cambridge, MA: Harvard University Press.

Davidson, Basil. 1988. The African Slave Trade. Boston: Back Bay.

Deetz, James. 1967. Invitation to Archaeology. New York: Doubleday.

Deloria, Vine. 1969. Custer Died for Your Sins. London: Collier-Macmillan.

Dentan, Robert. 1979. The Semai: A Nonviolent People of Malaysia. (Fieldwork Edition). New York: Holt, Rinehart and Winston.

De Waal, Frans, and Frans Lanting. 1997. Bonobo: The Forgotten Ape. Berkeley: University of California Press.

Diamond, Jared. 2004. Collapse: How Societies Choose to Fail or Succeed. New York: Viking.

Doughty, Paul L. 2004. Review of Stein, William. 2003. Deconstructing Development Discourse in Peru: A Meta-Ethnography of the Modernity Project at Vicos. New York: University Press of America. American Ethnologist 31(4):n.p.

Draper, Patricia. 1975. "!Kung Women: Contrasts in Sexual Egalitarianism. In: Toward an Anthropology of Women. Raina Reiter, ed. Pp. 77–109. New York: Monthly Review Press.

Drucker, Philip. 1955. Indians of the Northwest Coast. New York: Natural History Press.

Drury, Shadia B. 1999. Leo Strauss and the American Right. New York: St. Martin's Press.

Durkheim, Emile. 1995. Elementary Forms of the Religious Life. New York: Free Press.

Dyson-Hudson, Neville. 1966. Karimojong Politics. Oxford, UK: Clarendon Press.

Dyson-Hudson, Rada, and Eric Allen Smith. 1978. "Human Territoriality: An Ecological Reassessment." American Anthropologist 80(1):21–41.

Edgerton, Robert B. 1992. Sick Societies: Challenging the Myth of Primitive Harmony. New York: Free Press.

Eliade, Mircea. 1964. Shamanism. Princeton: Princeton University Press.

Ember, Carol, and Melvin Ember. 1971. "The Conditions Favoring Matrilocal Versus Patrilocal Residence." American Anthropologist 73:371–374.

Ember, Carol and Melvin Ember. 2002. Cultural Anthropology, 10th ed. Upper Saddle River, NJ: Prentice-Hall.

Evans, Karin. 2001. The Lost Daughters of China: Abandoned Girls, Their Journey to America, and the Search for a Missing Past. New York: Jeremy P. Tarcher.

Evans-Pritchard, Edward E. 1940. The Nuer. Oxford, UK: Oxford University Press.

Evans-Pritchard, Edward E. 1976. Witchcraft, Oracles and Magic Among the Azande (abridged ed.). Oxford, UK: Oxford University Press.

Fagan, Brian. 2004. Ancient Lives, 2nd ed. Upper Saddle River, NJ: Prentice-Hall.

Fallers, Louis. 1961. "Are African Cultivators to Be called Peasants?" Current Anthropology 2(2):108–110.

Feder, Kenneth, 2004. The Past in Perspective: An Introduction to Human Prehistory, 3rd ed. New York: McGraw-Hill.

Foster, George. 1987. Tzintzuntzan: Mexican Peasants in a Changing World. Prospect Heights, IL: Waveland Press.

Fox, Robin. 1967. Kinship and Marriage. Harmondsworth, UK: Penguin.

Frank, Andre Gunder. 1965. Capitalism and Underdevelopment in Latin America: Historical Studies of Chile and Brazil. New York: Monthly Review Press.

Frank, Andre Gunder. 1972. "The Sociology of Development and the Underdevelopment of Sociology." In Dependence and Underdevelopment. James Cockcroft, Andre Gunder Frank, and Dale Johnson, eds. New York: Doubleday. Pp. 321–398.

Frank, Andre Gunder. 1998. ReOrient: Global Economy in an Asian Age. Berkeley: University of California Press.

Frank, Andre Gunder, and Barry K. Gills, eds. 1993. The World System: Five Hundred Years or Five Thousand. London: Routledge.

Frank, Thomas. 2004. What's the Matter with Kansas? How Conservatives Won the Heart of America. New York: Metropolitan Books.

Frazer, James. 1958. The Golden Bough. New York: Scribner.

Freeman, Derek. 1983. Margaret Mead and Samoa: The Making and Unmaking of an Anthropological Myth. Cambridge, MA: Harvard University Press.

Freeman, Derek. 1989. "Fa'apua' a Fa'amu and Margaret Mead" American Anthropologist 91: 1017–1022.

Freud, Sigmund. 1913. Totem and Taboo: Some Points of Agreement Between the Mental Lives of Savages and Neurotics. New YorK: W.W. Norton.

Freud, Sigmund. 1943 [1917]. A General Introduction to Psychoanalysis. Garden City, NY: Garden City Publishing.

Fried, Morton. 1967. The Evolution of Political Society: An Essay in Political Anthropology. New York: Random House.

Fried, Morton. 1978. "The State, the Chicken, and the Egg or What Came First?" In Origins of the State. Ronald Cohen and Elman Service, eds. Philadelphia: Institute for the Study of Human Issues.

Gamble, C. 1986. The Paleolithic Settlements of Europe. Cambridge, UK: Cambridge University Press.

Gaulin, Stephen, and James S. Boster. 1990. "Dowry as Female Competition." American Anthropologist 92:994–1005.

Gee, H. 1995. "New Hominid Remains Found in Ethiopia." Nature 373:272.

Goldstein, Melvyn. n.d. Fraternal Polyandry and Fertility in a High Himalayan Valley in Northwest Nepal. Unpublished manuscript. <www.case.edu/affil/tibet/booksandpapers/fraternal.html>

Goldstein, Melvyn. 1987. "When Brothers Share a Wife." Natural History 96(3):39–48.

Good, Kenneth. 1997. Into The Heart: One Man's Pursuit of Love and Knowledge Among the Yanomami. Upper Saddle River, NJ: Prentice-Hall.

Goodall, Jane. 1986. The Chimpanzees of Gombe: Patterns of Behavior. Cambridge: Harvard University Press.

Goodenough, Ward H. 1963. Cooperation in Change. New York: Russell Sage Foundation.

Goody, Jack. 1976. Production and Reproduction: A Comparative Study of the Domestic Domain. Cambridge, UK: Cambridge University Press.

Gough, Kathleen. 1959. "The Nayars and the Definition of Marriage." Journal of the Royal Anthropological Institute 89:23–34.

Gough, Kathleen. 1968. "New Proposals for Anthropologists." Current Anthropology 9:403–407.

Hanson, F. Allan. 1970. Rapan Lifeways: Society and History on a Polynesian Island. Boston: Little, Brown.

Harner, Michael. 1972. The Jívaro: People of the Sacred Waterfalls. Garden City, NY: Natural History Press.

Harris, Marvin. 1974. Cows, Pigs, Wars, and Witches. New York: Vintage.

Harris, Marvin, and Orna Johnson. 2003. Cultural Anthropology, 6th ed. Boston: Allyn and Bacon.

Hart, C.W.M., Arnold R. Pilling, and Jane Goodale. 1988. The Tiwi of North Australia, 3rd ed. New York: Holt, Rinehart and Winston.

Hassan, Ferri A. 1981. Demographic Archaeology. New York: Academic Press.

Hatch, Elvin. 1983. Culture and Morality: The Relativity of Values in Anthropology. New York: Columbia University Press.

Haviland, William. 2002. Cultural Anthropology, 10th ed. New York: Harcourt.

Hayden, Tom. 2001. The Zapatista Reader. San Francisco: Last Gasp.

Heider, Karl. 1970. The Dugum Dani: A Papuan Culture in the Highlands of West New Guinea. Chicago: Aldine.

Heinberg, Richard. 2003. The Party's Over: Oil, War and the Fate of Industrial Societies. Boston: South End Press.

Heinzelin, Jean de, J. Desmond Clark, Timothy White, William Hart, Paul Renne, Gidey Wolde Gabriel, Youe Beyene, and Elisabeth Vrba. 1999. Environment and the behavior of 2.5-million year old Bouri Hominids. Science 284:625–629.

Herdt, Gilbert. 1987. The Sambia. New York: Holt, Rinehart and Winston.

Herdt, Gilbert. 1993. Sexual repression, social control, and gender hierarchy in Sambia culture. In Gender Hierarchies. B. Miller, ed. Cambridge, UK: Cambridge University Press, pp. 193–211.

Herrnstein, Richard, and Charles Murray. 1994. The Bell Curve: Intelligence and Class Structure in American Life. New York: Free Press.

Hinshaw, Robert. 1975. Panajachel: A Guatemalan Town in Thirty-Year Perspective. Pittsburgh: University of Pittsburgh Press.

Hodgson, Dorothy. 2004. Once Intrepid Warriors: Gender, Ethnicity, and the Cultural Politics of Maasai Development. Bloomington: Indiana University Press.

Hoebel, E. Adamson. 1960. The Cheyenne. New York: Holt, Rinehart and Winston.

Hoebel, E. Adamson. 1968 [1954]. The Law of Primitive Man: A Comparison in Legal Dynamics. New York: Atheneum.

Hurtado, A. Magdalena, Kim Hill, Hillard Kaplan, and Jane Lancaster. 2000. The epidemiology of infectious diseases among South American Indians. Paper read at the 2000 meeting of the American Anthropolgical Association.

Hoselitz, Bert. 1960. Sociological Aspects of Economic Growth. New York: Free Press.

Hsu, Francis. 1971. Psychological Homeostasis and Jen: Conceptual Tools for Advancing Psychological Anthropology. American Anthropologist 73:23–44.

Immerman, Richard H. 1986. The CIA in Guatemala: The Foreign Policy of Intervention. Austin: University of Texas Press.

Johanson, Don. 1974. Lucy: The Beginnings of Humankind. New York: Simon and Schuster.

Johnson, Chalmers. 2004. The Sorrows of Empire: Militarism, Secrecy, and the End of The Republic. New York: Metropolitan Books.

Jonas, Susanne, and David Tobis. 1974. Guatemala. New York: NACLA.

Jones, Chester Lloyd. 1940. Guatemala: Past and Present. Minneapolis: University of Minnesota Press.

Kaplan, David. 1965. "The Mexican Marketplace: Then and Now." Paper presented at Proceedings of the Annual Spring Meeting of the American Ethnological Society. Seattle: University of Washington Press.

Kardiner, Abram, and Ralph Linton. 1939. The Individual and His Society. New York: Columbia University Press.

Kelly, Raymond C. 1977. Etoro Social Structure: A Study in Structural Contradiction. Ann Arbor: University of Michigan Press.

Kerbo, Haroold R., and John A. McKinstry. 1998. Modern Japan. New York: McGraw-Hill.

Khare, Ravindra. 1984. The Untouchable as Himself: Identity and Pragmatism Among the Lucknow Chamars. New York: Cambridge University Press.

Kinzer, Stephen. 2003. All the Shah's Men: An American Coup and the Roots of Middle East Terror. Hoboken, NJ: Wiley.

Klein, Naomi. 2000. No Logo. New York: Picador.

Kluckhohn, Clyde. 1967. Navajo Witchcraft. Boston: Beacon Press.

Koch, Klaus-Friedrich, Soraya Altorki, Andrew Arno, and Letitia Hickson. 1977. "Ritual Reconciliation and the Obviation of Grievances: A Comparative Study in the Ethnography of Law." Ethnology 16:269–284.

Kroeber, Alfred L. 1948. Anthropology. New York: Harcourt, Brace, and World.

Kroeber, Albert L., and Clyde Kluckhohn. 1952. Culture: A Critical Review of Concepts and Definitions. New York: Vintage/Random House.

Lancaster, William. 1997. The Rwala Bedouin Today. Prospect Heights, IL: Waveland Press.

Lansing, Stephen. 1983. The Three Worlds of Bali. Westport, CT: Praeger.

Leach, Edmond. 1961. Rethinking Anthropology. London: Athlone Press.

Leakey, Mary, and R. L. Hay. 1979. "Pliocene Footprints in Laetoli Beds at Laetoli, Northern Tanzania." Nature 278:317–323).

Leakey, Meave, Fred Spoor, Frank H. Brown, Patrick N. Gathogo, Christopher Klarle, Louise N. Leakey, and Ian McDougall. 2001. "New Hominid Genus from Eastern Africa Shows Diverse Middle Pliocene Lineages." Nature 410:433–440.

Leakey, Richard, and Roger Lewin. 1995. The Sixth Extinction. New York: Doubleday.

Leavitt, G. C. 1990. Sociobiological Explanations of Incest Avoidance: A Critical Review of Evidential Claims. American Anthropologist 92:973.

Lee, Richard. 1993. The Dobe Ju/'hoansi. Fort Worth, TX: Harcourt, Brace.

Lee, Richard. 2003. The Dobe Ju/'hoansi, 3rd ed. New York: Thomson.

LePage du Pratz, Antoine-Simon. 1958. Histoire de la Louisiane. Paris: np. [Originally published as a series in Journal Deconomique between 1651 and 1653.]

Lett, James W. 1987. Human Enterprise: A Critical Introduction to Anthropological Theory. Boulder, CO: Westview Press.

Lett, James W. 1990. A Field Guide to Critical Thinking. Skeptical Inquirer 14(2):154–160).

Levi-Strauss, Claude. 1963. Structural Anthropology. New York: Basic Books.

Lewis, Avi, and Naomi Klein. 2004. The Take. Ottawa: National Film Board.

Lewis, Oscar. 1951. Life in a Mexican Village: Tepoztlan Restudied. Urbana: University of Illinois Press.

Little, Kenneth. 1965. "The Political Function of the Poro, Part 1." Africa 35:349–365.

Little, Kenneth. 1966. "The Political Function of the Poro, Part 2." Africa 36:62–71.

Long, Bruce. 1987. "Reincarnation." Encyclopedia of Religion. Vol. 12. Pp. 265–269. New York: Macmillan.

Magnani, Esteban. 2003. El cambio silencioso: Empresas y fábricas recuperadas por los trabajadores en la Argentina. Buenos Aires: Prometeo Libros.

Malinowski, Bronislaw. 1922. Argonauts of the Western Pacific. New York: Dutton.

Malinowski, Bronislaw. 1927. Sex and Repression in Savage Society. New York: Meridian Books.

Maloney, William. 1987a. "Dharma." Encyclopedia of Religion, vol. 4. Pp. 239–332. New York: Macmillan.

Maloney, William. 1987b. "Karma." Encyclopedia of Religion, vol. 8. Pp. 261–266. New York: Macmillan.

Manz, Beatrice. 1987. Refugees of a Hidden War. New York: State University of New York.

Marano, Lou. 1982. "Windigo Psychosis: The Anatomy of an Emic-Etic Confusion." Current Anthropology 23:385–412.

Marett, Robert. 1914. The Threshold of Religion. London: Metheun.

Marshall, Lorna. 1965. The !Kung Bushmen of the Kalahari Desert. In Peoples of Africa. James Gibbs, ed. Holt, Rinehart and Winston, pp. 241–278.

Marshall, John. 1974. Bushmen of the Kalahari. New York: National Geographic Society.

Martin, M. Kay, and Barbara Voorhis. 1975. Female of the Species. New York: Columbia University Press.

Mauss, Marcel. 2001 [1925]. The Gift: The Form and Reason for Exchange in Archaic Societies. London: Routledge.

McClelland, David. 1961. The Achieving Society. New York: Free Press.

McDowell, Paul V. 1974. Political and Religious Change in a Guatemalan Factory Community. Ph.D. Dissertation, University of British Columbia.

McDowell, Paul V. 1980. "The Decline of the Civil-Religious Hierarchy: The Case of Cantel." NorthSouth: Canadian Journal of Latin American Studies 35(10):17–35.

McDowell, Paul V. 1994. "The Commercialization of the Guatemalan Economy, 1871–1944: Political and Military Dimensions." in New Developments in Institutional Economics. James M. Acheson, ed. Lanham, MD: University Press of America.

McMahon, Frank, and Judith H. McMahon. 1983. Abnormal Behavior: Psychology's View. Homewood, IL: Dorsey Press.

Mead, Margaret. 1950. Sex and Temperament in Three Primitive Societies. New York: Mentor.

Mead, Margaret. 1961 [1927]. Coming of Age in Samoa: A Study of Adolescence and Sex in Primitive Society. New York: Morrow.

Mead, Margaret, John Rickman, and Geoffrey Görer. 2001. Russian Culture. New York: Berghahn.

Meggers, Betty. 1996. Amazonia: Man and Culture in a Counterfeit Paradise, Rev. ed. Washington, DC: Smithsonian Press.

Meggitt, Mervyn. 1964. "Male-Female Relationships in the Highlands of Australian New Guinea." American Anthropologist 66:204–214.

Meggitt, Mervyn. 1977. Blood is Their Argument: Warfare Among the Mae-Enga. Palo Alto, CA: Mayfield.

Middleton, John. 1960. Lugbara Religion. Oxford, UK: Oxford University Press.

Mooney, James. 1965. The Ghost Dance Religion. Chicago: University of Chicago Press.

Moselle, Boaz 1995. "Allotments, Enclosure, and Proletarianization in Early Nineteenth-Century Southern England." Economic History Review 47(3):482–500.

Murdock, George Peter. 1949. Social Structure. New York: Free Press.

Murphy, Robert F., and Leonard Kasdan. 1959. "The Structure of Parallel Cousin Marriage." American Anthropologist 61(1):17–29.

Nader, Laura. 1991. Harmony Ideology: Justice and Control in a Zapotec Mountain Village. Stanford, CA: Stanford University Press.

National Research Council, Committee on Mineral Resources and the Environment.

National Research Council. 1975. Mineral Resources and the Environment. Washington, DC: National Academy of Sciences.

Newark, Tim, and Angus McBride. 1991. Women Warlords: An Illustrated Military History of Female Warriors. London: Blandford.

Olivera, Oscar, and Tom Lewis. 2003. Cochabamba! Water War in Bolivia. Boston: South End Press.

Oakley, Kenneth Page. 1949. Man the Tool-Maker. London: British Museum.

O'Grady, William, John Archibald, Mark Aronoff, and Jamie Rees-Miller. 2001. Contemporary Linguistics: An Introduction, 4th ed. Boston and New York: Bedford and St. Martins.

Oliver, Douglas. 1955. A Solomon Island Society: Kinship and Leadership Among the Siuai of Bougainville. Cambridge, MA: Harvard University Press.

Otterbein, Keith. 1974. "The Anthropology of War." Honigman, John, ed. Handbook of Social and Cultural Anthropology. Chicago: Rand McNally, pp. 923–958.

Otterbein, Keith. 1989. The Evolution of War: A Cross-Cultural Study. New Haven, CT: Human Relation Area Files.

Park, Michael Alan. 2002. Biological Anthropology. New York: McGraw-Hill.

Parrinder, Geoffrey. 1983. World Religions: From Ancient History to the Present. New York: Hamlyn.

Parsons, Talcott. 1960. Structure and Process in Modern Societies. New York: Free Press.

Perelman, Michael. 2000. The Invention of Capitalism: Classical Political Economy and the Secret History of Primitive Accumulation. Durham, NC: Duke University Press.

Petersen, Kurt. 1992. The Maquiladora Revolution in Guatemala. New Haven, CT: Orville Schell Center for International Studies.

Piaget, Jean. 2000. The Psychology of the Child. New York: Basic Books.

Pinker, Steven. 1994. The Language Instinct: How the Mind Creates Language. New York: Harper Collins.

Plattner, Stuart. 1989. "Economic Behavior in Markets." in Economic Anthropology. Pp. 209–211. Stuart Plattner, ed. Stanford: Stanford University Press.

Pocha, Jehangir. 2005. "The Axis of Oil." In These Times 29(7):20–21.

Polanyi, Karl. 1944. The Great Transformation. Boston: Beacon Press.

Polanyi, Karl. 1971. Primitive, Archaic, and Modern Economies: Essays of Karl Polanyi. Boston: Beacon Press.

Polanyi, Karl, Conrad Arensberg, and Harry Pearson. 1957. Trade and Market in the Early Empires. Chicago: Gateway.

Pospisil, Leopold. 1963. The Kapauku Papuans of West New Guinea. New York: Holt, Rinehart and Winston.

Price, T. Douglas, and Gary M. Feinman. 2004. Images of the Past, 4th ed. Palo Alto, CA: Mayfield.

Redfield, Robert. 1973 [1926]. Tepoztlan: A Mexican Village—A Study of Folk Life. Chicago: University of Chicago Press.

Redfield, Robert. 1989. The Little Community and Peasant Society and Culture. Chicago: University of Chicago Press.

Robbins, Lionel M. 1937. An Essay on the Nature and Significance of Economic Science. London: Palgrave.

Roberts, Sam. 1993. "Fighting the Tide of Bloodshed on Streets Resembling a War Zone." New York Times, November 15:B12.

Rohner, Ronald, and Elizabeth Bettauer. 1986. Kwakiutl: Indians of British Columbia. Prospect Heights, IL: Waveland Press.

Ross, John. 2000. The Zapatista Chronicles 1994–2000. Monroe, ME: Common Courage Press.

Rostow, Walt W. 1991 [1960]. The Stages of Economic Growth: A Non-Communist Manifesto. Cambridge, UK: Cambridge University Press.

Sahlins, Marshall. 1961. The Segmentary Lineage: An Organization of Predatory Expansion. American Anthropologist 63:322–343.

Sahlins, Marshall. 1968. Tribesmen. Englewood Cliffs, NJ: Prentice-Hall.

Sahlins, Marshall. 1972. Stone Age Economics. Chicago: Aldine.

Sandstrom, Alan R. 1991. Corn is Our Blood: Culture and Ethnic Identity in a Contemporary Aztec Indian Village. Norman: University of Oklahoma Press.

Sangree, Walter. 1965. The Bantu Tiriki of Western Kenya. In Peoples of Africa, James Gibbs, ed. New York: Holt, Rinehart and Winston, 41–80.

Savinar, Matt. 2004. The Oil Age is Over: What to Expect as the World Runs Out of Cheap Oil, 2005–2050. Santa Rosa, CA: Matt Savinar Publications.

Schele, Linda, and Mary Ellen Miller. 1986. The Blood of Kings: Dynasty and Ritual in Modern Art. Fort Worth, TX: Kimball Art museum.

Schildkraut, Enid, and Carol Gelber. 1987. Golden Stool: Studies of the Asante Center and Periphery. New York: Natural History Press.

Scupin, Raymond. 2003. Cultural Anthropology: A Global Perspective, 5th ed. Upper Saddle River, NJ: Prentice-Hall.

Segal, Nancy L. 1997. Same-Age Unrelated Siblings: A Unique Test of Within-Family Environmental Influences on IQ Similarity. Journal of Educational Psychology. 89(2):381–390.

Service, Elman. 1962. Primitive Social Organization: An Evolutionary Perspective. New York: Random House.

Service, Elman. 1975. Origins of the State and Civilization: The Process of Cultural Evolution. New York: W.W. Norton.

Service, Elman. 1978. Profiles of Ethnology, 3rd ed. New York: Harper Collins.

Shannon, Thomas. 1988. An Introduction to the World-System Perspective. Boulder, CO: Westview Press.

Small, Meredith. 1992. "The Evolution of Human Sexuality and Mate Selection in Humans." Human Nature 3(2):133–156.

Small, Meredith. 1995. What's Love Got to Do with It? The Evolution of Human Mating. New York: Anchor Books.

Smith, Adam. 1977 [1776]. An Inquiry into the Nature and Causes of the Wealth of Nations. Chicago: University of Chicago Press.

Stanner, William Edward Hanley. 1979. "The Dreaming." In Reader in Comparative Religion, 4th ed. William A. Lessa and Evon Z. Vogt, eds. Pp. 513–523. New York: Harper and Row.

Stavrianos, Leften S. 1974. Global Rift. New York: Quill.

Stenning, Derrick. 1965. "The Pastoral Fulani of Northern Nigeria." In Peoples of Africa. James L. Gibbs, Jr., ed. Pp. 361–402. New York: Holt, Rinehart and Winston.

Steward, Julian. 1955. The Theory of Culture Change: The Methodology of Multilinear Evolution. Urbana: University of Illinois Press.

Steward, Julian, and Louis C. Faron. 1959. Native Peoples of South America. New York: McGraw-Hill.

Stewart, Omer. 1987. Peyote Religion: A History. Norman: University of Oklahoma Press.

Strathern, Andrew, and Pamela J. Stewart. 1999. Collaborations and Conflict: A Leader Through Time. Belmont, CA: Wadsworth.

Swadesh, Morris. 1964. "Linguistics as an Instrument in History." In Language and Society. Dell Hymes, ed. pp. 575–584. New York: Harper and Row.

Talmon, Yonina. 1972. "Mate Selection in Collective Settlements." American Sociological Review 29:491–508.

Tannen, Deborah. 1990. You Just Don't Understand: Women and Men in Conversation. New York: Morrow.

Tax, Sol. 1952. Penny Capitalism: A Guatemalan Indian Economy. Chicago: University of Chicago Press.

Thomas, Elizabeth Marshall. 1959. The Harmless People. New York: Knopf.

Thornhill, Nancy. 1993. Cited in Haviland, William A. and R. J. Gorman, eds. Talking About People. Mountain View, CA: Mayfield.

Thornhill, Nancy. 1993. The Record History of Inbreeding and Overbreeding. Chicago: University of Chicago Press.

Trompf, Garry W. 1991. Melanesian Religion. Cambridge, UK: Cambridge University Press.

Turnbull, Colin. 1963. The Forest People: A Study of the Pygmies of the Congo. New York: Simon and Schuster.

Turnbull, Colin. 1965. "The Mbuti Pygmies in the Congo. In Peoples of Africa. James Gibbs, ed. Pp. 279–318. New York: Holt, Rinehart and Winston.

Turnbull, Colin. 1983. The Mbuti Pygmies: Change and Adaptation. New York: Holt, Rinehart and Winston.

Tylor, Edward Burnett. 1976 [1871]. Primitive Culture: Researches into the Development of Mythology, Philosophy, Religion, Language, Art, and Custom. New York: Gordon Press.

Tylor, Edward Burnett. 1888. On a Method of Investigating the Development of Institutions. Journal of the Royal Anthropological Institute 18:245–270.

Underhill, Ruth M. 1977. Social Organization of the Papago Indians. New York: Columbia University Press.

U.S. Environmental Protection Agency. 2005. Ozone Depletion. <www.epa.gov/docs/ozone/science/sc_fact.html>

Vogt, Evon Z. 1969. Zinacantan: A Maya Community in the Highlands of Chiapas. Cambridge, MA: Harvard University Press.

Wallace, Anthony F. C. 1956. "Revitalization Movements." American Anthropologist 58:264–281.

Wallace, Anthony F. C. 1970. Culture and Personality. New York: Random House.

Wallace, Anthony F. C. 1972. "Mental Illness, Biology, and Culture." In Psychological Anthropology. Francis Hsu, ed. Cambridge, MA: Schenkman. pp. 363–402.

Wallerstein, Immanuel. 1974. The Modern World-System: Capitalist Agriculture and the Origins of the European World-Economy in the Sixteenth Century. New York: Academic Press.

Ward, Carol, Meave Leakey, and Alan Walker. 1999. "The new hominid species Australopithecus anamensis". Evolutionary Anthropology 7(6):197–205.

Weber, Max. 1977. The Theory of Social and Economic Organization. New York: Free Press.

Weiner, Annette. 1988. The Trobrianders of Papua New Guinea. Belmont, CA: Wadsworth.

Werner, Dennis. 1979. "A Cross-Cultural Perspective on Theory and Research on Male Homosexuality." Journal of Homosexuality 4:345–362.

Westermarck, Edward. 1894. The History of Human Marriage. New York: Macmillan.

White, Douglas. 1988. "Rethinking Polygyny, Co-Wives, Codes, and Cultural Systems." Current Anthropology 29(4):529–533.

White, Leslie. 1959. The Evolution of Culture. New York: McGraw-Hill.

Whiting, John W. M., and Irvin Child. 1953. Child Training and Personality: A Cross-Cultural Study. New Haven, CT: Yale University Press.

Whorf, Benjamin Lee. 1956. Language, Thought, and Reality: The Selected Writings of Benjamin Lee Whorf. Cambridge, MA: MIT Press.

Whyte, Martin K. 1978. The Status of Women in Preindustrial Societies. Princeton, NJ: Princeton University Press.

Wilkinson, Daniel. 2002. Silence on the Mountain: Stories of Terror, Betrayal, and Forgetting in Guatemala. Boston: Houghton Mifflin.

Wilson, Monica. 1951. Good Company: A Study of Nyakyusa Age Villages. Boston: Beacon Press.

Wolf, Eric R. 1957. Closed Corporate Communities in Mesoamerica and Central Java. Southwestern Journal of Anthropology 13(1):1–18.

Wolf, Eric R. 1959. Sons of the Shaking Earth. Chicago: University of Chicago Press.

Wolf, Eric R. 1966. Peasants. Englewood Cliffs, NJ: Prentice-Hall.

Wolpoff, Milford. 1999. Paleoanthropology, 2nd ed. New York: McGraw-Hill.

Woodward, Ralph Lee. 1999. Central America: A Nation Divided. Oxford, UK: Oxford University Press.

Worsley, Peter. 1968. The Trumpet Shall Sound: A Study of Cargo Cults in Melanesia. New York: Schocken.

Wu, Frank. 2002. "The Best "Chink" Food: Dog Eating and the Dilemma of Diversity." Gastronomica 2(2):38–45.

Wynne-Edwards, Vero C. 1962. Animal Dispersion In Relation to Social Behavior. Edinburgh: Oliver and Boyd.

Wynne-Edwards, Vero C. 1986. Evolution Through Group Selection. Oxford, UK: Blackwell.

INDEX